MILESTONES IN GUJARATI LITERATURE

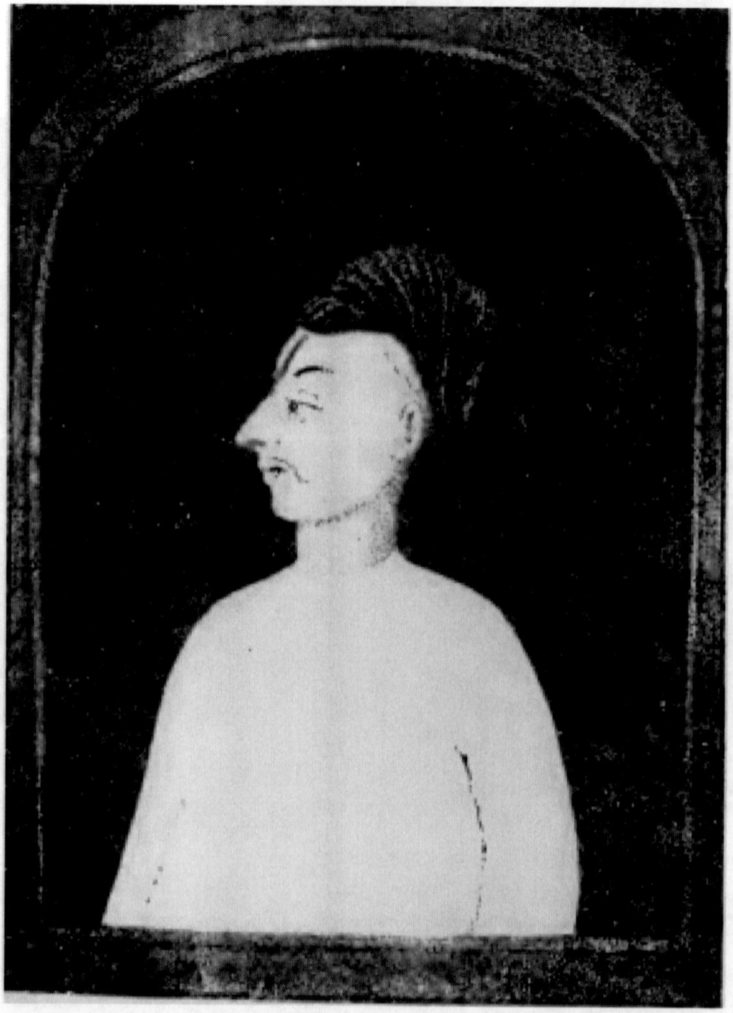

DAYÂRÂM

MILESTONES IN GUJARATI LITERATURE

KRISHNALAL M. JHAVERI

GYAN

Published by

Gyan Publishing House
5, Ansari Road
Daryaganj, New Delhi-110002
Phone: 011-47034999, 9811692060
E-mail: books@gyanbooks.com

Distribution Network
gyanbooks.com
India, USA, Canada, UK, Australia, France

ISBN: 9788121237796 (PB)
First Published, 1914

2nd Impression 2020

Printed at: Gyan Press, Delhi.

Milestones in Gujarati Literature
Author: Krishnalal M. Jhaveri

PREFACE

TO THE SECOND EDITION

Since 1914 when the first edition of this book was published a great deal of research work has been done. This has thrown new light on many questions relating to the Literature of Gujarāt. Accordingly I have revised the text in many places and made additions to bring it up to date.

In this I have been greatly helped by my friend Mr. Ambālāl B. Jāni, B. A., whose study of old Gujarāti Literature is extensive and profound. Mr. Natvarlāl I. Desāi, B. A., has also greatly helped me in this connection.

I cannot sufficiently thank Rev. W. Graham Mulligan, M. A., of the Irish Presbyterian Mission, Ahmedābād, for his help in preparing the manuscript for the Press. He has taken great interest in my work, and, in the light of his own close study of Gujarāti and English Literature, has been able to make valuable suggestions which I have adopted.

Bombay,
18th June 1938

KRISHNALAL M. JHAVERI.

PREFACE

TO THE FIRST EDITION

There being no such book in English, the idea of writing a sketch of the history of Gujarāti Literature was first suggested to me by my colleague, Mr. A. K. Donald, a gentleman who takes great interest in vernacular literature. My original idea was to include both periods, classical and modern, in one volume, but as I proceeded with the work, the subject grew upon me, and in spite of trying my best to condense the materials, I was unable to carry out my original plan, and had to leave the modern period over for another volume.

The book is written at intervals snatched from a busy official life, and owing to lack of leisure many shortcomings have crept into it: of this I am fully conseious.

The MSS. were submitted to my friend, Mr. Narsinhrāo Bholānāth Divatiā, B. A., a gentleman of acknowledged authority on Gujarāti Language and Literature, and to my eldest brother, Motilāl, whose study and knowledge of our literature is remarkably deep and accurate, and they have made many valuable suggestions and corrections. Similarly the Rev. Mr. Johnson, B. A., of the Irish Presbyterian Mission at Broach, and Mr. A. K. Donald, have rendered me great assistance by suggesting suitable alterations in the language and arrangement of the work. Mr. Donald has besides kindy contributed a foreword. To all of them I am deeply grateful.

With a view to secure a wider public than the inhabitants of Gujarāt and Kāthiāwād, I have thought it fit to print the vernacular text in Bālbodh characters instead of Gujarāti, Bālbodh being read over the whole of India.

The picture of Kavi Dayārām has been furnished by Mr. Manilāl Ichchārām Desāi, B. A. I am obliged to him for the loan.

Bombay,
September 1914.

KRISHNALAL M. JHAVERI.

vernacular spoken by ten millions must have a literature, and it is the duty of educated Gujarātis to improve the language, and enrich the literature, because it is only by means of instruction through the vernacular that those ten millions of people and their progeny can be brought to a higher level of education and wellbeing. Those Gujarātis who have access to modern learning through English, should endeavour to place before their less fortunate brethren those treasures in Gujarāti dress, but this is only one part of their task. Gujarāti authors must give voice to the ideals of the Gujarāti people; where they are low, they must try and raise them. They must use the novel, the drama and the satire to unmask the self seeker and parasite. They must place before the Gujarātis models of noble characters, so that the young may be constrained to strive to lead the noble life. In this way only, can Gujarāti authors earn the lasting gratitude of their countrymen.

A. K. DONALD.

CONTENTS

CHAPTER I

INTRODUCTION (1-21)

CHAPTER II (22-29)

EARLY JAIN LITERATURE AND, FORM OF LANGUAGE

CHAPTER III (30-61)

BHAKTIMĀRGA AND POETS OF THE FIFTEENTH CENTURY

CHAPTER IV (68–73)

POETS OF THE SIXTEENTH CENTURY

CHAPTER V (74–199)

POETS OF THE SEVENTEENTH CENTURY

CHAPTER VI (200–228)

POETS OF THE EIGHTEENTH CENTURY

CHAPTER VII (229–333)

POETS OF THE FIRST OF THE NINETEENTH CENTURY

APPENDIX to CHAPTER VII (328–333)

CHAPTER VIII (334-354)

THE INDIGENOUS LITERATURE OF KÂTHIÂWÂD

APPENDIX (355-376)

FOLKLORE LITERATURE IN GUJARĀT

ERRATA

Incorrect	Pages & Line	Correct
along	9, 26 f.	a long
Saurseni	12, 6	Śaurseni
हमतिआरतुं	16, 27 f.	हमजिआरतुं
Bhāndārs	20, 6	Bhandārs
,,	20, 8	,,
Swetāmbar	20, 17	Śwetāmbar
१	22, 13	1
Saṃvat	23, 5	Samvat
,,	23, 7	,,
Sāstri	23, 15	Śāstri
१	25, 13	1
२	25, 20	2
१	25, 21 f.	1
Sutrās	27, 5	Sutras
१	27, 13	1
Tālāja	43, 31	Talājā
Joshipur	43, 37	Joshipurā
Mādhavji's	52, 28 f.	Mādhavji
Presistently	60, 10	Persistently
tarnslation	62, 18	translation
works	73, 26 f.	work
ersort	77, 29 f.	resort
(p. 97–	89. 28 f.	(pp. 97–
Diwān	96, 25 f.	Rāo
घसता र	125, 19	घसता रे
गमे ?	125, 26 f.	गमे ?"

Incorrect	Pages & Line	Correct
it	128, 29	them
bulbuls nightingales	128, 25	bulbul-nightingales-
Rākhidās	135, 20 f.	Rakhidās
(Dhāmanwād)	137, 2	(Gatrād)
(Gatrād)	137, 2	(Dhāmanwād)
Sivdās	163, 2	Śivadās
"	163, 22	"
Sudra	166, 27	Śudra
but it is impossible to say when it was written	167, 23-24 f.	written in (V. S. 1660). See Forbes Gujarāti Sabhā Manuscript List part II pp. 1, 21, 402
yet		yet.
Kunti-prasānnākhyān	173, 8	Kunti-prasannākhyān
vorses	176, 6	verses
लाल	208, 16	लाळ
tilt	218, 26 f.	lilt
Jālā	243, 25 f.	Jalā
au thorof	250, 24 f.	author of
he welcomes	277, 19	She welcomes
(footnote P. 228)	292, 28 f.	no, P. 291

MILESTONES IN GUJARATI LITERATURE

CHAPTER 1

INTRODUCTION

The Gujarati language is the mother-tongue of about ten millions (1,08,49,984) of people in Western India.[1] It comes in rank after Hindi (Western and Eastern), Punjabi, Bengali, Marathi, Rajasthani, Kannad, Telugu and Oriya. It is used not only by Hindus, but by Parsis and Mahomedans alike, and has furnished for centuries a vehicle of thought and expression to these three communities, varying in religion but united in language.

Geographically Gujarat is separated from Kathiawad and Cutch, though linguistically it might be taken as if Gujarāt, Kathiawad and Cutch were one, excepting for the provincialism which is bound to exist in areas, widely differing from each other, in the origin and character of their inhabitants.

Historical Sketch

Gujarāt is the land of Gurjars. Vincent Smith considers them to have been "foreign immigrants, closely associated with, and

1 Besides it is being used by Gujarātis, who have settled down in Ceylon, Burma, Straits Settlements and various parts of Africa in large numbers.

possibly allied in blood to, the White Huns They founded a considerable kingdom in Rājputānā, the capital of which was Bhinmāl or Śrimāl, about fifty miles to the north-west of Mount Ābu. The minor Gurjar kingdom of Broach (Bharooch) was an off-shoot of this kingdom which conquered Kanauj at the beginning of the ninth century."[1] Roughly this kingdom was called Gujarāt or Northern Gujarāt and Rājputānā, and the Southern portion of the same territory was called Lāt[2] or Southern Gujarāt.[3] Kāthiāwād, the home of the Scythians or Kāthis, was originally known as Saurāshtra[4] or Ānarta आनर्त. Disregarding, the very ancient Yādav period, the earliest European record is that of the conquest of this province by Menander (Milinda) about 155–3 B. C. The Edicts of Aśoka (240 B. C.), and of the fourth Śaka Satrap Rudra Dāman (150 A. D.), cut on the rock at Girnār, and the construction of the Sudarśana Lake, by Tushāspha, the Persian Viceroy of Aśoka's grandfather,

1 Early History of India, 2nd Edition, p. 303.

2 "Lāt is said to be the name of a country lying to the West of the Narmadā. It probably included Broach, Baroda and Ahmedabad. and Khaira also according to some."–V. S. Apte. Also Vadnagar, (Ānandpur) according to Hieun Tsang. The boundaries of Lāt have differed at different times.

3 Shāstri Vrajlāl thinks that Broach was the capital of the Lāt Kingdom.

4 At present Saurāshtra is the official name of one of the four divisions of the Political Agency of the province, and includes the territories of the Nawab Saheb of Junāgadh.

Chandragupta, have given Kāthiāwād an important place in the History of Ancient India. The Śakas, a nomadic Central Asian tribe living somewhere north of the Upper Jaxartes, migrated to India about the middle of the second century B. C., and, traversing via Taxilā and Mathurā, the province of Sind, "carved out for themselves a dominion in the Peninsula of Saurāshtra or Kāthiāwād, and some of the neighbouring districts on the mainland." Although they became converts to one or other form of Hindu religion and assumed Indian names,[1] the practices of these foreigners were distasteful to the natives of India, and the Āndhra Kings seem to have conquered the Śakas, but the province of Kāthiāwād again became detached, and along with Sind, Cutch and other Western provinces, passed under the sway of Rudra Dāman, a Śaka Satrap (circa 145 A. D.). The reign of this tribe lasted till about 390 A. D. when Chandragupta II, Vikramāditya, finally overthrew the dynasty. Then the Kings of Kanauj, who belonged to the Gurjar stock of Rājputs, ruled Kāthiāwād, control over which implied also control over Gujarāt and Mālwā. They lost these somewhere about 914 A. D. In Gujarāt the Solankis (Chālukyās)[2] founded an independent king-

1 Vide "Gujarāti Language and Literature" by N. B. Divatiā. Vol. 1, p. 24.

2 These Chālukyās held a considerable kingdom in the Deccan with their capital at Kalyān. Their kingdom flourished for nearly four ot five centuries, with reverses of fortune.

dom with their capital at Aṇhilwād (961 A. D.), Mulrāj being the founder. The first faint traces of the invasion of India by the followers of Islam became visible about this time, and the sack of Somnāth (1024 A. D.) by Mahmud of Ghazni brought the peninsula into prominent historical relief.

Eastern Kāthiāwād boasted of the famous Vallabhi dynasty, which was founded by Bhattārka[1] towards the beginning of the sixth century (509 to 766 A. D.). Their reign lasted till 770 A. D., when the Ārab invaders from Sind overthrew them. Chinese travellers have described the glories of Vallabhipura[2], which ranked in learning with the famous University of Nālanda in Bihār. It was a wealthy city, a centre for the study of Buddhist philosophy. Aṇhilwād Pātaṇ rose on the ruins of Vallabhipura, and it retained its place as the chief city of Western India till Ahmedabad came into prominence in the fifteenth century under Mahomedan rule. The Chāvdās (746 to 942 A. D.), Chalukyās (942 to 1244 A. D.) and Wāghelās (1219 to 1304 A. D.) represented the last traces of native Hindu rule over Gujarāt. Alauddin Khilji dealt the first direct blow to this rule, and then Mahomedan supremacy prevailed till the Marāthās in the eighteenth century overran the province and founded

1 It is not certain whether he was a Gurjar; but he was a foreigner all the same.

2 Modern Valā.

a kingdom at Baroda. How the present British Government took the province from the Marāthās is matter of recent history.

Geographical Boundaries

The limits of modern Gujarāt, i. e., that part of the country in which Gujarāti is the current language of the inhabitants, may roughly be taken as follows:—

It is bounded on the north by the river Banās, which rises near Udaipur and is lost in the Raṇ (desert) of Cutch; on the south by the Damaṇ or Damaṇgangā river, which flows into the sea near Damaṇ; on the east by the province of Mālwā, and the Western Ghāts or Sahyādri range; and on the west by the Gulf of Cutch and the Arabian Sea or Indian Occan.[1]

Linguistic Boundaries

For linguistic purposes North Gujarāt may be taken to be bounded by Sirohi and Mārwār, Thar and Pārkar in Sindh and Cutch also; South Gujarāt by the Damaṇgangā and Thāṇā District; East Gujarāt from Dharampur to the eastern frontier of Pālanpur.[2]

1 Kavi Narmadāshankar has described the boundaries thus:—

उत्तरमां अम्बामात,
पूरवमां काळीमात;
छे दक्षिण दिशमां करन्त रक्षा कुन्तेश्वर महादेव,
ने सोमनाथ ने द्वारकेश ए, पश्चिम केरा देव.

2 'Gujarāt and Its Literature,' by K. M. Munshi pp. 1–2.

Dialects

Though the current saying is that "Speech changes every twelve Kos",[1] there are two principal dialects of modern Gujarāti, viz., Cutchi and Mārwādi. Cutchi is the spoken language of the people of Cutch. They have got no other written language save Gujarāti, which is used for all sorts of written communications, and for the keeping of accounts.

The Mārwādis are scattered over a very large part of Gujarāt, and they speak a peculiar dialect which is an admixture of Brijbhāsba with Gujarāti, and written in characters which are nothing else than a modification of Gujarāti characters, with the vowel marks either omitted or displaced.[2]

Extent of use of Gujarāti

Those who speak this language belong to the three great religions of India,–Hindu, Mahomedan and Zoroastrian. Baniās, Jains, Lohānas, Bhātias, Rājputs, Kolis and Bhils, Memons, Borās, Khojās and Musalmans, along with Parsis, have helped to carry the use of the Gujarāti

1 बार बार गाउए बोली बदलाय.

2 For instance the Mārwādis and even little educated Gujarātis would write कक अज मर गय छ which would read when the vowel marks are supplied काका अजमेर गया छे (Uncle has gone to Ajmer), or काका आजे मरी गया छे (Uncle has died today). Written Persian also partakes of this peculiarity. It is said that the following languages (dialects) have been absorbed into the main language: Surti, Kāthiāwādi, Pārsi Gujārāti, Khārwā, Ghisādi, Anāvalā, Bharuchi, Charotari, Memon, Nāgri, Pātidāri, Bhātiā. Vol 8, Part 1, Census of India (1931) p. 317.

language beyond the borders of India. Natives of Gujarāt are to be met with in Burma, Ceylon, South and East Africa, Siam, Manilla, Hong-Kong, Shanghai, Kobe, Mauritius, Fiji Islands and Straits Settlements, and recently in London and Paris, Berlin, Hamburg, Amsterdam, Vienna and even New York, and though scattered over such a wide area, they are using their mother tongue for purposes of trade and commerce. Indeed, in Burma and Zanzibar and Lamu and Mombassa, even the judicial courts have had to recognise the existence of this language by the appointment of Gujarāti interpreters, and South and East Africa now maintain weekly journals and dailies published in Gujarāti and English. In East Africa they have even founded a Gujarāti Literary Society[1].

Nature of the language

The language is easy and does not present many obstacles to the student. As a conversational language, it is concise, simple, and well-adapted for social and domestic intercourse. Though not possessing a large vocabulary it is flowing and forceful. "To express abstruse metaphysical and scientific disquisitions, it has to borrow largely from Sanskrit. Its simplicity consists in the following particulars. The conjugations of its verbs are few, and less complex than those of English, Sanskrit and Arabic; and it is not overloaded with auxiliaries,

१ गुजराती साहित्योत्तेजक मंडळ—नैरोबी.

articles, prepositions and adverbs. The letters are few and without any combinations except the diacritical or vowel marks. Some of the letters, particularly, च छ झ ठ ड ण त थ द भ together with the nasal and guttural sounds are somewhat difficult for the foreigner to pronounce with accuracy."[1] This characteristic it shares in common with all those vernaculars of India which are derived from Sanskrit, for instance, Bengāli, Hindi, and Marāthi.

Characters, Spelling and Pronunciation

Gujarāti characters are borrowed from Sanskrit, or rather are Sanskrit themselves with a slight modification, the most outstanding being that the top line of each letter is done away with in Gujarāti. The table given below will show at a glance the original and the modified alphabet.

VOWELS

Sanskrit	Gujarāti	Sanskrit	Gujarāti
अ	અ	ऋ	ઋ
आ	આ	ए	એ
इ	ઇ	ऐ	ઐ
ई	ઈ	ओ	ઓ
उ	ઉ	औ	ઔ
ऊ	ઊ	अं	અં

1 For the above I am obliged to the Preface in Mirza Mahomed Cauzim's Dictionary (1846).

CONSONANTS

क	ક	द	દ
ख	ખ	ध	ધ
ग	ગ	न	ન
घ	ઘ	प	પ
ङ	ઙ	फ	ફ
च	ચ	ब	બ
छ	છ	भ	ભ
ज	જ	म	મ
झ	ઝ	य	ય
ञ	ઞ	र	ર
ट	ટ	ल	લ
ठ	ઠ	व	વ
ड	ડ	श	શ
ढ	ઢ	ष	ષ
ण	ણ	स	સ
त	ત	ह	હ
थ	થ	ळ	ળ[1]

The mode of writing these symbols is phonetic, i. e., every sound is represented by a symbol.[2]

1 There is no ળ (ळ) in Sanskrit excepting in the Vedas, अग्निमिळे पुरोहितम्– but only લ (ल). ळ appears in Gujarāti where ल occurs in Sanskrit generally, e. g., कमळ in Gujarāti but कमल in Sanskrit.

2 This is a fit place to notice the great difficulty experienced by foreigners in correctly pronouncing certain words of the Gujarāti Language. There are no marks to distinguish a short sound from along

Mode of Writing

The mode of writing these characters has passed through two intermediate stages after parting company with Sanskrit.

The first is the *Bālabodh* or *Devanāgari* mode, where the Sanskrit mode itself was reproduced with the top-line for each letter kept untouched; and then to obviate the necessity of drawing a small head-line for each symbol after writing its body, a whole or entire line, covering the length of the slate, tablet or paper was drawn beforehand and the symbols written underneath (like the Modi form of writing Marāthi); the latest or most recent mode is to write bald characters without a top-line.

one, when one and the same word pronounced short or long means two different things: e. g., ગોળ pronounced *gol* (the o being long as in *old*) means 'round in shape', while pronounced short as *Gaul*, it means 'treacle.' Similarly though many words are pronounced with an aspirant they may have no provision made in them for writing it: e. g., મારા (mine) is pronounced *Māhrā* મ્હારા though the "h" is not written. There are also great defects in the mode of the spelling of words, for which there are no uniform rules existing. This question is closely connected with that of the correct pronunciation of words, and is engaging the close attention of Gujarāti scholars. Much discussion has taken place but no definite conclusions have yet been arrived at. A Committee was appointed by the Sāhitya Parishad, and it has submitted a report (April 1912) in which an effort is made to lay down some guiding principles in respect of this subject. The Vidyāpitha of Ahmedabad, however, has lately published a જોડણીકોશ; the standard of spelling followed in it is likely to be adopted by a majority of writers, and thus solve the difficulty to a large extent.

Devanāgrí हुं घेर जाउं छुं
Modified હુ ઘેર જાઉ છુ
Modern હું ઘેર જાઉં છું

The correct mode of writing the language is to separate each word from the other by means of a slight distance, but this is generally done only by the educated class. Merchants and other less educated people do not observe this rule. Nor have they yet left off entirely the second mode of writing, i. e., drawing a line overhead. In fact, children are taught to write in that fashion yet, as it serves to guide their hand and keep it straight. In business correspondence and account books this mode is still current.

Origin of the Language

The origin of the language is traced to Sanskrit, i. e., later or Purānic Sanskrit, as distinguished from the language of the Vedās, which is called Mahā Sanskrit. "With the rise of Magadha and the advent of Gautama Buddha, who preferred to preach to nations in the spoken tongue, the Pāli language was recognised as the spoken tongue of Northern India"[1] (circa 500 B. C.) "In the centuries following the Christian Era, the Pāli became gradually replaced by the Prākrits, the spoken dialects of the people. The heroines of Kalidās speak Prākrit, and while Dushyanta makes love in Sanskrit, the beauteous

1 The अर्धमागधी of the Jains.

Śakuntala responds to his love in the softer Prākrit. Vararuchi, one of the "nine gems" of Vikramāditya's court, is the earliest grammarian who recognises the Prākrits in his Grammar, and he distinguishes four distinct dialects of the Prākrit,[1] Viz., *Mahārāshtri*, *Sauraseni*, *Pāiśāchi*, and *Māgādhi*. We may fix the date of this literary recognition of the Prākrit dialects at 500 A. D. The different Prākrits have been modified into the different spoken dialects of modern India."[2] Some say, Gujarāti comes through Śauraseni which was prevalent near Mathurā, from where it passed on to the West, i. e., to the shores of the Indus and thence to Mārwād and Gujarāt, and is thus related to Punjābi, Sindhi and Mārwādi; others think that it is closely related to the Mahārāshtri group. Anyhow, one thing is certain that in its earliest form, where it begins to resemble the present dialect, it is met with in what is called अपभ्रंश.[3] Though it is not noticed by Vararuchi, we find it noticed by Chand, who in his book "Prākrit

1 Prof. A. MacDonell says in his History of Sanskrit Literature, "Between the beginning of our era and about 1000 A. D. mediaeval Prākrit, which is still synthetic in character is divided into four chief dialects. In the West we find *Apa-bhranśa* (decadent) in the valleys of the Indus, and *Çaurseni* in the Doab, with Mathura as its centre. Subdivisions of the latter were *Gaurjari* (Gujarāti), *Avanti*, Western *Rajputāni* and *Mahārāshtri* (Eastern Rajputani)."

2 R. C. Dutt's Literature of Bengal.

3 Apabhramśa literally means deterioration or corruption, and hence a language which is a form of Sanskrit deteriorated or corrupted.

Lakshaṇa" mentions certain rules about it. Dr. Hœrnle, who has edited this book, says that Māgadhi was spoken in Bihār, Bengāl, Orissā and the North-East of Central India. In the North-West, in Western India and in some parts of Southern India, Sāmānya Prākrit (Mahārāshtri) was current. The Apabhramśa was spoken in those parts of Northern India which are situated to the east of the Indus, but from certain inscriptions and forms of words found on the Girnār and in earlier Gujarāti writers, it is possible to conceive also that Mahāsāshtri and Sauraseni were also prevalent there at one time. The Apabhramśa form of the language has been specially recognised in his Grammar by Hemachandrāchārya, the most literary of Jain Āchāryas, who flourished in the reigns of Siddharāj and Kumārpāla, but he has not told us whether it was current in his time in Gujarāt or not, nor has he stated where it was in use, but it is conjectured from the copious illustrations given by him of Apabhramśa that it must have been a spoken tongue in his time. This Grammar was composed in 1168 Samvat year (1112 A. D.), and therefore, there is very good reason to believe that even before then it was in general use.[1]

1 As to the state of the language and literature before the Apabhramśa and old Gujarāti period, see Jain Gurjar Kavio, Part 1, by Mohanlal Dalichand Desai (1926). He has been able to give a couple of instances of the spoken language in the 9th century of the Samvat era from a poem called Kuvalaya Mālā (V, S. 835) by Udyotan Suri.-Section VII, Chapter III of the Preface, p. 317.

Without going into minute details, it would not be improper to adopt the conclusion of Diwan Bahadur K. H. Dhruvā,[1] a most eminent philological scholar of Gujarāt, that the history of the language could be divided into three periods.

Three periods

1. From the tenth or eleventh century A. D., to the fourteenth. This might be called the Apabhramśa or old Gujarāti period.

2. From the fifteenth to the seventeenth century: this might be called the middle Gujarāti period.

3. From the seventeenth century onwards, modern or new Gujarāti period.

Thus it might be safely said that what Mr. Dutt calls "literary recognition" was accorded to old Gujarāti or Apabhramśa in about the tenth century, and so far as this part of India was concerned, it was the last modification of Prākrit.

Some Words

The following words are देशी or देश्य, i. e., they are not derived from Sanskrit, but were already prevalent in the country, when it came in contact with Sanskrit. A long list of these words is given by Hemachandra in his work called दशीनाममाळा. ढंकुण (a bug) the Prākrit equivalent being मक्कुण (Sanskrit मत्कुण) Gujarāti मांकण or मांकड; बोलवुं (to

1 See his Presidential Address p. 3, l. 32–36, Second Gujarātī Sāhitya Parishad, Bombay.

speak) is from बोल. रोडुं, झांखरुं, धाबळी, खोळीउं, खाबडुं, ढोबरुं, बाचको are pure देश्य words. The following words have come direct from Sanskrit without the intermediation of Prākrit:—

विजोग from वियोग
धीरज from धैर्य
करम from कर्म

A majority of words have come through the intermediate Prākrit, e. g ,

Gujarāti	Prākrit	Sanskrit
हइडुं	हिअअं (इं)	हृदयम्
सूडो	सुअडो	शुकः
घेलो	गहिअ(लो) / गहेलो	गृहीतः
आप	अप्पा	आत्मा
घउं	गोहुमो	गोधूमः
मेलुं	मइलं	मलिनम्

A number of words are used in their pure Sanskrit form: भय, पूर्व, पश्चिम etc.

The modern tendency is to use words in their pure Sanskrit form, ignoring the intermediate stages. A writer would now discard the form अरथ and use its Sanskrit original अर्थ, गर्दभ and not गरधब, नियम and not निम, so राज्य and not राज.

There is an admixture of Portuguese words like मोसंबी sweet lemon (lime), आफुस the alphonso variety of Mango, French words like पलटण a regiment, and also Marāthi, Persian and Arabic words in the language, the result of the province having passed under the political control of some of these nations, or having come in close contact at different times with those who spoke that particular language. Many English words have now found a permanent home in Gujarāti.

Early state of Literature in Gujarāt

Before giving some illustrations of the literature of the Apabhramsa, it would be just as well to see how Gujarāt stood in history and what sort of literature was in existence there before the rise of this vernacular literature, so that we might know what it inherited from the older culture. The Rājputs ruled over Gujarāt between A. D. 746 and 1298, and various Sanskrit works were written during that period both by the Brahmins and the Jains.[1] But about the tenth century Apabhramśa

1 It would surprise the present generation of Pārsis,—whose language was Pārsik (Pehalvi)-and who landed in Gujarāt in the eighth century-to learn that they too have contributed to the literature of Gujarāt in its early form, and that their religious books were translated from Pehalvi into Sanskrit and thence into Gujarāti. The "Arda Virāf Nāmā" was translated from Pehalvi into Sanskrit, and thence into Gujarāti; the poet calls the language "पराक्रस्त" (=प्राकृत), in another Nāmeh written by him-p. 3 of मोबेद रूस्तम पेशोतन हमतिआरनुं जरतोस्तनामुं by Meherbanu Behrāmgor and Behrāmgor T. Ankalesaria (1932). A manuscript copy of Arda Virāf Nāmā was made in Samvat year 1507 (A. D, 1451), by Behrām Lakhamidhar (mark the resemblance

began to come into use and several *Rāsās* in praise of Rājput Kings were written in it by Bhāts and Chāraṇs, and stories and poems in praise of wealthy and religious persons by Jain Sādhus. Their language was a mixture of Mārwādi, Vraj and other vernaculars, and the birth of Gujarāti was thus heralded by these court-poets in a language spoken by the people in contra-distinction to the learned language, Sanskrit, which was exclusively used by the Brāhmins and Jain Ácharyas. Pāli and Māgadhi respectively were used as learned languages by Bauddh and Jain religious writers. The use of Prākrit was considered vulgar by Brāhmins, and Prākrit works were being translated into Sanskrit; this exclusiveness was overcome after a very long time, and that too owing to political causes. Even then, Vraj and Hindi reigned supreme amongst the Prākrits, and as pointed out above, it was not until the tenth century that Apabhramśa or primitive Gujarāti could take a place among these more cultured tongues.

State of Literature during early Musalmān period

Even in the Musalmān period that followed the Rājput domination, say from A. D. 1298 to 1420, when the Mahomedans conquered Aṇhilwād, Cambay, Somnāth, Gondal, Junāgadh, Idar and ultimately laid the

of the latter name to a Hindu one). The "Minoi Khirad" was treated similarly in about 1613 Samvat year (1554 A. D.). See also p. 62 of the preface of Anklesariās' book where they refer to having seen a Mss. of the Khordāh Avestā translated into Gujarāti, about 600 years old.

foundation of Ahmedābād (1412 A. D.), the languages most in use were Sanskrit and Prākrit. The literature was almost entirely religious, and with the exception of only one non-Jain author it was wholly kept alive by Jain Sādhus. The Brāhmins and other classes were entirely silent. The sun of their glory had set with the fall of the Rājputs. The reason[1] given by Mr. G. M. Tripāthi as to why these Sādhus alone were able to keep burning the torch of literature, while there was darkness all round, is this: with the fall of Aṇhilwād and the consequent insecurity of person and property due to the advent of the Mahomedans, the energy of the Brāhmins, Baniās and other well-to-do classes, who alone could be thought in any way interested in letters, was absorbed in the anxions task of discovering places of security and settling in them. They entered, therefore, on an era of wandering, and scattered themselves over all parts of Northern India as far as Benāres and Mathurā.[2] This state of mind was not in the least calculated to foster a spirit of reading, writing, or study. On the other hand, the Jain Sādhus had got the protecting arm of their Gachchhās (गच्छ) over them, and were thus able to live quietly and peacefully and carry on undisturbed their studies in religion and

1 See his Presidential Address at the first Gujarāti Sāhitya Parishad, Ahmedabad, 1905.

2 Famines, earthquakes, floods, wars and similar natural calamities must have been other contributory causes of their migration.

literature. They were further able to preserve the purity of their language,[1] because, being ascetics, they were more or less removed from contact with those who were following worldly avocations, while Brāhmins, Baniās and others daily came in contact with their Mahomedan rulers on the one hand, and Bhils, Kolis and other aborigines on the other, with the result that the purity of their language was affected. Owing to such a combination of circumstances, the influence of Sanskrit and other learned languages and literature began to wane, and the birth of a new language, a mixture of Deśi (the language spoken by the masses), Prākrit, Hindi and cognate tongues, and its development, arrest our attention. The seeds of early Gujarāti literature were sown in the beginning of the fifteenth century. Southern India was as yet free from the inroads of the iconoclastic followers of Islām, and was able to pursue peacefully its great religious campaign, which culminated in the advent of such renowned Āchāryas, as Rāmānujāchārya and Madhvāchārya, the great refuters of Śankarāchārya's philosophy (about the twelfth century). The echoes of their preaching

1 Jains believe that the preservation of the purity of the language is a holy behest; its non-preservation a sin. Duhās, proverbs, and apopthegms, were largely used by Jain Sādhus in their discourses to the laity: variants in their text are not due to impurity of language but to the difference in the dialect of the locality where they were spoken or to passage of time. Even now some Jain Sadhus write in the old language.

and teaching penetrated into Gujarāt too about this time, and influenced its people.

Extensive unpublished Jain Literature

There is a number of Jain books, which can be counted by millions, which are still unpublished, lying untouched or uninspected in the several Bhāndārs, scattered all over the country. These are contained in the Bhāndārs of Pātaṇ, Cambay, Ahmedābād, Jesalmere and the libraries of several Apāsarās (Jain temples), as well as in the collections of private individuals. They thus remained concealed during the insecure days of Mahomedan rule, and the feeling that these books being sacred should not be exposed to public view is still held by many. The variety of this concealed literature and its wide extent can be gauged by a reference to a very useful book called the Jain Granthāvali (a list of Jain books), published by the Jain Swetāmbar conference of Bombay (1910 A. D.) as also to the two large volumes "Jain Gurjar Kavio", Parts I and II (1926 and 1931) and "A short History of Jain literature" (1933) by Mohanlal Dalichand Desai B. A., LL. B. The Jains were a great force in the time of Vanrāj, who was brought up by a Jain Sādhu Śilagunasuri,[1] and during the reigns of Siddharāj and Kumārpāl they far outstripped the Brāhmins, and attained to the zenith of their power.

1 The Modh Brāhmins believe that their fellow castemen of Modherā had brought up Vanrāj (vide धर्मारण्य of स्कन्दपुराण).

It was at this time that they wrote most, and produced the Pāṇini[1] of Gujarāti literature, Hemachandrāchārya. But the Brāhmins regained their position during the reign of Ajayapāl and his descendants, and beat them back, and were able to create such a prejudice against them that they have left a saying to this effect; that if you are pursued by a mad elephant, though a Jain temple be near, it is better to be killed than take protection therein: हस्तिना ताड्यमानोऽपि न विशेज्जिनमन्दिरम्.

1 Hemchandrāchārya states in his well-known Grammar सिद्धहैम that he wrote it at the request of Siddharāj. It is said that Siddharāj was so much pleased with it that he arranged to have it brought to his Darbar, on his own adorned elephant, in a procession and worshipped it as if it were सरस्वती, the Goddess of Learning herself.

CHAPTER II

EARLY JAIN LITERATURE AND FORM OF LANGUAGE

Early Jain Works and Rāsās.

Rāsās are a peculiar poetical form of composition affected by Jain Sādhus, with the object of instructing the people in religion and morals, and hence, they were written in a tongue which they (the masses) could understand.[1] A useful list of about three to four hundred Rāsās is published by a Jain author, Mansukhlal Kiratchand Mehta.[2] They range in date from fourteen hundred Vikrama Samvat (even earlier)[3] to nineteen

1 बालस्त्रीमन्दमूर्खाणां नृणां चारित्र्यकांक्षिणाम्
अनुग्रहार्थं तत्त्वज्ञैः सिद्धान्तः प्राकृतः कृतः ।
(सिद्धसेन दिवाकर)

2 Mr. Mohanlal Dalichand Desai's two large volumes of Jain Gurjar Poets, already referred to, also deal very comprehensively with Rāsās (13th to 18th century of the Vikrama Era).

3 A Rāsā called सप्तक्षेत्री रास composed in Samvat year 1327, and another work, called उपदेशमाला by Ratnasinhsūri are instances in point. The following couplet from the उपदेशमाला shows the state of the language then-i. e., about Samvat year 1347, when it is said to have been composed.

विजय नरिंद जिणिंद, वीरहत्थी हिंवय लेविणु,
धम्मदास गणिनामि गमि, नयरिहिं विहरू पुणुं.

A King called Vijaya was initiated (into Sādhuship) by Virjinendra, and he was thereafter named Dharamdās Gaṇi. Śri Jain Śwetāmbar Conference Herald. January-February, 1913. p. 33.

hundred (A. D. 1344 to A. D. 1800). They incidentally throw a great light on the history of Gujarāt, political, literary and social. The earliest (excluding those mentioned in the foot-notes) of such Rāsās are क्षेमप्रकाश written about (Vikrama Saṃvat) 1410 by Jayānandsuri and भारतबाहुबलीरास by Guṇaratnasuri, हंसराज वछराज and शीळरास in Saṃvat year 1411 by Vijayabhadra, गौतमस्वामी or रास by Udayavant Vijayabhadrasuri in 1412, and मदनरेखा(मयणरेहा) in 1413 by Harsevak.

Illustrations of Apabhramśa poetry

The following instances of poetry written in Apabhramśa which are generally referred to by those who are interested in this branch of literature, are taken from (I) Hemchandra's writings and from the Essay on Gujarāti language written by the late Śāstri Vrajlāl Kālidās, a pioneer in this department.

सन्ता भोग जु परिहरइ तस कन्तए बलि किस ।
तस दई वेण विमुंडियुं जस बल्लि हउ हंसीस ॥

We should sacrifice ourselves for a husband who eschews enjoyments even though they are near: God himself has shaved the head of one who is bald: those who have got no enjoyments near, perforce forego them (i. e., there is no sacrifice involved in doing so).

Mr. Mohanlal Dalichand Desai mentions a still earlier Rāsā (Samwat year 1241) भरतेश्वर बाहुबलीरास of Bali Bhadra Suri. Jain Gurjar Kavio. Vol. I. p. I.

काती करवत कापतां, वहिलउ आवइ छेह ।
नारी विंध्या टलवलइ, जाजीवइ ता देह ॥

Those who are wounded by a knife or saw, die soon; but the bodies of those who (whose hearts) are pierced by women writhe as long as they live.

आगि दाधा पाल्हवइ छेद्या वाधइ वृक्ष ।
नारि हुताशनि जाळिया छार उडउयिया लक्ष ॥

Trees burnt by fire sprout leaves again, trees which are cut down grow again, but (millions of) men scorched by women are blown about like ashes.

अट्ठोत्तरसु बुद्धडी रावणतणइ कपालि ।
एकू बुद्धि न सांपडी लंका-भंजण-कालि ॥

Rāvaṇ was endowed with very great intellect (7,800 kinds of intelligence) but not even one (of them) was of any use to him at the time when Lankā fell.

These are extracts from Munjrājprabandh, written by Merutung Āchārya, in A. D. 1305. The Gautamrāsā written in Samvat year 1412 (A. D. 1356) contains two छन्दs called [1]वत्थु(वस्तु)छन्द and भाषाछन्द. The former, Mr. Mansukhlal Ravjibhai, another scholar of Jain literature, suspects to have been written by some one before the fourteenth century and inserted in the poem. It reads thus:—

1 वत्थु(वस्तु) means a summary or substance. It describes by way of a preface what the reader is to expect in that particular part of the composition. This summary is given in Prākrit, while the Chhand or real composition is written in the Gujarāti of the period.

वस्तु छंद–इण अनुक्रमे इण अनुक्रमे नाणसंपन्न,
पन्नरहसय परवरिय हरिय दिय दुजिणनाह वन्दे;
जाणवि जगगुरु वयण तिह नाण अपाण निन्दे,
चरम जिणेसर इम भणे, गोयम म करिस खेऊ;
छेह जई आपण सही, होसुं तुला बेउं.

This is another extract from the same **work written** in the

भाषा छंद–जिम सुरतरुवर सोहे शाखा,
जिम उत्तम मुख मधुरी भाषा;
जिम वनकेतकी महमहे ए,
जिम भूमिपति भुयबल चमके;
जिम जिनमन्दिर घंटा रणके,
तिम गोयम लब्धे गहगहे ए.[1]

At the end the author writes

चउदहसय बारोत्तर वरसें,
गोयम गणहर केवळ दिवसें;
किउं कवित उपगार करो,
आदिहिं मंगळ एह पभणिजे;
परव महोच्छव पहिलो लीजें,
ऋद्धि वृद्धि कल्याण करो.[2]

१ रायचन्द्र जैन काव्यमाळा, गुच्छक पहेलो, पानुं २८.

2 **To those who** are interested in this Rāsā, the following longer **extract is sure to give delight.** It is a beautiful picture of scenes of **nature, and well depicted.**

जिम सहकारे कोयल टहुके,
जिम कुसुम वने परिमल महके,
जिम चंदन सुगंधनिधि;

जिम गंगाजल लहेरे लहेके,
जिम कयणाचल तेजे झलके,
तिम गोयम सौभाग्यनिधि;

In the following Samvat year i. e., 1413 Harmunī (or Harsevak) wrote his मयणरेहा:

गाम कुकडीये कर्यो चोमासो,
संवत् चौदा तेरोमांयो;
कथा कारण आ रास ज कीधो,
हरसेवक चित्त लायो;
साधां रे तमे मुळ सांभळज्यो
चरित मयणरेहारो;
तिण उपरी कांई अधिका ऊछो,
मिच्छा दुक्कड मारो.

In 1450 (A. D. 1394) a book called Mugdhāvabodh Auktik was written in Gujarāti by a Jain to explain the rules of Sanskrit grammar. The language is not exactly Apabhramśa but at the same time it is not the modern Gujarāti:

जेह तउ हुं तउ थउ थकउ इत्यादि बोकि वईजेहे वस्तु नई परित्याग सूचीई अपादान.

In the same year Śri Somasundaraji wrote a Rāsā called Ārādhanā Rāsā.

जिम मानसरोवर निवसे हंसा,
जिम सुरवरसिरिं कयणे वतंसा,
जिम महुयर राजीपदनी;
जिम रयणायर रयणें विलसे,
जिम अंबर तारागण विकसे,
तिम गोयम गुण केलिवनी.

पुनिमनिशि जिम ससियर सोहे,
सुरतरुमहिमा जिम जग मोहे,
पुरव दिसि जिम सहसकरु,
पंचायण जिम गिरिवर राजे,
नरवर घर जिम मयगल गाजे,
तिम जिनशासन मुनिपवरु.

Instances of early Gujarāti Prose

About Samvat year 1455 (A. D. 1399) Śri Muni Sundar Suri wrote a Rāsa called "Śānta Rāsa," both in prose and poetry. In the next century Jain Sādhus translated many Sutrās into Gujarāti. A specimen of prose written in Samvat year 1529 (A. D. 1463) is taken from the Introduction to the Narma Kośa.

पाडलीपुर नगर तिहां नंदनउ शत्रु चंद्रगुप्त राजा तेहनउ प्रधान चाणिक्य प्रतिबिम्बथकउ राज्य भोगवई; परं भंडारी द्रव्य नहि तेहभणी, देवता आराधी पासा पामी स्वर्णथाल भरी जुवटई बईठु; जे के, मझनइं जीपइ ते थाल सोनैईए भरिउं लिउ अनई तुम्हेवु एक दीनार दिउ. एम देवतादत्त पासे करी जीपवा लागउ किवा हरईकोई देवतादत्त पासे हुं ते जीपई पणि मानवजन्म हारविउ दोहिलउ पामई.'

Nature of works written during this period

Instances of prose and poetry written during this period can be multiplied from sources some of which have now been revealed through the studies of Gujarāti Jains, who have taken a leading part in unearthing

1 Śastri Vrajlāl Kālidas gives some instances of earlier prose written somewhere between 1400 and 1481 A. D. from books treating of (1) Rituals (2) Medicine and (3) Jewels, from which only short extracts are selected, as there is no very outstanding line of cleavage between them and the more recent extract given above.

` लघु बालक दंत विना मरइ ।तहनुं सूतक दिन १ । ।क्षोर कर्म्म करीउं हुई ।तहनुं सूतक. दिन ३ ॥ २ ॥ करंज मूल गाई तणइं मूत्रसूं पीजइ हरस जाइ। छास सुउं पाकउं बीलुँ पीजइ हरस जाइ ॥३॥ मोतिनुं पहिलउ आगर सिंधलद्विप जाणिवउ बिजइ आगर आरब ।दश जाणिवउ. त्रीजइ आगर पारसीक ।दश जाणिवउ। चउवउ आगर बावर (सं० बर्बर) ।दश जाणिवउ।

their old manuscripts, but, beyond emphasizing the fact that there was a goodly amount of (old) Gujarāti literature in existence, not in a crude form, or a form which marks the early struggles of a rising literature, but in a form which could be taken to be an advanced–if not a finished–one for the circumstances then obtaining, they would not be of great use to us for our present purposes. Religious topics, popular tales,[1] biography, rituals, medicine and other useful subjects were intelligently treated by these writers, and the common popular belief till now obtaining, that with Narsinh Mehtā (A. D. 1414–1481) began the rise of Gujarāti literature, and that he should therefore be honoured as the Father of that literature, has to be abandoned, and the date of its rise pushed back several centuries.

Form of language can be traced backwards

A scientific treatment of this subject is beyond the scope of a manual like this. But the form assumed by the language now current, tracing it step by step backwards from middle and old Gujarāti to Prākrit and Sanskrit, grammtically, is not an impossible thing, as is shown by scholars of the calibre of the late Rao Bahadur Sir Ramanbhai Nilkanth, Dewan Bahadur Keshavlal H. Dhruva and the late Mr. N. B. Divatia. Pho-

1 Instances of stories written in prose by Jain Sādhns in the XIV and XV centuries are to be found at pp.-92-96 of 'Gujarāta and Its Literature' (1935) by K. M. Munshi.

netic changes, the formation of new words by analogy, and various other elements which contribute to the evolution of a language have also influenced Gujarāti at various periods of its growth, and the curious reader would find much to interest him in the works of these scholars.[1]

1 The following is a short table given to show changes introduced into Sanskrit words in their passage from Sanskrit into Gujarāti through Prākrit.

सं.	पनस	पिबति	तीक्ष्णम्
प्रा.	फणसो	पिअइ	तिक्खं
जुनी गु.	......	पिअइ	”
गु.	फणस	पीए	तीखुं

CHAPTER III

BHĀKTI MĀRGA AND POETS OF THE FIFTEENTH CENTURY

Religion the main-spring of early poetry

It has been remarked somewhere that poetry and religion are inseparable in India. This is eminently true of early Gujarāti poetry. The trend of it, even before the time of Narsinh and Mirānbai, was religious. The Rāsās have their origin in the desire of the Jain Sādhus to teach religion and morals to the masses through a tongue spoken by them, and the poems treating of the social and domestic concerns of the people are very few in number compared with those relating to morals and religion.[1] Consequently, when we emerge on the period, beginning with 1400 A. D., where we have got more solid ground to rest upon in the shape of more known and more popular works, we must not

1 Mr. Ambālāl B. Jāni, B. A., in his Introduction (pp. 10-12) to Shri Harililā Shodash Kalā-(1930, published by the Gujarāt Vernacular Society, Ahmedabad)-the work of an old Gujarāti poet Vishnudas Bhim-cites a number of works on non-religious subjects, such as (i) history (ii) folk and other stories (iii) Śringār (erotics) (iv) Purāṇas, Rāmāyaṇa, Mahābhārat and Ākhyāns (v) Shiv-Śakti Bhakti and (vi) philosophy, all written between Samvat years 1388 and 1600. This, he does, with a view to show that religion and particularly the loves of Rādhā and Krishṇa alone did not furnish the subject matter of the compositions of the time. Writers both Jains and non-Jains did not confine themselves only to these subjects.

be surprised to find a continuity in the subject-matter of poetical compositions. Religion in various forms, constituted the staple food of most of these singers. The Jains praised their own saints, Māhāvir and the Tirthankars, and among non-Jains, worship assumed the form of devotion to Lord Krishṇa and was called the Bhākti Mārga. Rāma and Shiva were also devoutly sung by poets like Bhālaṇ and others.

Bhakti Mârga or Krishṇa worship

A very able exposition of this subject is made by Mr. L. J. Sedgwick, I. C. S., in a lecture printed in Vol. XXIII, No. LXV of the Journal of the Bombay Branch of the Royal Asiatic Society (1910). He describes Bhakti to be "personal faith in a personal God, love for him as for a human being, the dedication of everything to his service, and the attainment of Moksha[1] by this means, rather than by knowledge or sacrifice, or works." Leaving the Upanishads aside, he finds the first germ of this cult in the Bhagvad Gitā, and specially in Chapter IX (26-29) which he translates thus:—

1 The same idea, but in a more developed form had been put forward in 1892 by a Gujarāti scholar of acknowledged ability, Mr. Govardhanrām M. Tripāthi, B. A., LL. B., in his "Classical Poets of Gujarāt and their Influence on Society and Morals." He thus describes Bhakti: "The soul and spirit of this new religion was Bhakti, a word which, with its numerous associations, has no English word for it. Worship, prayer and even devotion are words which fall short of the full connotation of Bhakti. It means, standing in the presence of God, serving Him, loving Him, being loved by him, talking to Him, seeing Him, and in fact enjoying the Deity."

"He who with Bhakti makes me (Krishṇa) an offering of a leaf, a flower, a fruit or water, I accept it (lit: eat it) because it is offered with Bhakti, and comes from one whose personality is pure. Whatever you do, whatever you eat, whatever you sacrifice, whatever you give away, whatever penance you perform, O Son of Kunti, do it as if offered to me. Thus you will be released from the bonds of Karma with their fruits both pleasant and unpleasant, and being released, and having your personality filled with renunciation and Yoga, you will attain to me. I am alike in the case of all living things. One is not hateful to me, nor another dear. But they who worship me with Bhakti, they are in me and I am in them."[1]

This idea marks the first stage of this cult, namely, "the conception of personal dedication of self, and the things of self to God. The idea of mutual affection was still to be evolved." It came centuries after.

The second wave of Bhakti came about a thousand years later, and it took a literary shape. In the mean-

१ पत्रं पुष्पं फलं तोयं यो मे भक्त्या प्रयच्छति ।
तदहं भक्त्युपहृतमश्नामि प्रियतात्मनः ॥ २६ ॥
यत्करोषि यदश्नासि यज्जुहोषि ददासि यत् ।
यत्तपस्यसि कौंतेय तत्कुरुष्व मदर्पणम् ॥ २७ ॥
शुभाशुभफलैरेवं मोक्ष्यसे कर्मबन्धनैः ।
संन्यासयोगयुक्तात्मा विमुक्तो मामुपैष्यसि ॥ २८ ॥
समोऽहं सर्वभूतेषु न मे द्वेष्योऽस्ति न प्रियः ।
ये भजन्ति तु मां भक्त्या मयि ते तेषु चाप्यहम् ॥ २९ ॥

while the worship of Krishṇa, the boy cowherd, had taken a strong root in a very large portion of the Indian continent. Various views have been put forward to explain the origin of this personality. Some say he was a syncretism. They speculate that Krishṇa was the result of several contradictory characters being combined into one: a drunken brawler and robber of Dwārkā, a dark sungod, a wild lovable hero of the North-West valleys and the child of Mathurā,–these five persons blended made up one divine Krishṇa. This is the opinion of a European scholar quoted by Mr. Sedgwick. It is a theory which no Indian mind will be prepared to accept without doing great violence to its sentiment.

Attempts have also been made to connect Krishṇa with the worship of the divine child of Christianity. But it is not material for us to find out and account for the origin of this phase of emotional religion in India. The fact is there that about eleventh century it had spread largely over India. In South India Rāma seems to have received the attention of Bhaktas; in North India, Central India and Bengal,[1] Krishṇa; in the Deccan and West Karnātic, Vitthala. The names are different, (Rāma, Hari, Krishṇa, Vitthala) but the

1 Jayadev, the famous Bihāri poet wrote his immortal Gita Govinda, a rhapsody on the amours of Krishṇa and Rādhā in the twelfth century. It is translated into English by Sir Edwin Arnold as the Song of the Lord.

spirit in which the Bhakti is offered to them is the same. The effects of this wave, a highly developed Bhakti, which now meant mutual affection, partaking of physical emotion, and what is more important, ignoring all caste distinctions (even a low caste man can obtain this best of all spiritual treasures by Bhakti) seem to have touched Gujarāt somewhere about the end of the fourteenth and beginning of the fifteenth century, and produced the two celebrated singers Mirān Bāi (1403–1470) and Narsinh Mehtā[1] (1415–1481).

1. From his Presidential speech delivered at the inaugural meeting of the first Gujarāti Literary Conference at Ahmedābād in 1905, Mr. Govardhanrām Tripāthi seems to be of opinion that this flame of Bhakti began to burn in the bosoms of Mirān Bāi and Narsinh Mehtā of its own accord, i. e., they were both uninfluenced by the preachings or teachings of any outsider. Vallabhāchārya, the great founder of the Krishṇa-worship cult on the western side of India, came later (he was born in 1479 A. D.), and Chaitanya, who spread Vaishnavism in Bengal, was born a few years after (1485). Surdās who wrote on Rādhā and Krishṇa in Hindi also flourished later, so that he is of opinion that these two poets struck out a path for themselves independently of any teachings from outside Gujarāt—a circumstance not very likely. As against this is to be considered the following theory of his put forward in his Classical Poets (p. 19): "It seems the missionaries of the new religion of Bhakti were roaming about the whole of Gujarāt at this time [he is describing the time in which Mirān Bāi and Narsinh Mehtā wrote] and charming the people with a religion, which, while it allowed people like Mirān to pass an ascetic life, peopled their brains with the fairyland visions of Krishṇa."

Mr. Ambālāl B. Jāni B. A, in his Introduction to the Hari Līlā Shodash Kalā, Mr. K. M. Munshi, in Gujarāt and Its Literature, and Dr.

Fifteenth Century: Mirān Bāi, the premier poetess of Gujarāt

Colonel Todd, the celebrated historian of Rājputāna, thus alludes to Mirān Bāi: "Kumbho (the brave Rānā of Mewār who succeeded to his father's throne in A. D. 1491) married a daughter of Mairtā (correctly Medtā), the first of the clans of Mārwār. Mirān Bāi was the most celebrated princess of her time for beauty and romantic piety. Her compositions were numerous, though better known to the worshippers of the Hindu Apollo, than to the ribald bards. Some of her odes and hymns to the deity are preserved and admired. Whether she imbibed her poetic piety from her husband or whether he caught from her the sympathy which produced the "sequel to the Song of Govinda" (Gita Govinda), we cannot determine. Her history is a romance and her excess of devotion at every shrine of the favourite deity with the fair (sex) of Hind from the Yamunā to the "World's end" (Dwārkā), gave rise to many tales of scandal."

N. A. Thoothi, in the Vaishanavas of Gujarāt (1935), amongst others, have treated this subject elaborately and from a point of view different from that given here. Mr. Ambālāl B. Jāni has tried to prove that the cult of Krishṇa as well as Vishnu Bhakti were firmly established in the province long before the time of Narsinh Mehtā, that the Dwārkāpitha itself was not the exclusive stronghold of Shankar and that the Shankarāchāryas of this Pitha preached Vishnu Bhakti, as they were not the detractors of Vishnu, because Nārāyan was their greatest Guru (परम गुरु). Vide pp. 20-23 of the Introduction to Vol. I, Hari Lilā Shodash Kalā.

Incidents in her life

There is a great conflict of opinion as to the time when Mirān Bāi was born and lived. The generally received date is somewhere near A. D. 1403. She is said to have lived for 67 years, and died in A. D. 1470. In her case, however, very scant correct biographical details can be had, because whatever little we know about her is hedged round with romantic incidents; for instance, it is said that Emperor Akbar and his famous musician Tānsen went to visit her. Now that would take her down to the sixteenth century A. D. The historian of Mewār, Deviprasād, and the famous poet of the same province, Kavi Śāmaldās, try to make her out to be the wife not of Kumbho, but of Bhojrāj. Some make her the daughter-in-law of Rāṇā Sanga who fought so valiantly against Bābar. The question as to whose wife she was is not of any importance,[1] for she did not

1. The story is current-it may be an apocryphal one-that Mirān and her child companions were playing a game of वरवहु i. e., playing at being husband and wife. Mirān in order to give an air of reality to the play asked her mother to marry her. The latter did not like the request and placed before her an idol of Lord Krishṇa and said "Marry Him." Since that time it is said that Mirān considered herself wedded to Krishṇa. When she became of marriageable age, her mother told her that she would be given in marriage to Rāṇā Bhojrāj. She replied "Mother! my husband is Krishṇa. You yourself have given me in marriage to Him." In spite of her protest, however she was given away, in marriage, as proposed by her mother. All the same, she ever afterwards, remained devoutly attached to Krishṇa.

agree with her husband and her husband's people. She was brought up as a follower of Vishnu (Krishṇa), while her husband and his people worshipped Śiva, and the dispute occurred on the very first night after her marriage. From some of her songs one would gather that she had made up her mind to marry only the Lord of her heart, Krishṇa, and that she did not want to have any corporeal husband, but that against her wishes she was joined in wedlock to the Rānā of Mewār; for, as soon as she was asked by her husband's sister to bow to Mahādev, the presiding deity of the family, she refused to do so, and said that she had dedicated herself to Krishṇa. The Rāṇā goaded by his sister then tried various means to bring his fair spouse to book, but all to no purpose. Similarly Mirān also tried to persuade him to adopt her tenents of belief but the Rāṇā was found to be obdurate, and she ultimately left his protection and went to Dwārkā, where she passed the rest of her life in serving Krishṇa, and consorting with his followers, mostly Sādhus.

Even in her husband's house, she would behave in that way, and this naturally gave rise to a great deal of scandal, which the Rāṇā ultimately wanted to put a stop to by giving her poison. She took it, but by a miracle it was changed to nectar. The following verses of hers mention some of these coercive measures adopted by her husband.[1]

"Govind (Krishṇa) is my Lord and for the whole world I feel a dislike. I adore my Rāmji, none other is worth anything in my eye. In the palace of Mirān Bāi live those (Sādhus) who love Hari. Hari lives away from the falsehearted (men like the Rāṇā), but He always lives near my Sādhus. The Rāṇā sends a letter to

1. गोविन्दो प्राण अमारो रे, मने जग लाग्यो खारो रे;
मने मारो रामजी भावे रे, बीजो मारी नजरे न आवे रे.
मीरांबाईना महेलमां रे, हरि संतननो वास;
कपटीथी हरि दूर वसे, मारा संतन केरी पास. गोविन्दो.
राणोजी कागळ मोकले रे, दो राणी मीराने हाथ;
साधुनी संगत छोडी द्यो, तमो वसोने अमारे साथ. गोविन्दो.
मीरांबाई कागळ मोकले रे, देजो राणाजीने हाथ;
राजपाट तमे छोडी राणाजी ! वसो साधुने साथ. गोविन्दो.
विषनो प्यालो राणे मोकल्यो रे, देजो मीरांने हाथ;
अमृत जाणी मीरां पी गयां, (जेने) सहाय श्री विश्वनो नाथ. गोविन्दो.
सांढवाळा सांढ शणगारजे रे, जावुं सो सो रे कोश;
राणाजीना देशमां रे मारे, जळ रे पीधानो दोष. गोविन्दो.
डाबो मेल्यो मेवाड रे, मीरां गई पश्चिम मांय;
सरव छोडी मीरां नीसर्यां, जेनुं मायामां मनडुं न कांय. गोविन्दो.
सासु अमारी सपुमणा रे, ससरो प्रेम संतोष;
जेठ जगजीवन जगतमां मारो, ना व लि यो नि र्दो ष. गोविन्दो.
चुंदडी ओढुं त्यारे रंग चुवे रे, रंग बेरंगी होय;
ओढुं हुं काळो कांबळो, दुजो डाघ न लागे कोय. गोविन्दो.
मीरां हरिनी लाडणी रे, रहेती संत हजूर;
साधु संगाथे स्नेह घणो, पेला कपटीथी दिल दूर. गोविन्दो.

be delivered into the hands of Mirān in which he asks her to give up the company of the Sādhus and live with him. Mirān sends a reply to be delivered into the hands of the Rāṇāji, requesting him to abdicate his throne and live in the society of the Sādhus. The Rāṇā sent a cup full of poison to be given to Mirān, and she drank it off, taking it to be nectar, and she had the assistance of the Lord of the world. O camel-man ! equip your camel, I have to travel hundreds of miles. I consider it (now) a sin even to drink water in the territory of the Rāṇāji. She left Mewār to her left, and (Mirān) went towards the West. She left her all because she had no love for the world (Māyā). सुषुम्णा[1] is my mother-in-law and contentment in religious love my father-in-law, Jagjivan (God) is my husband's elder brother and Spotless Hari is my husband. When I wear my wedding garment, its dye drips (disappears) and the colour fades in course of time; hence I prefer to wear a black blanket that will not alter (lit., which nothing can stain again).[2] Mirān was the favourite of Hari and lived with Sādhus (Saints). She had great love for them but her heart was turned away from that insincere person."

1. A particular but imaginary artery of the human body said to lie between इडा and पिंगला, two of the tubular vessels of the body, according to the anatomy of the Yoga Philosophy.

2. Married life being likely to come in the way of her union with God, she desired to renounce the world.

Her husband tried to gain her heart by decking her with jewels and gorgeous raiment, but she pushed these gifts aside. "I will die in a hut unadorned and without earthly treasure. My crown of glory is borne on the brow of him to whom I am devoted–my beloved Krishṇa, Lord of my heart." Her love for her husband was, she sings in a song, like that for a piece of cactus. Under these circumstances living together was impossible and she lived apart, where she passed her whole time in the company of Sādhus. This considerably scandalised the Rāṇā and as stated above he wanted to do away with her. Poison proved ineffectual. He then tried to put her to death with his dagger, but as soon as he raised it, he saw four Mirāns instead of one, and he could not make up his mind as to which it was who was his wife. He then sent her a venomous cobra concealed in a basket, which usually contained the idol of Krishṇa, but even this device failed, and then it was that Mirān deported herself from Mewār and went to Dwārkā.

Her Verses

Mirān Bāi was not a born Gujarāti, but a Mārwādi Rājasthāni, and she must have acquired a knowledge of the language after she came to Dwārkā.[1] Her verses are found

1. Another view is that Mirān did not compose verses in Gujarāti but in Rājasthāni, and in the process of passing from mouth to mouth, they assumed their present (Gujarāti) form. If Mss: of her verses older than those obtainable at present are found, considerable

composed in Hindi also. No seperate collection of her Gujarāti compositions exists, but they lie scattered about in various books and number about two hundred and fifty. Mirān Bāi's great popularity especially with the fair sex, has produced a crowd of imitators, who have passed off their own verses under her name. Unless this is assumed, it would be difficult to account for the extreme modernity of the language, phrases and idioms, and for the frequent recurrence of the same phrases and idioms in some of the poems which are counted amongst her compositions.

Like the Persian Sufi, who sees in God his beloved, Mirān saw in Krishṇa her beloved, and she dedicated herself completely, body and soul, to him.[1]

light would be thrown on this question, viz., that in Mirān and Narsinh Mehtā's time a common language was current in Gujarāt and Marwād Rājasthān, called old Western Rājasthāni, and that this was the language used by them in their compositions. Mr. Manjulāl Majmudār, a noted research scholar, tells me that he has heard Narsinh Mehtā's Prabhātiās recited in the early morning on Jodhpur Railway Station, by a Mārwādi lady fellow passsenger in her own language. He has alluded to it in a paper–नरसिंह महेतानां पदोनो मारवाडमां प्रचार–read before the 12th Session of the Gujarāti Sāhitya Parishad at Ahmedabad (1936).

1. For example take the following lines:

प्रेमनी प्रेमनी प्रेमनी रे, मने लागी कटारी प्रेमनी.

जळ जमुनामां भरवा गयां'तां, हती गागर माथे हेमनी रे. मने.

Characteristics of her poetry

Mirān Bāi's songs on the surface seem to be mere erotic verse. But this interpretation is never put upon them in Gujarāt. The object of her devotion is no earthly lover but her ideal Krishṇa. The songs are really the ejaculations of a devout soul trying to express in the terms of human love her ardent desire to be united with her deity. Mothers and daughters sing them together in the Garbās,[1] which men and women gather together to witness, and no one thinks that there is anything improper or harmful in listening to the sweet garbis[2] of Mirān Bāi being sung or repeated. On the contrary, they are always listened to with enthusiasm. She is one of those very few poets, whose verses and names have become household words in Gujarāt.[3]

काचे ते तांतणे हरिजीए बांधी, जेम खेंचे तेम तेमनी रे. मने.
मीरां कहे प्रभु गिरधर नागर, शामळी सुरत शुभ एमनी रे. मने.

For further specimens of such songs, see pp. 17, 39, 43, 52 and 53 of "The Story of Mirā Bāi" by Bankey Behari (1935).

1. A Garbā is a singing party or a musical seance, where men but oftener women, move round and round in a circle and sing to the accompaniment of a rhythmical and uniform clapping of the hands.

2. A garbi means a song or poem generally recited by ladies.

3. A very instructive article on her works is to be found in the Māgh, Chaitra and Vaiśākh (V. S. 1966) issues of the "Vasant" written by Bhānusukhrām N. Mehtā, B. A. Her life is also written by the late Mr. T. M. Tripathi, B. A., in the Brihat Kāvya Dohan, Vol. VII. (1913 A. D.).

With Narsinh Mehtā (1414–1481)[1] we enter upon firmer biographical ground.

Narsinh Mehtā

He was a Nāgar Brāhmin of Junāgadh (said to have been born at Talājā[2] under Bhavnagar and then migrated to Junāgadh twenty years later) in Kāthiāwād, and was left an orphan in the care of his cousin and his cousin's wife. The caste to which he belonged was composed entirely of the worshippers of Śiva, while he had from early life taken to Krishṇa worship. He used to spend much time with Sādhus, encamped on the outskirts of the town, and sing and dance in their company, sometimes in the garb of a woman to personate the Gopi (cowherdess) of Vraj accor-

1. Great difference of opinion exists about the time when Narsinh Mehtā lived and died. Various views have been expressed by scholars like Mr. Ambālāl B. Jāni, Dr. Ānandshankar Dhruva, Mr. K. M. Munshi, Mr. Durgāshankar K. Shāstri and Mr. Natverlāl I. Desāi. They have all been examined and summed up by the late Mr. N. B. Divatiā, in Thakkar Vasanji Mādhavji lectures delivered under the auspices of the Bombay University on Gujarāti Language and Literature (1932), pp. 42–47. He favours the opinion of Dr. Ānandshankar Dhruva, "who shifts Narsinh Mehtā to a later (e. i., later than A. D. 1480) period, especially because the period assigned by orthodox opinion rests entirely on hearsay." Till the controversy ends finally, the orthodox view may be adopted. specially as Dr. Dhruva's opinion is not conclusive but recommendatory. Vide Introduction to Shree Hari Lilā Shodash Kalā by Ambālāl B. Jāni, Schedules I, II and III. pp. 78–85.

2. A Cave called Narsinh's school (निशाळ) has been discovered in the Tālājā hills. Narsinh Mehtā by J. P. Joshipura, p. 11.

ding to some, and according to others, dance with women themselves. This naturally scandalised his family and caste-men, and his father-in-law broke off his betrothal with his daughter. But later on, he was married to another girl and when the time came for him to live the life of a householder, it found him penniless and entirely dependent on his cousin. The latter's wife taunted him with his utter uselessness. She said "even the washing stone of a washerman was more useful." He took it to heart and went away to a retired place called Gopnāth under Bhāvnagar, on the sea-shore, and there worshipped Mahādev with a vow that he would go back to his home only if the god fulfilled his wishes. Pleased with his devotion and austerity, the god took him to Dwārkā, where he was shown that most famous incident, rarely seen by human eyes, in the life of Krishṇa, viz., the Rās Līlā[1] (Krishṇa's dance with sixteen thousand Gopis). This settled his future as a specially favoured devotee of Krishṇa, and he returned to his home fully inspired and invigorated, and thanked his cousin's wife for

1. A variant of this incident is given by the late Shāstri Vrajlāl Kālidās in his नागरोनुं पुरावृत्त. He says that the Shankarāchārya of Dwārkā pleased with his devotion took him there and showed him the Rās Lilā. Thus the Shankarāchārya would be the Guru, to initiate him into Vaishanavism. Diwāli issue of the "Gujarāti", 1923: नरसिंह महेतानुं जीवनचरित्र, pp. 51-52.

the taunt which resulted in his obtaining a vision of the Lord.[1]

His domestic life

Thereafter he separated from his cousin and began to live with his wife and had by her two children, a son Sāmal and a daughter Kunwar Bāi. He lived in a state of chronic poverty. He passed the whole day in devotional singing and dancing, and did nothing to earn a livelihood. His wife Mānek Bāi by means of taunts and by retiring at times to her father's house, often tried to induce him to do something but he was incorrigible. His only answer was "I was always like this."[2] The children grew up and had to be married, and for that purpose the impecunious devotee of Krishṇa depended on him, and the tradition is that

1. भाभीए भाग्य उदे कर्यों, मने कह्यां ते कठिण वचन,
त्यारे नरसैंयो निरभय थयो, पाम्यो ते जगजीवन.

2. एवा रे अमो एवा रे वळी तमो कहो छो तेवा रे,
भक्ति करतां जो भ्रष्ट कहेशो तो करशुं दामोदरनी सेवा रे.
× × × ×
जेनुं मन जे साथे बंधाणुं पहेलुं हतुं घर रातुं रे,
हवे थयुं छे हरिरसमातुं घेर घेर हींडे छे गातुं रे.
× × × ×
शुं कहेशे दुरीजन लवतां रे,
सामळीआसुं रंगभरी रमतां कुटुंब सउ कोइ रूठुं रे;
जो रूठो तो रूठजो, मारे नंदकुंवरसुं काम रे,
कुटुंब सहु कोय केडे लागां जण जण आगळ लवतां रे.

The above are some of the lines betraying the general state of his feelings.

he did help him and got both his son and daughter married.

-and misfortunes

Soon after this difficulty was over, Narsinh Mehtā's wife died and she was followed by her son.[1] His daughter had already gone to her husband's house, and he felt at one bound, discharged from all his worldly obligations, and free to follow unreservedly the bent of his mind. The poem he wrote at this time breathes all the spirit of a bird liberated from its cage. The verses[2] have become proverbial amongst Gujarātis to show the relief a man feels when he gets rid of all his obligations, leaving him free to worship Gopāl

Association with Dheds

It was at this time that the most famous incident in his life occurred. According to him, in the sight of Krishṇa, all his devotees were equal, be they low caste Dheds or high caste Brahmins. He was

1. His son died leaving behind a widow Sursenā. She was a great devotee of Krishṇa like her father-in-law and is said to have helped him at the हारप्रसंग in invoking Dāmodar (Krishṇa).

2. भलुं थयुं भागी जंजाळ सुखे भजीशुं श्रीगोपाळ

Looking at the verses in relation to their context, the incident in connection with which they have been composed may be some other one than the death of his wife. They are meant to convey his strong devotion to Krishṇa worship and feeling of equality with fellow devotees of Krishṇa to whatever caste or creed they belonged.

called upon to put this belief to a practical test. The Dhed caste, as a rule, is religious, and shows its devotion by the singing of Bhajans[1] and dancing, individually and collectively. The Dheds of Junāgadh requested Narsinh Mehtā to go to their quarter[2] and join them in their devotional exercises of singing and dancing, and he complied at once with the request.[3] He passed the whole night in close association with this untouchable community, and paid the penalty by being out-casted.[4]

1 Psalms or devotional hymns.

2 This Dhedwādā must have been situated at the foot of the Girnār hill, near the Dāmodar Tank.

गिरि तळाटी ने कुंड दामोदर त्यां म्हेताजी न्हावा जाय,
ढेड वरणमां दृढ हरिभक्ति ते म्हेताने लाग्या पाय.

3 In describing this incident he sings,

पक्षापक्षी त्यां नहि परमेश्वर समदृष्टिने सर्व समान.

Where there is favouritism, there is no God; to one who looks equally upon all, all are equal. Recalling the words of the Gitā

विद्याविनयसंपन्ने ब्राह्मणे गवि हस्तिनि ।
शुनि चैव श्वपाके च पण्डिताः समदर्शिनः ॥ अ. ५ श्लोक १८

To learned men, all are equal: a learned and modest Brāhmin, a cow, an elephant, a dog and a Chāndāl.

4 His persecution at the hands of his caste fellows was so cruel that even the patient devotee had to pray that he should not be reborn in the Nāgar caste—

निर्धन ने वळी नात नागरी, मा देइश प्रभु अवतार रे,
× × × न आपे वाटकी छाश रे.

Poverty and the Nāgar caste, O God! do not give me my rebirth therein........the Nāgars are so miserly (or even spiteful)

He was formally debarred from attending caste-dinners. One night Krishṇa appeared to him in a dream and urged him to attend one caste-dinner at any rate. He did attend one and began to sing songs in praise of Krishṇa. Thereupon he was driven out and then his caste fellows, to their horror saw that in the rows of diners, there was one Dhed sitting between every two of them. But when they asked Mehtā to sit with them this illusion disappeared. They felt ashamed of their conduct and acknowledged the sincerity of Narsinh Mehtā's belief and took him back into their fold.

A miracle

The ruler of Junāgadh, Ra' Mandlik (the third) was a worshipper of Śiva and his mother of Krishṇa. She is said to have occassionally helped Narshinh Mehtā. But her son did not like this, and matters were brought to a crisis by the king inviting Narsinh Mehtā to enter into a religious contest with Bhim, a Vairagi, other Sanyasis and Brahmins at the temple of Dāmodar. Narsinh Mehtā was dubbed a hypocrite and a cheat, because he danced and consorted with women under the guise of Rās Lilā. He was called upon to furnish some sign of his God being a true

that they would not give away a cup of sour milk even.......Giving away small quantities of sour milk to persons asking for them is the common practice of those who keep milch cattle.

and living God, in other words to show some miracle. The miracle did come and Krishṇa presented himself as a corporeal being in the court of the king and garlanded his devotee.[1] The king's mother died sometime after, and whatever little help Narsiṅh Mehtā used to get from her, was stopped. His caste-men never afterwards ill-treated him, and he died at the age of sixty-six. They, however, expiated their sins against him by at least performing his last rites without any hesitation, and they are even now expiating them by proudly proclaiming that the Chaucer of Gujarāti Literature came of their caste.

More miracles

There are twenty miracles mentioned in the sketch of Narsinh Mehtā's life given by the late Mr. Ichhārām S. Desāi. Some of them have been given above. However, two further examples must suffice. On one occasion Krishṇa apprearing in the market with the name and in the garb of a Bania,-Śamalshah,-accepted in Dwārkā a Hundi written by Narsinh Mehtā for Rs. 700/- in favour of some pilgrims, in order to keep his honour unblemished. On another occasion he (Krishṇa) fully supplied

1 This miraculous event is said to have happened in V. S. 1512. Mohammed Begadā conquered Junāgadh in V. S. 1529. Narsinh Mehtā is stated to have left Junāgadh and lived at Māngrol where he died.

the presents to be given to his daughter's relatives-at-law when her first pregnancy ceremony was to be observed in Unā. The four most outstanding ones have been versified by Premānand, who succeeded him, two hundred years after, in language so sweet and simple, that today every man and woman in Gujarāt sings them.[1]

Narsinh Mehtā's Chorā

At Majevadi Darwājā in Junāgadh there still stands enclosed by a building a Chorā (platform) which is known as Narsinh Mehtā's Chorā. There is an image of his favourite god there, and the place is looked upon as a cherished monument of a great religious poet, and latterly, on the day of his anniversary, (Māgsar Sud Seventh), devout and educated Nāgars have begun to recall his influence and his work by means of celebrations of various kinds, literary and religious.

His works

His chief works are, Hāramālā (some persons question his authorship of this work),[2] Sudāmā Charitra, Chāturi

1. They are १. कुंवरबाईनुं मामेरुं, २. नरसिंह महेताना बापनुं श्राद्ध. ३. शामळ्दासनो विवाह. ४. नरसिंह महेतानी हुंडी. (Narsinh Mehtā has also written poems on the first, third and fourth subject). Some critics are of opinion that Premānand has also written हारमाळा with certain पद्s of Narsinh Mehtā.

2. Some scholars who have examined the problem in its various details are of opinion that those verses (Padas) that express

Śhodaśi, Chāturi Chhatriśi, Śāmaldās no Vivāh, Dāṇalīlā, Govind Gaman, about 2,000 Padas[1] on Devotion and Erotics (Śringār), and SuratSangrām.

The tradition is that he has in all composed, one and a quarter lac Padas. When he had finished one lac, death came to him, but his soul would not leave his body till the 25,000 had been finished. His widowed daughter-in-law[2] then seeing the pain he was in, promised to compose them for him and publish them in his name. Thus assured, he died peacefully and she fulfilled her promise. Others say he was reincarnated as the famous Lālā Bhagat of Sāylā, and finished them, and some believe that Dayārām, who came in the nineteenth century, was in his former birth Narsinh Mehtā. A third legend prevalent in Kāthiāwād and North India makes him a reincarnation of Pipā Bhakta,[3] a devotee of Rāmānand.

and Tradition

deep devotion and ardent, heart-rending feelings towards Krishṇa are composed by Narsinh Mehtā himself, but that the story is written by some other writer, who wove the whole incident into his Padas. Vishwanātha Jāni's composition (A. D. 1652, V. S. 1708) is the first one obtainable of its kind.

1. Hymns known as सहस्त्रपदिरास, वसन्तनां कीर्तनो, हींडोलानां पदो, etc.

2. The same who is referred to in the footnote to page 46.

लक्ष सवा तणां नाम किरतन, नरसैंयाने मन लाग्युं मीठुं. (शामलशाहनो विवाह)

3. Pipā Vāv under Bhāvnagar is said to be the place which is named after him.

His works can roughly be divided into two kinds:- Śringār (Love-poems) and Bhakti (Devotional poems). The Śringār was meant ultimately to merge into Bhakti, though to the lay mind which contemplates only the outward significance of the words, it is difficult to comprehend how the sentiments and actions so openly described could be construed into devotion. As a sample of pure Śringār,[1] there have been selected a few verses, the translation of which seems open to least objection. The occasion described is as follows: A lady messenger, called Lalitā, was sent by Krishṇa to call his beloved Rādhā, and succeeded in enticing her to meet Krishṇa alone.

Nature of his works

"The Prince took her with him and brought her to the grove. A retired spot was selected, and a bed was prepared. They then began to enjoy themselves. Krishṇa took her close to his bosom, kissed her on the cheek.

Śringār

1. The whole poem of सुरतसंग्राम is based on the sentiment of spiritualising the ordinary or material relations between man and woman; the principle is also inculcated that there is no (भेद) difference or distinction as between the devotee and the object of devotion. They are or become one (तदाकार). The influence of Jayadev's Gita Govinda is clearly visible in it. On the subject of Jayadev influencing Narsinh Mehtā, see pp. 49-55 of N. B. Divatiā's Thakkar Vasanji Mādhavji's Lectures on Gujarāti Language and Literature (1932).

The ardent and impassioned lover began to enjoy the pleasures of carnal enjoyment.[1]

There are others in which, what is called **उघाडो शृंगार**[2] is too fully treated to be considered suitable for translation here. All the little arts that a woman would use to excite the carnal passions of man, are there described, as practised by the Gopis to win over Krishṇa. He furnishsd the key, however, to the interpretation of these sentiments. Sings he: "Listen you, women! I have led a life of continence from birth. I am not known (as such) to the bulk of mankind, a ṛare person knows it. Even the Vedas cannot fathom me (my mystery). Nārada, Sanaka and others extol me. The credit of knowing me belongs either to the Gopis of Vraj, or to the poet Jayadev (the author of Gita Govinda) who knew what love for me means."[3] Once Krishṇa is said to have gone to give water to Narsinh

1. कुंज समीपे आविया कुंवरीने तेडी कुमार,
एकान्त स्थाने रची शय्या मळी करे रे विहार.
भूधरे भीडी हृदेशुं, चुंबन लीधुं गाल,
रसीओ ते रस प्रीते पीए, कंद्रप रस रसाळ.

2. Erotic songs wherein love is depicted undisguised or without regard to the rules of decorum.

3. सुणो तमे नारी, अमे ब्रह्मचारी, अमने ते कोई एक जाणे रे;
वेद भेद लहे नहि मारो, सनकादिक नारद वखाणे रे;
एक जाणे छे व्रजनी गोपी, के रस जयदेवे पीधो रे.
नरसिंह–शृंगारमाळा.

Mehtā when thirsty in the shape of a beautiful woman. He says that on looking at such a woman you are to drop from your eyes the scales of physical passion, and if you do so, you will find in her none other than Lord Krishṇa.[1]

Narsinh's and Mirān Bāi's Śringār

The love songs of Mirān Bāi are indeed sweeter in language and chaster in sentiments, at least in their expression, than those of her male contemporary. They breathe all the gentleness of a woman's heart, and are restrained in their tone, the poetess being naturally unable to get rid of the limitations of her sex. As a result, her compositions are far more in vogue, and, as a matter of course, more generously read and recited by the generality of people.

Bhakti Verses

Narsinh's pure devotional and philosophical (Bhakti) verses stand, however, on a different footing. They are resonant with all the echoes of the the religious philosophy of India, and go to show how far, in spite of Krishṇa worship, Narsinh Mehtā was saturated with that philosophy. He says to man: "Pray to God, give up your love for the world, consider your origin. Who are you? To whom have you attached yourself? Without knowing

1. व्यभिचार मूकी, जुवो विचारी, ए तो नरसैंयाचा स्वामी रे.

its significance, you say this is mine, this is mine. If you observe it well, you will find that even your body is not yours; even if you want to keep it, it will not abide, it will perish as a certainty. The body leaves its old connections and forms new ones.[1] Son, wife and family disappear. You are always, night and day, thinking of wealth, which acts as a great barrier to salvation. The One dear to the heart was near you, but you recognised Him not and now you have lost this game. Your waiting has come to naught. You were asleep, but why could not the words of holy men awake you? Narsinh says, it is a great shame that you did not wake. If you had awakened, the misery of life after life (i.e., of being born again and again) would have gone."[2]

Based on the following line,

1. In practice it is the other way: the soul severs its connection with the body and forms fresh connections with new bodies.

2. समरने श्री हरि, मेल्य ममता परी, जोने विचारीने मूळ तहारुं,
तुं अल्या कोण, ने कोने वळगी रह्यो, वगर समजे कहे महारुं महारुं–समरने

देह तहारी नथी जो तुं जुगते करी, राखतां नव रहे निश्चे जाये,
देह संबंध तजे, नवनवां बहु थशे, पुत्र कलत्र परिवार वहाये–समरने

धन तणुं ध्यान तुं अहोनिश आदरे, ए ज तारे अंतराय म्होटी,
पासे छे पियु अल्या, तेने नव परखियो, हाथथी बाजी गई थयो रे खोटी–समरने

भरनिद्रा भर्यो, रोंधी घेर्यो घणो, संतना शब्द सुणी कां न जागे,
न जागतां नरसैंया लाज छे अतिघणी, जन्मोजन्म तारी खांत भागे–समरने

"श्री वल्लभ, श्री विट्ठल, भूतल प्रगटीने पुष्टिमारग ते विस्तर करशे."
occurring in one of his Padas, the view is put forward, that Narsinh Mehtā was the fore-runner (वधैयो) of Vallabhāchārya and that therefore his Bhakti was of Vallabh's type: पुष्टिमार्ग. But Mr. Ichhārām Desāi and Mr. N. B. Divatiā are conclusively of opinion that the line is an interpolation.[1]

There are other wellknown poems expounding the same theme as well as तत्त्वज्ञान, but it is not possible to quote them all here.[2]

Popularity of poems

There are numbers of other poems couched in more philosophical language than that used here, and there are a few composed in simpler language, and called Matutinals or morning songs. The peculiarity about these latter is, that they are intended to be sung or chanted, the first thing in the early dawn; and are replete with praises of Krishṇa,

1. See pp. 65-67, N. B. Divatiā's Vasanji Mādhāvji Thakkar Lectures on Gujarāti Language and Literature (1932).

2. Their first lines are:

(१) ज्यां लगी आतमातत्व चीह्नयुं नहि, त्यां लगी साधना सर्व जूठी.
(२) निरखने गगनमां कोण घूमी रह्यो, ते ज हुं, ते ज हुं शब्द बोले.
(३) जागीने जोउं तो जगत दीसे नहि, उंघमां अटपटा भोग भासे.
(४) वैष्णवजन तो तेने कहीए जे पीड पराई जाणे रे.

No. (iv) has now become wellknown all over India. Wherever Gāndhiji goes, it forms an invariable item in the programme of his daily congregational prayers.

and pieces of advice on philosophical texts, and their tone is one of sweet reasonableness, though they appear to be cast in the mould of reproach to humanity for its remissness. If the very first word that a man utters when his eyes open be of God and about God, nothing but good will come to him. This is the *motif* with which they are written. Some of these are extremely popular, being both sonorous and melodious and it is not unusual for early-risers to hear one another reciting these प्रभातीयां[1] with great fervour. This is not a new thing with Hindus. The Abhangas of Tukārām are utilised in exactly the same way by the natives of the Deccan, and the late Mr. Justice Rānade always used to wake up, as his wife tells us in his Life, at four o'clock in the morning with some verse or other of Tukārām on his lips.

and their philosophical meaning

The deep philosophical meaning which underlies some of his poems, and which forms the most prominent feature of others, is not discussed here in detail. For instance, the allegory of the Rās Lilā, the dance of the Gopis[2] with Krishṇa, a vision which the poet was permitted to see in

1. Morning songs. Narsinh Mehtā's प्रभातीयां s are considered unique in the language.

2. Milkmaids or cowherdesses of Vraj, translated as "Sylvan Maids" by Sir Edwin Arnold.

Swarga[1] by the grace of Śiva, is to be understood as the dance of the human heart with Hari. The subject is rather abstruse for the common reader.

His style

In his style there is nothing antique or pedantic. In discussing philosophy, he is not so hard as Akho, while in his Śringār he is not so happy as Dayārām, nor so lyrical as Mirān. The language in which he wrote is not preserved.[2] Occasionally terminations like the genitive चा point to an old form of Gujarāti which preserved it in common with Marāthi, both languages being traceable to a common stock.[3]

Bhālaṇ

There are two minor poets who belong to this period: Bhālaṇ (A. D. 1439-1539)[4] and Bhim (A. D. 1484). Bhālaṇ was by caste a Śrimāli Brāhmin and belonged to

1. The paradise.

2. In the footnote, ante p. 40, in respect of the language in which Mirān Bāi wrote, reference has been made to that of Narsinh Mehtā also. The original text has assumed the present form in passing from mouth to mouth. The quarterly (त्रैमासिक) of the Forbes Gujarāti Sabhā (1936–1937) has published a Ms. of the Hāramālā copied out in V. S. 1733. It supports the view advanced here.

3. See p. 60. Appendix to Lecture III of Mr. N. B. Divatiā's Thakkar Vasanji Mādhavji Lectures. He says "This termination began in the Prākrita stage......it was the common property of old Gujarāti and Marāthi, and that while it disappeared in later Gujarāti it stuck on and still survives in modern Marāthi."

4. These dates are not universally accepted. Mr. Rāmlāl Chunilāl Modi in his monograph on Bhālaṇ, Sayāji Sāhitya Mālā Series (1919) places them as A. D. 1434–1514 (p. 155, Schedule K.)

Pātaṇ. As the capital of Gujarāt was at this time free from any political disturbance, the neglected study of Sanskrit was again taken up, and it is from this point of view that the works of both these comparatively obscure poets deserve mention. They had so far advanced also in their love for Gujarāti, that instead of composing in Sanskrit, as their study of it would have prompted them to do, they rather worked the other way. They rendered Sanskrit works into Gujarāti. They took incidents from Sanskrit works and presented them in their own language i.e., language current in their time.

Bhālaṇ thus rendered the celebrated romance-Kādambari[1] of Bāṇa Bhatt into Gujarāti, and Bhim the synopsis of Bhāgwat by Bopdeva.[2] The former is a secular work, while the latter is religious; what prompted Bhālaṇ thus to wander from the beaten path of religious poetry, we are unable to say. But he has tried his pen in that direction also, and his poems comprise different incidents in the lives of Rāma, Krishṇa and Śiva. The conclusion he wants to impress on the reader is that, although they appear to be different, still the Bhakta of the one is the

1. Diwān Bahādur K. H. Dhruva has published the first part of this work with critical notes.

2. Bopdeva calls it Harililā Vivek; it gives in the form of *Sutras* a synopsis of the whole of the Bhāgwat.

Bhakta of the other, and that he is after all, one God with different names. His long poems, viz., Chandi Ākhyān[1] (narrative of the godess Chandi or Kāli) and Nalākhyān have no special merit, and verse for verse the latter is greatly inferior to that of his successor Premānand in expression, style and narration. The same remark applies to the language of Bhālaṇ as to that of Narsinh Mehtā, regarding the use of words taken from the old common stock; for instance, the word आई for mother is presistently used by him. Bhālaṇ's works are many.[2] In some he has traversed the same ground which Premānand traversed some centuries later. He is most remembered by one of his songs, beginning with सांभळ रे तुं, सजनी मारी रजनी क्यां रमी आवीजी[3] where the secret meeting of a Gopi with Krishṇa and their nocturnal adventures are exposed by means of certain tell-tale signs on the body of the former. The dialogue is full of vivacity and replete with exchanges of repartee between the Gopi and her friend, who finds her secret out.

1. A poetic translation of सप्तशती of मार्कण्डेयपुराण.

2. दशमस्कन्ध; नळाख्यान; सप्तशती; रामायण; शिवभीलडी संवाद; कादम्बरी; ध्रुवाख्यान.

3. This very garbi is attributed to Dayārām also. Narsinh Mehtā, however, seems to have described the identical situation in one of his Padās, which Bhālaṇ copied. Pp. 119-122, Bhālaṇ by Rāmlāl Chunilāl Modi (1919).

Bhim

Bhim was a Modha Brāhmin of Sidhpur Pātaṇ,[1] and his poetry is principally taken up with the Bhāgwat of Bopdev (V. S. 1541). In the Gujarāti current in his time he says that he narrates the story of the Bhāgwat on the strength of Bopdeva, and is trying to quench the thirst of the people as from a well on the shores of a lake.[2]

Padmanābha and his historical work

The historical poem of Padmanābha, a Visalnagarā Nāgar Brāhmin, merits special mention.[3] Written in A. D. 1456 (Samvat year 1512) at Zālor in

1. (i) Siddha Kshetra Prabhās Pātaṇ in Kāthiāwād. pp. 98-100 Introduction to Hari Lilā Shodash Kālā by Ambālāl B. Jāni (1930).

(ii) For a very good notice of Bhim, see pp. 230-31, The Vaishanavas of Gujarāt, by Dr. N. A. Thoothi.

2. पण्डित बोपदेव द्विज एक किधु हरिलीलाविवेक;
तिणि आधारि मि करी कथा, सरोवरजमलु कुउ यथा.

p. 212 Hari Lilā Shodash Kalā, by Ambālāl B. Jāni, B. A. (1928). These lines are typical of the methods followed by the writers then; here, for instance, Bhim takes as the basis of his work Bopdeva's Index of the incidents in the Bhāgwat and weaves several such incidents into a narrative (कथा) in his own language.

His other work प्रबोधप्रकाश (V. S. 1546), however, looks more like a translation of Krishṇa Mishra's (Sanskrit) play प्रबोधचन्द्रोदय which has been published by the Gujarāt Vernācular Society. Based on this Sanskrit play is प्रबोधचिन्तामणी a work rendered into Gujarāti by Jayashekhar Suri also. Bhim says that his object in rendering these works into Prākrit (the current language) was to make them available to the Śudras and women who cannot read difficult books (कठिन ग्रंथ). P. 120 Ibid.

3. (i) Padmanābh's work has overshadowed that of his predecessor, Shridhar Vyās, called Raṇamall Chhanda-the poem of (Rāv)

Western Mārwād, Kahānad De Prabandha is unqiue in early Gujarāti literature. It describes in great

Raṇamall, the Ruler of Idar. It recites in heroic terms the defeat of Zafar Khān, the Subedār of Pātaṇ at the hands of Raṇamall, whose territories he had invaded. It seems to have been composed about A. D. 1398. It is one of the very few historical or rather epic poems written in early Gujarāti literature. In vigour of style and in its vivid description of the display of martial prowess by the Rāthod Rājputs it stands unmatched. Diwan Bahadur Keshavlāl H. Dhruva in his प्राचीन गुर्जर काव्य (1927) has edited it and reviewed its merits at length. It further shows how even at that early period Persian words–at least military and financial (revenue) terms–had found a permanent home in Gujarāti Literature. The whole poem is full of such words as:

फुरमाण, सुरताण, माल, हलाल, खान, खिजमत, आलमि हैराण्, खुदालम, फोज, सिहर, (a city), लसकर, तेजी, खानखुद, हाल, दीवाणी, बक्षी.

Mr. K. M. Munshi has referred to this poet on p. 101 of Gujarāt and Its Literature. The tarnslatiou given there of the verse quoted in footnote 1 is wrong. The verse quoted means, "Obey the firman of Sultān and forthwith hand over the royal treasure, (which Raṇamall had looted). The verses intended to be translated are:

साहस वसि सुरताण दल समुहरि जिम चमकन्त;
तिम रणमलइ रोस वसि मूछ सिहरि फुरकन्त.

(ii) Besides the principal poets referred to in this Chapter, there were several others also who have left works worth notice. Their compositions (a) वसन्तविलास, (b) सीताहरण, (c) उषाहरण and (d) प्रबोधचिन्तामणि have been edited by Diwān Bahādur Keshavlāl H. Dhruva in प्राचीन गुर्जर काव्य (1927). (a) Is considered by him to have been composed in the commencement of the XV century A. D., its composer is not known. As it does not, however, anywhere contain praise of the Jain sampradāya nor is called faggu as would have been the case ordinarily, it is supposed to have been written by a non-Jain. (But see the article written by Sārābhai Manilāl

detail the invasion and conquest of Gujarāt and Kāthiāwād by Alaf Khān, the renowned lieutenant of Alāud-din Khilji, in the preceding century. The extinction of Hindu rule from Anhilwād Pātaṇ, the sack of Somnāth Pātaṇ, the varying fortunes in war of both the combatants, the supreme courage displayed by the Rājputs who were able to beat back some three or four times the vast armies from the North, the helplessness of the Hindus in the face of their water-supply being cut off by the pollution of the water in the lake by the blood of slaughtered cows, and the ultimate betrayal by some faithless Rājput of Kahānad De, the Prince of Zālor, who with-

Nawāb in the Forbes Gujarāti Sabhā Quarterly Vol. I, No. IV Jan. March, 1937, pp. 442–447 where he sets out his contention as to the author being a Jain Āchārya). It is full of descriptions of the joys of spring time. (b) The Ms. of this poem was picked up by the Diwān Bahādur from the odds and ends sold at the (Gujari) Bazār of Ahmedābād held every Friday. It describes incidents in the life of Rāma and has been written by a Bania poet Karmaṇ Mantri in A. D. 1470. Mr. D. P. Derāsari has dealt with this poet at some length in a paper he read at the Fifth session of the Gujarāti Sāhitya Parishad, held at Surat. (c) Is from the pen of a Khadāytā Brāhmin, Janārdhan Travādi. It was finished in A. D. 1498. It is of a very ordinary type, (d) Is a composition in the Gujarāti current when it was written by a Jain poet Jayashekhar Suri, who had also composed a similar poem in Sanskrit called प्रबोधचिन्तामणि for those who knew that learned language. It is said to be the oldest poetic allegory in Gujarāti, and the Diwān Bahādur surmises that it must have been based on the प्रबोधचंद्रोदय नाटक of Krishṇa Mishra. It must have been written somewhere in the commencement of the 15th century A. D. It is called त्रिभुवन दीपक प्रबंध also (about V. S. 1557).

stood a seige by Alāud-din for twelve years, are described with great force by the poet. Indeed while reading some of his lines you feel the blood coursing more rapidly in your veins, in sympathy with the patriotic feeling running through the graphic narration of certain events, such as the defiant answer sent by Kahānad to Alāud-din that he would not allow the army of a Mahomedan King to pass through his territories for the purpose of invading a Hindu kingdom, or the state of utter panic in Delhi when the Sultan was informed that Kahānad De had defeated and destroyed his army.

Description of the rout

A few lines from the description of this rout and panic shows both the state of the language at the time as well as the style of the poet.

जे जे तुरक नासी ढवल्या
एक ठामी जइ अंगळि मिल्या
एक उघाड वस्त्र–विहीण
भूखई करी एक थाइ खीण
एक घूमन्ता जाइ घाइ
एक डोली उपाडया जाइ
× × ×
मल्लुखान अंधारं करी
वस्त्र एक मुखि अंतरि धरी
× × ×

भागा तणी वात इम सुणि
ठाम ठाम रोइ तुरकणी
× × ×
एक फाडइ पहिरणि सुथणी
पाए नेउर भाजइ घणी
एक लाखइ एकाउलि हार
एक उतारइ सवि सिणगार
× × ×
एक तणा बंधव भरतार
एक तणा फुटरा कुमार

"Those Mahomedans who were able to escape gathered together in one place in the forest. Some were stripped naked, others worn out with hunger. Some were tottering on account of wounds, others had to be carried in Doolies......Alaf Khān entered (Delhi) in darkness with a cloth over his face......Everywhere did the Mahomedan ladies (in Delhi) weep, hearing the news of the plight.........Some (ladies) tore their shirts, others their skirts (trousers). Many broke the anklets on their feet, some threw away their precious pearl-necklaces and others took off their ornaments.........Some had lost their brothers and husbands while others had lost their handsome sons."

Preservation of his language

It will be seen that the original language (technically called old Gujarāti, Prākrit, the language of the people),[1] in which Padmanābha wrote is preserved in this poem, while that of his contemporaries Narsinh Mehtā and Mirān Bāi, has undergone such a change that it is impossible to distinguish it from modern Gujarāti. The reason is that the work never became popular. It did not lose its original form in being communicated from mouth to mouth, as was the case with the works of Narsinh Mehtā and Mirān Bāi. Indeed it was rescued from oblivion by Dr. Bühler in A. D. 1875–76, who secured a

1. See footnotes to p. 40 and p. 41.

manuscript copy written by two Jain Sādhus in A. D. 1550. The Jains took it to be some work written by a Jain (and its name Kahānad De Prabandha lent colour to that belief, as Prabandhās are mostly written by Jains) and they kept it in their Bhandār at Tharād, near Pālanpur. Its importance as a philological find was never appreciated till very recently.[1]

Keshavdās Harderām

The Dashamskandh (X Chapter of the Bhāgwat) has attracted a number of poets; one of them was Keshavdās Harderām of Prabhās Pātaṇ, a Kāyasth by caste. He wrote his Dashamskandh in V. S. 1529.[2]

End of first epoch

The first epoch of Gujarāti poetry closes here. The devotion of the Bhakta to Krishṇa, sung both in lyrical and philosophical verse, is a marked feature of the period, though not the only one.[3] Narsinh and Mirān Bāi, both quarelled with their nearest and dearest to devote themselves to Krishṇa and each was rewarded

1. The poem has been critically edited by Dāhyābhāi P. Derāsari Esq. Barrister-at-law, who read a valuable paper on the subject at the Third Gujarāti Sāhitya Parishad at Rājkot in A. D. 1909. I am indebted to that paper for the above summary.

2. This work as कृष्णक्रीडाकाव्य has been published by Ambālāl B. Jāni B. A., through the help of The Forbes Gujarāti Sabhā, with a valuable Introduction by Natvarlal I. Desai, B. A.

3. See ante p. 30 footnote.

with the beatific vision, the description of which they have sung in numbers, which still appeal to the hearts of men and women of Gujarāt.

Opinion of Prof. B. K. Thākore

As to the poetic value to be attached to some of the poems of Mirān Bāi and Narsinh Mehtā, Prof. B. K. Thākore rightly notes, "that all Gujarātis with one voice acclaim (accept) that they are "inspired: a Prasādi (gift) of the third eye of Shiva, a rare phenomenon".[1]

1. See p. 124, Lyric (1928) by Prof. B. K. Thākore.

CHAPTER IV

POETS OF THE SIXTEENTH CENTURY

The sixteenth century, till recent researches were made was taken to be a period of comparative barrenness. But in reality that is not so. The Hākems of Gujarāt were slowly becoming independent of the central Pathān authority at Delhi which itself was weakening. The most powerful of these rulers, Sultān Mohammed Begdā, also lost ground and political anarchy was the result. Akbar conquered Gujarāt in 1573 A. D., but even then the state of internal disturbance could not be put an end to. The times were too unfavourable for the gentle plant of poetry to grow or prosper. Still we have got a fair number of poets to rescue the period from the reproach of utter barrenness. Till researchers brought to light the works of other poets, Vasto, Vachharāj and Tulsi were considered to be the three notable poets of the period.

Vasto

Vasto was a Dodiā Koli[1] of Borsad in the Kairā district. His profession was that of an agriculturist, but early in life, he renounced the world and its ways, and remained

1. He himself says so:

वरतो कहे हुं विप्रनो दास,
डोडीआ कुळ बोरसदमां वास.'

बृहत्काव्यदोहन Vol IV p. 288 (शुकदेव आख्यान. कडवुं ८४)

a bachelor passing his time in travelling as a pilgrim in the company of Sādhus and Sannyāsis all over India. His two poems, Śukadevākhyān (V. S. 1624) based on a portion of Shānti Parva of the Mahābhārat and Subhadrā Haraṇ, a part of the Mahābhārat and the Bhāgwat, follow the literary trend of the period. They are narrative poems. His third work is "Sādhu Charitra" praising the devout lives of Saints and Sādhus like Narsinh Mehtā, Mirān Bāi and Nabhāji. Besides this there are Padās written by him.

Vachharāj

Vachharāj was the follower of the famous religious leader Kabir of Upper India, and hailed from Jambusar, a place of some importanace near Broach. His poem, Rās Manjari (V. S. 1635), is a collection of stories, which show the innate intelligence of the gentler sex when it comes to serving their own ends. Towards the end of this poem[1] he advises his reader not to feel sorry (मा धरशो खेद) at what he has narrated, as it portrays the difference (भेद) between soul and body. It is a secular piece and foreshadows the line which Sāmal Bhatt was to follow so brilliantly later.

Tulsi

Tulsi, a poet of note in his time, was a Sāraswat Brāhmin of Kundanpur, in Kāthiāwād, and he has narrated

1. See p. 246, Vol. IV, बृहत्काव्यदोहन.

(V. S. 1604)[1] the sad experiences (in चंद्रावळाs, a famous Kāthiāwādi छन्द) of little Dhruva who was banished from his home, and who by observing the strictest of penances in the forest, pleased God. The tale of Dhruva, like a number of other incidents in the Bhāgwat, the Rāmāyan and the Mahābhārat, has formed the staple of many poems, early and late.[2] In these works, however, "one clearly feels the quickening of the genius of the next century which was to burst upon the country with a regular shower of great poets, and with a variegated luxuriance of beautiful and powerful poetry."[3]

Ganapati

Besides the three poets mentioned above, a poet who wrote with taste and vigour, has recently been unearthed by

1. विप्र सारस्वत कुन्दनपुर गाम, माधवसुत तुल्सी तेहनुं नाम.

× × × ×

सरव नार तणो शणगार आद अंत ने वेद विचार.

ध्रुवाख्यान, p. 82 Vol. IV, बृहत्काव्यदोहन.

This is a peculiar way of noting the year of the composition of a poem. The number of ornaments worn by a lady is 16; that should form the first (आद) number. The final (अन्त) number is 4 the Vedas being four in number. The middle number nought (o) is not pronounced.

2. He himself has treated the भीष्म and अश्वमेध Parvas of the Mahābhārat in the same fashion.

3. The Classical Poets of Gujarāt, by G. M. Tripāthi.

the late Mr. Chimanlāl D. Dalāl, M. A.,[1] who had very creditably made the subject of old Gujarāti his own. The name of the poet is Ganapati, son of Narsā, a Kāyastha by caste, and an inhabitant of Āmod near Broach. He forestalled Sāmal and wrote a narrative poem, called the Mādhavānal Kāmakandalā Dogdhak, consisting of twenty-five hundred couplets divided into eight parts. It was composed in Samvat year 1574 (A. D. 1518). The story is narrated in a more pleasing way than Sāmal, and throws some light on the manners and customs of the time.

Kushalalābh

Another poet, a Jain Sādhu by name Kushalalābha Vāchak, who has written many books of poems including Māru Dholā Chopāi (Samvat year 1616, A. D. 1560), has tried his hand at the same story, and has called his composition Mādhavānal Kāmakandalā Rās.[2] Both these works are written in old Gujarāti, and they furnish proof of the fact that Sāmal was not a pioneer, in this branch of Gujarāti literature, but had more than one predecessor, whose works must have furnished him with materials for his own poems.

1. See the monthly periodical, Sāhitya, for August 1914.

2. Rao Bahādur Hargovandās Dwārkādās Kāntāvālā, who published this Rās in the pages of the Sāhitya monthly (from June 1914), gives Samvat year 1616 and A. D. 1560 as the date of its composition.

Other Jain poets

Besides Kuśalālabha Vāchak there were other Jain poets of some fame who flourished during this period. Lāvaṇya Samay (A. D. 1485) who wrote the well-known Vimala Prabandh (about A. D. 1512),–a biography of Vimalshā, the minister of Bhim I,–was one of them. Nayasundar (about A. D. 1560–1620) has composed a Rās on the popular subject of Nala Damayanti and other works. Samaya Sundar and Rishabhadās also contributed handsomely to the literature of the period.

Prose

Prose–writing had till now, made very little headway. Jain writers, however, began to pay some attention to it. Lāvaṇya Samaya has told us that at the age of sixteen "he began to compose excellent Rāsās with parts in prose".[1] The Panchtantra was translated into prose and also the Rāmāyana, Yoga-vāśistha and Bhagwad Gitā.[2] Tabā (टबा) was the term by which prose works were known in Jain literature.[3]

1. Gujarāt and Its Literature p. 164.

2. Ambālāl B. Jāni's HariLilā Shodash Kalā, Introduction, pp. 11-12.

3. A Short history of Jain Literature by Mohanlāl D. Desāi.

Nākar

Nākar[1] was a Disāvāl Baniā belonging to Barodā and he is the author of many poems, out of which seven only are published.[2] They are the Hariśchandrākhyān, (V. S. 1572), ŚivaVivāh (the marriage of Śiva), Dhruvākhyān, Chandrahāsākhyān, LavaKushākhyān, Mrigalisamvād, and Bhilādi nā Bār Mās. Bhaktamāl like the work of Nabhāji treats of the Saints of Gujarāt and resembles the Sādhu Charitra of Vasto. He composed them in plain, simple language with the express view of making a present of them to Brāhmins, who recite them before their audiences and so earn their livelihood. They were so recited. He thought this would bring him religious merit.

1. Nākar, who was believed to belong to the seventeenth century is now transfered to this century, as the dates of his compositions supplied by Nākar himself place him there. Vide Ambālāl B. Jāni's Introduction to Vol. VIII of the बृहत्काव्यदोहन. In his opinion which is founded on the study of his works, published and unpublished, the poet flourished in Samvat year 1550-60 and must have been alive till V. S. 1630. He is also inclined to think that for some of the best works of Premānand, such as the Nalākhyān, the material has been supplied by Nākar's verses. Vishṇudās and Shivdās whom he considers to have lived in the same century as Nākar are however, placed in the seventeenth century as a major part of their works was acccomplished during that century.

2. See बृहत्काव्यदोहन Vol. VIII वैश्य कवि नाकर pp. 56-57, for a detailed list of his works arranged by Ambālāl B. Jāni.

CHAPTER V

POETS OF THE SEVENTEENTH CENTURY

Akhā and his early life

The first of the brilliant group of three, dominating this century is Akhā (1615–1675 A. D.), styled Bhagat[1] (a devotee of God), a goldsmith by caste. He came to Ahmedābād, from a village called Jetalpur nearby.[2] Early in life the death of his sister weaned him away from the pleasures of the world, and sowed in him the seeds of that Vairāgya (retirement from the world) which influenced his life to such a great extent. Several incidents, coming one in the wake of another, set him absolutely in opposition to the ways of the world. The belief in Gujarāt, crystallised into a proverb[3], is that a goldsmith will not let even his own sister escape without stealing a little gold from the quantity entrusted to him, for making ornaments. A lady, whom he loved more than his sister, once gave him some gold to be made into a necklace. It was worth Rs. 300. Out of affection for her, he add-

1. More correctly a ज्ञानी भक्त.

2. In the locality known as Khādiā (in Ahmedābād) where he resided, there still exists a room known as Akhā's room (अखानो ओरडो).

3. "सोनी सग्गी बेनने पण (चोरवामांथी) न छोडे."

ed Rs. 100 from his own pocket, and made an ornament worth Rs. 400. The lady was very much pleased with the jewellery, but on talking over the matter with a friend, it was suggested that it was not possible to find a goldsmith who would act so very much against the instinct of his craft. Accordingly the necklace was tested by being broken up, and it was found that it contained gold worth more than Rs. 300. She went back to Akhā to get it made whole, and on being pressed for information as to how the ornament came to be broken, she made a clean breast of the whole affair. Akhā was convinced that there was no room for good men in the world, and that it consisted wholly of dishonest men and rogues who would not appreciate honesty in others.

Renouncing the world–

As the head of the royal mint at Ahmedābād, he was the victim of the machinations of some of his caste-people, who charged him with alloying the silver with baser metals in minting coins. The Subā first put him into prison and then, enquiring into the matter, found that he was innocent. He was set free, but he took the incident so much to heart that he determined to leave the world and its sharp practices. He threw his implements into a well, sold off all his belongings, and started in search of a good, virtuous Master (गुरु), who would show him the Right Path. In Ahmedābād, where he commenced his search he failed to find such a guru. He then proceeded to Benāres[1] and Allahābād (प्रयाग), visiting Gokul enroute. The head of the Vallabhāchārya Mandir (temple) there attracted his attention, and he sat at his feet hoping to glean some good things from him. As Akhā was rich he was well received, and fed on all the good things which are proverbially to be had in a Vaishnav temple, as the Prasād (food-offering) of the Thākorji (god).[2] His spiritual cravings were however starved, and he left the place to go to Vraj and Mathurā where he had the same experience. On reaching Benāres, he sat at the feet of many Saints and Sādhus, but found none proof against mammon and woman. He stayed a long time there, and stumbled upon one who gave him the right teaching. Near the sacrosanct Ghāt of Maṇikarṇikā, in an unpretentious hut, he once

In search of a Guru

1. Besides being a place of pilgrimage Benāres was the centre of India's learning and culture and the meeting-place of the representatives of all the Sampradāyas. It was usual for any Hindu who wanted to acquire culture and learning to go to Benāres.

2. It is said that Akhā was aware of this and therefore when invited to sit down to dine he put his costly turban and dress on the dining stool, instead of himself taking his seat on it.

heard a Sannyāsi (ascetic), Brahmānand by name,[1] explaining the tenets of the Vedānta philosophy to only a single disciple. This was a very unusual event in that sacred city, overflowing with students and where the humblest of gurus could muster at-least one hundred disciples. He used to hide be-hind the thin walls of the hut at the reading time, and listen attentively to the lecture.[2] This he did for twelve months, and he was thereupon satisfied that he had discovered his guru. He tried to see if wealth or women would tempt him, and was convinced in the end, that he was proof against both. He, therefore, resolved to put himself under him, and this he did in a very unusual manner. It is usual in these recitals or lectures for the hearer to respond by a gut-

-and finding one

1. See pp. 15-16 of AkhāKrit Kāvyo, Part I by Diwān Bāhādur Narmadāshankar D. Mehtā B. A. (1931).

At a place called Kahānwā, near Jambusar in the Broach district, there is an (Institute) Āshram, (known as Bungalow) founded with Akhā as the guru, and presided over by Swāmis in the direct line of descent of the Shishyas (disciples) of Brahmānand-a guru of Akhā.. It is a storehouse of Akhā's unpub-lished writings, some of which are edited critically by Sāgar and recently published by the Gujarāt Vernacular Society, Ahmedābād.

2. He was a goldsmith by caste and profession and not a Dwija, and was therefore afraid that he would not be accepted as a disciple by any Swāmi or Brāhmin. He had therefore to ersort to secrecy.

tural sound,[1] or shake of the head to the words of the reader. This is supposed to encourage the reader, as he knows that his audience is wide awake and following him. When the audience is large, some naturally go to sleep and fail to respond. But there are others to make up for the silence and the sleepers are not noticed. But where the audience consists of only one individual, he has to keep awake. In spite of all the guru's efforts this particular hearer happened to go to sleep on a particular day, and, as it was necessary to keep up the interest of the reading, Akhā from behind the wall gave his response. This startled the guru, and on searching about, he discovered Akhā. He was asked the reason of his strange conduct, and explaining the situation he requested to be received as a pupil. As a proof of his earnestness he repeated the whole of the Kathā (story) he had listened to for the last twelve months. The Swāmi, convinced of his great faith in him, took him as his disciple, and during the three years that he lived there Akhā studied under him the PanchDaśi, the Adhyātma-Rāmāyan, the Bhagwad Gitā, the YogaVāsiśtha, the Rāmāyan, the Mahābhārat and other highly technical works on the philosophy of the Vedānta, like the Upanishads.

1. Like हरे, हरे, हा जी corresponding to "Âmen".

Interview with old guru

On his way back to Ahmedābād he again visited Gokul.[1] His object was to see how his old guru Gokulnāth, the opulent Vaishnav Mahārāj, would receive him now that he had parted with his worldly wealth, and was rich in the matter of knowledge only. It turned out as he had anticipated. The doorkeeper failed to recognise him and prevented his ingress. He refused to believe that he was Akhā who, he said, was a very wealthy Śethiā, and not a beggar like the individual before him. Hearing this discussion, the Mahārāj looked out from his window, and he too, although he recognised Akhā, repudiated all acquaintance with him. He could very well see that it was his wealth that the Mahārāj had coveted and not him. In his association with different sects of ascetics (Bāvās, Vairāgis, Sādhus) while at Ahmedābād and outside, he had always observed their conduct very carefully and the hypocrisy and loose morals of these people had so disgusted him, that he had determined to spend the whole of his life in exposing them.[2] On

Akhā's opinion of ascetics

1. The former edition mentioned Jeypore, as the place where the Mahārāj lived. Historically Jeypore was founded later. This discrepancy was pointed out by Mr. Natvarlāl I. Desāi, B. A.

2. He describes himself as "Akha Sonaro" Akhā the Goldsmith. Just as a goldsmith distinguishes between sterling and inferior gold, so Akhā brings to light and exposes human insincerity and hypocrisy.

the other hand, he had come across some good men too, and he has not failed to render unto them the meed of praise they properly deserved. While in his works the exposure of deceitful Sādhus and hypocritical Saints predominates, it is not unusual to find those who have passed his test alluded to in terms of great admiration.

Akhā had imbibed many principles of the Vedānta philosophy of Śankaracharya.[1]

Akhā's works: their abstruse philosophical nature

His works are, Akhegitā, Chitta-Vichār-Samvād, Panchikaraṇ, Guru-Śishya-Samvād, Anubhava-Bindu, Shat Padi (Chhappās), Kaivalya Gitā, Brahma-Lilā (in Hindustāni), Parampada-Prāpti and Panchdaśi-Tātparya, which are all, as their very names imply, treatises on Vedānta philosophy.[2] They are very abstruse, and fail to yield their secrets or even their ordinary meaning to the uninitiated reader. He has as his style clearly shows, addressed all of

1. There was prevailing in Gujarāt, a threefold influence in matters of thought and religion: (i) Sāmpradāyic i. e., of religious teachers such as Śankar, Rāmānuja, Vallabh, Madhva, (ii) Paurānic: mythological and (iii) of Saints like Rāmānand, Kabir, Nānak and Dādu. Akhā's philosophy was an amalgam of all the three. He had absorbed सांप्रदायिक तत्त्वज्ञान, Paurānic lore and also the mysticism अगम निगमनी गूढ रीति of Saints like Kabir.

2. Besides these large works he has written a good-many instructive Padās.

them to the general public, but, in doing so, forgotten that the masses had not gone so far in search of the Parabrahma as he had done, nor so deep into the mysteries of the Kaivalya and other Vedāntic principles as himself. Besides, all philosophy, and especially so hard and abstruse metaphysics as Sankar's Vedānta philosophy, is difficult to versify. The poetising of this subject hardly ever renders it attractive, and for this reason, these works of Akhā have failed to command universal attention. But the fact is otherwise in the case of his seven hundred and forty six Chhappās (six lined stanzas),[1] and sixty Padās in which he has taught some very wholesome lessons about the world and its ways. He has mercilessly but justly unmasked the worldly wise, those so called leaders of the different religious sects, the Sādhus and the Saints, the ascetics and the anchorites, steeped in the Māyā (illusion) of the world, and painted the unfavourable aspect of wealth, women, progeny, and attendants, friends and relatives, their hollowness and

Exposure of hypocrisy,

1. An earlier poet Māndaṇ Bandhāra (a fuller) had written Chhappās, which are described as Shatpadi (a poem of six lines) in old manuscripts. See Māndaṇ's रावणमंदोदरीसंवाद (S. V. 1565-78). Hindi language is full of this kind of verse. Māndaṇ's work has been referred to at pp. 232-233 of Dr. Thoothi's "The Vaishnavas of Gujarāt." Besides these Akhā wrote verses resembling Prabhātiās (but inferior to Narsinh Mehtā's), कुंडळीया, सोरठा and साखी.

their lip-loyalty, in such startling but true colours, that this particular part of his work has permeated the masses, and many of his telling verses have become common literary property, and passed into ordinary household language. His tenet was that your wife, your children, your friends, your relatives and your attendants, all fawn upon you because of your wealth; as soon as that disappears, they desert you. The world and its love, the sansār and its hate, its likes and dislikes, are all unreal. The ways of the world are unreal. The Sādhus and Sannyāsis are unreal and hypocrites. The one Real Being is the Parabrahma, and to him should we all turn, leaving "the trappings" of the world to take care of themselves.

and preaching the unreality of the world

Akhā was not a very cultured but a (बहुश्रुत) individual. His language therefore is far from classical. It is like rough unhewn stone, albeit for some purposes it is exceedingly effective. For satire, caustic criticism, telling examples and similies, and fearless exposure, he is hard to beat.[1] In this respect he is unequalled

Akhā's style

1. Prof. B. K. Thākore calls Akhā's caustic criticisms (टीका) "burning tongues of the flame of a fire not found in this world' (अलौकिक). Prof. Thākore mentions the Bible, the Korān and the commencement of the Bhāgwat, detailing the signs of Kaliyug, as matching Akhā's prophetic satire. Lyric. p. 124.

in Gujarāti. He lashes vice, with a heavy whip but the range of his satire is limited, he repeats himself. Thus a selection of his satires is more edifying than a complete collection. There is also to be noted the obscurity of a great many of the phrases and words he uses, and the unfamiliar sources of Vedāntic metaphysics, from which he draws most of his similies. These two factors have constituted him, so far as the greater part of his compositions is concerned, a poet for the select few. His verses are devoid of wit. You feel they are the product of a man, severe and austere, who is moved to indignation at the immorality, hypocrisy, and vice prevalent around him. He resembles Juvenal in his power of epigram and in the force of his attacks on contemporary superstition and vice. Society in Gujarāt has not changed greatly since his time, and some of his descriptions are as true today as they were when they were written.

As examples of his verses, satirical and ordinary, the following should suffice.

And satire

After finding out the real nature of the Mahārāj at Gokul, whose name was Gokulanāth, he said, "I made Gokulanāth my guru (preceptor), which was like putting reins on an old bullock (who eats your food but does not answer to the goad). He (the guru) would take away your wealth but not the uneasiness of your mind. What good can such a guru do?"[1]

"He has with great zest proclaimed himself a guru, (but) how can a man with a stone round his neck, float?"[2] He means to say that if the teacher himself has the stone of ignorance round his neck how can he swim, much less make others swim?

Pilgrimage

He did not believe in the spiritual benefits of mere pilgrimages. He said, "at the feet of Harijan (a pious man, one who has known God) are a million places of pil-

1. गुरु कीधा में गोकुळनाथ, घरडा बळदने घाली नाथ,
धन हरे, धोखो नव हरे, ए गुरु कल्याण शुं करे?

A variant to this couplet is suggested at p.8 of the Introduction to AkhāKrit Kāvyo, part 1, by Diwān Bahādur Narmadāshankar D. Mehtā:

गुरु कर्या में गोकुलनाथ, नगुरा मनने घाली नाथ,
मन मनावी सगुरु थयो, पण विचार नगुरानो रह्यो.

The variant is found in the oldest manuscript of प्रपञ्च अंग. The verses convey the idea that in accordance with custom I made Gokulnāth my Guru and put reins on my guruless mind. In order to placate myself I thus became an individual with a guru, but after experience, my thoughts remained guruless all the same i.e., independent, without the shackles of a guru.

This no doubt seems to be the correct version though ineffective as satire.

2. गुरु थई बेठो होंसे करी, कंठे पहाण शके केम तरी?

grimage."[1] He came to this conclusion from experience gained as a widely travelled pilgrim.

His union with Brahma

He had reached the highest stage that a Vedāntin aspires to. He had known the unity of Jiva and Iśwara, he had reached the final beatitude, and become one with the Brahma. He said, "everyone is undergoing penance (तप) to get to Hari, but Akhā moves in Hari (i.e., in Hari he lived, moved and had his being) by himself without the help or mediation of penances."[2] Also, "you become your own guru, there is none other to whom to pray. Leaving off concentrating upon externals, turn your devotion inside, i.e., inside your own heart.[3] (Know thyself)."

Views on language

In his opinion Sanskrit, the language of the learned, had no magic in it. Prākrit or even vernacular was equally good, when used effectively, and so he used the latter as the vehicle for the expression of his thoughts. His aim was to teach the masses, and open their eyes to the follies practised round about them. If that

1. तीर्थ कोटी हरिजनने चरण.

2. हरि पामवा सौ तप करे, अखो हरिमां मेळे फरे.

3. गुरु था तारो तुं ज, नथी कोइ बीजो भजवा,
बाह्य सुरतने टाळ्य, वाळय अंतरमां सेवा.

was attained, then it was all right, and so he said,[1] "Why do you stick to (this or that) language, O idiot? He who succeeds on the battlefield (irrespective of the weapons he uses) is a hero."[2]

His illustrations

In developing some of his themes, he uses very homely illustrations. A man who pays no heed to what is taught to him or what he has heard, he likens to a leaky leather-bag going down a deep well.[3] A vainglorious man who happens to have a little sprinkling of knowledge is likened to a quarrelsome daughter-in-law who has become the mother of a son (this event, it need not be said, enhances her status greatly in a Hindu family).[4] He is "like a fighting bull, grazing his fill in clover in the monsoon, or like a mad dog. Everyone is afraid of such a man, says Akhā, because, forsooth, he is like a monkey drinking wine (which

1. भाषानें शुं वळगे भूर, जे रणमां जीते ते शूर.

2. A very lucid exposition of the views of Akhā on the comparative value of Sanskrit and Prākrit (the language of the people) will be found at pp. 12 and 13 of Akhā Bhakta and his poetry, a paper read before the Second Session of The Gujarāti Sāhitya Parishad at Bombay, (1907 A. D.) by Ambālāl B. Jāni.

3. ऊंडो कूवो ने फाटी बोख, शिखव्युं सांभळ्युं सघळुं फोक.

4. ओछुं पात्र ने अदकुं भण्यो, वढकणी वहुए दीकरो जण्यो,
मारकणो सांढ ने चोमासुं महाल्यो, करडकणा कुतराने हडकवा हाल्यो.

increases its mischievous tendency)."[1] "He hearkened to the Kathā (sacred reading) so long that he became deaf; still he did not know who Brahma was."[2] "He (a fool) worships all stones as gods."[3]

Dislike of being called a poet

Akhā has protested against his being called a poet.[4] He styles himself a philosopher, a knower (Jnāni), but still his Chhappās have placed him, much against his will, in the rank of poets.

Ignorance of prosody or indifference

It is difficult to say whether Akhā had studied that particular branch of literature called छन्दःशास्त्र (prosody). None of his poems are composed in any recognised metre. He tried to write in a popular strain ignoring the छन्दs (classical metres). His Chhappās are not the Chhappās recognised by prosody but are another name for Chopāis, rounded off with six instead of four lines (cho-four, pāis-lines).

1. मरकट ने वळी मदिरा पीए, अखा एथी सौ को बीहे.

2. कथा सांभळी फुट्या कान, तोए न आव्युं ब्रह्मज्ञान.

3. केटलाएक मूरखने पडी ए टेव, पत्थर तेटला पूजे देव.

4. ज्ञानीने कविमां न गणीश, किरण सूर्यनां केम वरणीश ?

He says elsewhere: what is the use of Akhā being a poet, if what he advises is not practised?

अखो शुं कविपणुं करे, जो वात कशी ना पहोंचे ठरे.

Akhā begins a new epoch in literature

His pithy epigrams and terse phrases proved of great help to him in the line of work he had laid down for himself. His work was more of a destructive than constructive nature, and the careful student will note that with him, therefore, began a new epoch in Gujarāti literature. He is the leader of that school of poetry which parted company with Bhakti, and which ceased to lay the foundation of its work only on the worship of Krishṇa. We miss in him and in those who follow him that singleness of purpose which saw in the cow-herd of Brindāban, the Lord of the Universe, and which saw salvation merely in devotion (दासत्व) to Hari. Henceforth poetry became, so to speak, secular, and ceased to minister to religion. Akhā revelled in philosophy, Premānand in delineation and description of human and physical nature, and Sāmal in story-telling. The verse literature of Gujarāt thus made an entirely new and welcome departure, beginning with Akhā.[1]

1. (i) Swāmi Brahmānand of Benāres had defied conventioa in accepting non-Brāhmin pupils, not one but four : Akhā, Gopāl, Butiā and Narhar. They all tried their hand at poetry. Gopāldās with Gopāl Gitā (V. S. 1706) at Ahmedābād. Butiā wrote verses (Padās) on Jnān and Vairāgya and Narhar versions of Gitā and Yoga Vāśisth (V. S. 1677). The characteristics of their work are thus summed up in doggerel:

Premānand : his merit

The laurel crown is ungrudgingly placed on the brow of Premānand, who followed Akhā. If any single individual has uplifted the language and literature of Gujarāt from the mire of obscurity, if any one writer has rescued it from the stigma of being a non-Sanskritic and therefore plebeian literature, fit only for barbarians, if by a vow solemnly made and religiously kept, any single poet has brought it in line with the much-renowned and ultra-cultured literatures of Sanskrit and Prākrit, it is Premānand. It is said of him that he had taken a vow not to

अखाए कर्यो डखो, गोपाळे करी घेंश;
बुटे कर्यो कूटो, नरहरने कहे शीरावा बेस.

डखो, घेंश, कूटो, are articles of every-day food of the country people. It is difficult to find their English equivalents; hardly any literary significance should be attributed to the couplet. See pp. 17. AkhāKrit Kāvyo, Part I. by Diwān Bahādur Narmadāshankar D. Mehtā.

(ii) A very interesting and instructive exposition of Akhā's philosophy and poems will be found in Dr. Thoothi's "The Vaishanavas of Gujarāt" pp. 238-242. He doubts that there was any Brahmānand at all who was Akhā's teacher. The Brahmānand referred to by him is a philosophical concept, and that he plays a pun on the word. (Ibid pp. 239-240).

(iii) The late Mr. N. B. Divatiā in lecture V. of the lectures delivered as the Thakkar Vasanji Mādhavji lectures on Gujarāti Language and Literature (p. 97-127) deals comprehensively with Akhā's work-"Sparks from the Anvil."

put on a turban,[1] till he had purged Gujarāti of the charge of inferiority, of having no literature worth the name as compared to Sanskrit. He kept his vow, and by his own genius created one, which for its richness and variety even today stands unequalled.

How he acquired gift of poetry

Premānand, or as he calls himself Bhatt Premānand (A. D. 1636–1734) was a Brahmin by caste and native of Barodā. His parents died when he was a child, leaving him in a state of poverty. For the gift of poetry, he too, like Narsinh Mehtā before him, and like his illustrious successor Dayārām, is said to have been indebted to divine agency. Till the age of fourteen or fifteen he was illiterate, but he was fortunate in being employed as attendant to a pious man who had come and settled in the neighbourhood of the Kāmanāth Mahādev temple of Barodā. The day before the holy man left Barodā he told Premānand he was going away, and invited him to see him early in the morning before he left. Like the Persian poet Hāfiz, who was called by the Prophet Khizar in similar circumstances, Premānand did not go to him in time and the Saint had left. Still by dint of running Premānand was able to catch up with him. The Saint thereupon blessed

1. See यक्षप्रश्नोत्तर by his son Vallabh, p. 265. Prāchin Kāvyamālā Vol. 21.

him for his services, and said: "Go home, you will be able to compose poems in Prākrit. If you had come earlier, I would have bestowed on you the ability to compose poems in Sanskrit."

Another tradition and it is one which is supported by the testimony of his distinguished pupil and son–Vallabh, is that the boy Premānand happened to cultivate the acquaintance of a learned Sannyāsi, Rāmacharaṇ Harihar by name, who had lodged in the temple of Kāmanāth at Barodā.[1] Rāmcharaṇ took him as his companion to different parts of India. Premānand was diligent and acquired a vast amount of learning in the course of his wanderings. He mastered Sanskrit and Hindi. In spite of the vituperations of Akhā, who disregarded the vogue of composing in Sanskrit and Hindi, Hindi was the

1. He was a Nāgar Brāhmin of Pātaṇ, before he became a Sannyāsi. See the lines of Vallabh beginning with–

एवे मळी आव्या सिद्ध, पृथ्वीमां प्रसिद्ध पूरा,
नमी पूछ्युं तेमने में, भलो त्यारे भावियो;
निष्कलंकी भाषा कोई बतावीए नरवर,
पूजक हुं थाउं तेनो व्यग्र मन अति छे.

युधिष्ठिरवृकोदरसंवादः मंगलाचरण. प्राचीन काव्यमाळा ग्रंथ २३.

And also, the characteristic reply of the Yogiraj:

उमर गूकी अने डुंगरने पूजे केम?

Why leave worship of your own threshold (i.e., Gujarāti) and go to a mountain (i.e.,) foreign languages (Hindi)? p. 15 of Premānand Jiwankalā in Subhadrāharaṇ by Ambalāl B. Jāni (1924).

recognised language of the cultured and the learned, and Premānand also at the outset fell a victim to the prevailing fashion. His first compositions were in Hindi. He showed them with great delight to his preceptor Rāmacharaṇ, who was a Gujarāti by birth. The Swāmi said, "Are you not proud of your own mother-tongue? Why do you compose poems in Hindi? It is to be greatly regretted." This touched him to the quick, and it was at this time that he took the vow not to put on his turban until he had enriched his mother-tongue.

Purāṇ-reciters of Gujarāt

In Gujarāt there is an institution of Purāṇ-reciters called गागरीआ भट्ट or माणभट्ट. They are Brahmins, and their business is to recite at night before large audiences, with suitable comments and illustrations accompanied by music, soul-stirring epics like those of the Mahābhārat and the Rāmāyan. The verses are mostly their own, composed impromptu and while singing them, they keep time by means of striking an iron ring, worn on their little fingers, against a large, round, narrow-necked copper vessel called गागर or माण. Even at the present day the institution exists, though it is not so flourishing as of yore. A clever reciter carries the audience with him by his manner of reproducing the incidents vividly before them. Any night, in the streets of Broach, Surat, Ahmedābād or Barodā, one can see the Bhatt now swaying his audience by means of his apt illustrations, and again exciting them to the very highest pitch of feeling, by himself sympathetically half-rising from his seat, in narration of a spirited dialogue, like that of Duryodhana and Bhim or Karṇa and Arjuna, when they meet face to face. These Purāṇ reciters were a great power in the land before modern education and printing presses brought books to the homes of the people. A light or two, a couple of attendants to supplement the music of the reciters, and either cap the verse or join in the chorus and a platter to collect the coins as one hearer after another came forward to do obeisance to the Bhatt, completed the paraphernalia of these itinerant story-tellers. If they were sweet-voiced and eloquent they attracted large audiences and made a lot of money. Their recitals were so instructive too, that even educated men did not disdain to attend them; and those who have listened to one of them mourn their gradual disappearance. This was the profession of Premānand, and when he died at the ripe age of ninety eight he left behind him, eight houses besides a considerable sum in cash representing his accumulated savings. He also spent a large amount in giving caste-dinners.

Premānand's earnings from Purāṇ recitation

Places where Premānand lived

He divided his time chiefly between Barodā, Surat and Nandarbār, to which last place he went towards the end of his life. It is presumed that he was supported by the rulers of Naṇdarbār, but of this no mention is made in his works.

Rivalry between Premānand and Sāmal, a myth

It was at one time believed that Premānand and Sāmal were contemporaries and bitter rivals. It has now been shown that Sāmal came when Premānand was far advanced in age and that therefore rivalry between them was impossible. Moreover their literary interests lay in quite different fields. Premānand wrote and recited before audiences made up of men and women of the higher classes on the lines of a Paurāṇic Vyās, basing his work on mythological आख्यानs; while Sāmal composed verses and stories of marvel and miracle for the benefit of the lower strata of society, Thākardās (minor Thākors) and the masses. They have each of them set out their objects in their own writings.[1]

Low estimate of Gujarāti in his time

Premānand's desire to add to and improve the literature of Gujarāt was keen. The very low estimate formed of Gujarāti at the time in compa-

1. Ambālāl B. Jāni in Premānand Jivankalā pp. 92-94 and 106-109; Subhadrāharaṇ (1924), has something to say on this matter.

rison with its sister vernaculars is rather humorously epitomised in the following hackneyed couplet:

अबे तबे के सोळ ही आने, अठे कठे के बार;
इकडं तिकडं आठ ही आने, शुं शां पेसे चार.

Abé Tabé (Urdu or Hindustani for 'here and there') is worth sixteen annas in the rupee, and Athé Kathé (Mārwādi for the same words) twelve. Ikdam Tikadam (Marāthi for the same) eight annas and Śun Śān, (Gujarāti equivalent for 'what') only four pice (one anna.)[1]

Foundation of a mixed literary club

This characteristically low place assigned to Gujarāti, Premānand could not brook, and not only by his own pen did he create a treasure-house of interesting and instructive literature, but he brought into existence a literary club of sympathetic spirits of both sexes, numbering about one hundred, pledged to carry forward the banner he had unfurled. Of these, fifty-two were actual workers in the field, twelve being women.[2] Out of

1. This also indicates that there were politically three reigning influences in Gujarāt at that time.

2. It is said Vallabh has thus alluded to them in Premānand-Kathā, which has not yet seen the light of the world. See ग्रंथनिरीक्षण pp. 2-3 प्राचीन काव्यमाळा Vol. 9.

छे नव दास अने भई चार ज, रत्न भलां द्वय शिष्य कहावे;
छे भव राश अने बई बार ज, रत्न मळां त्रय वि(वै)श्य कहावे.

these, six have left a name and considerable poetry, viz., Virji, Haridās, Dwarkādās, Ratneshwar, Vallabh and Sundar. Two of them Vallabh–Premānand's own son–and Virji were his favourites.

Premānand's love for Gujarāti

We shall pass on to a consideration of the poet's works after alluding to one very notable instance of that affection for his mother-tongue which endured till his dying-day. One of his best poems, viz., the Daśama Skandha (Tenth Chapter of the Bhāgwat, containing the history of the child-life of Krishṇa) was yet unfinished, and he felt his powers failing rapidly. He thereupon summoned to him his four most advanced pupils. Vallabh, Ratneshwar,[1] Virji and Sundar, and called upon each of them to compose a sample couplet bearing on the subject matter of the Tenth Chapter. The couplets of the first three he felt to be far superior to that of Sundar, but each of them at the end of the couplet had described himself as a poet, as was the invari-

छे वीर पंच ज, जी गणीए त्रण, नंद चतुरथ नाम सुहावे;
छे वीर वल्लभ, शें भणीए गण ? एक ज प्रेमनुं नाम पुहावे.

Some critics doubt Premānand's having founded a club of pupils, but differing from them. Diwān Bahādur K. H. Dhruva, Diwān Bahādur H. D. Kāntāwālā, Ambālāl B. Jāni and others do affirm the above view.

1. Ratneshwar has composed Dashamskandh in V. S. 1739 (A. D. 1683). It has been published by the late Pandit Gattulālji, in 1871 A. D.

able practice of poetry writers. Premānand himself had never taken this title for himself. He modestly called himself simple Bhatt or Vipra Premānand, and if any one addressed him as a poet, he did not like it. Sundar had deliberately omitted this appellation, and so the scales turned in his favour, and the dying behest of the illustrious master to complete his poem, –Bhāgvat–Daśam–was laid on him.[1]

and scheme of development

The literary programme said to have been laid down by Premānand was that he himself should write poetry like or on the model of Sanskrit and Prākrit, his son Vallabh, Hindi; Ratneshwar, Marāthi; Virji, Urdu and Persian; while Sundar was to compose Sanskrit Paurānic tales. He is reputed to have established a Pāthshāla to teach poetry, and had fifty two disciples in it according to a statement attributed to Vallabh, his son referred to above.

1. Sundar completed the Daśam in V. S. 1796. However, it is to be noted here that, neither Sundar himself nor Premānand has made any reference to having an incomplete Daśam Skandh been entrusted to him for completion anywhere in that work. But at the end of the fifty third chapter Sundar merely states that he is completing this work from where it was left incomplete. e, g.,

अध्याय बावनथी अधूरो रे, हरिकृपाए थयो पूरो रे.

As the year of the completion of Daśam by Sundar (V. S. 1796) is taken as a landmark in determining Premānand's death year, the above point has to be made clear.

His poetry objective

The modern fashion is to divide poetry into subjective and objective. Premanand's handiwork would fall under the second category.

His works

His poetical works, already published, alone come to nearly thirty six in number.[1]

1. 1. स्वर्गनिसरणी (His first poem); 2. लक्ष्मणाहरण* (A. D. 1664); 3. ओखाहरण (A. D. 1667); 4. चंद्रहासआख्यान (A. D. 1671); 5. अभिमन्युआख्यान (A. D. 1671); 6. मदालसाख्यान (A. D. 1672); 7. ऋष्यशृंगाख्यान (A. D. 1673); 8. हुंडी (A. D. 1674); 9. हारमाळा (A. D. 1678); 10. द्रौपदीस्वयंवर (A. D. 1680); 11. मांधाताख्यान (A. D. 1681); 12. श्राद्ध (A. D. 1681); 13. सुदामाचरित्र (A. D. 1682); 14. श्रीमद्‌भगवद्‌गीता (A. D. 1682); 15. मामेरुं (A. D. 1683); 16. सुधन्वाख्यान (A. D. 1684); 17 शामळशाहनो विवाह; (A. D. 1684); 18. रणयज्ञ (A. D. 1685); 19. नळाख्यान (A. D. 1685); 20. द्रौपदीहरण (A. D. 1689); 21. हरिश्चंद्राख्यान (A. D. 1692); 22. देवीचरित्र† (A. D. 1696); 23. सुभद्राहरण (A. D. 1702); 24. मार्कण्डेयपुराण (A. D. 1692-1709); 25. अष्टावक्राख्यान (A. D. 1710); 26. दाणलीला;

* Premānand was dissatisfied with लक्ष्मणाहरण. He had taken on a wager to compose in one day, a work, which would take only 2½ ghadis to peruse. He won the bet, but being composed in a hurry, the various रसs and अलंकारs were not to his taste.

† Devicharitra (सप्तशती-चंडीपाठ) was composed in answer to a challenge, that there was no merit in reproducing the Markandeya Purāṇ, which was easy enough. Devicharitra was comparatively difficult. Premānand, therefore, wrote it to show that he was at home in that branch of the Purāṇas too.

Subject-matter of poems: their popularity

The poems are of two kinds: domestic subjects and semi-religious or Paurānic subjects. He had to choose the former because of his being twitted by fellow Purāṇis (Reciters of the Purāṇas) whose vested interests were being jeopardised,[1] that he was no poet, but one who repeated what had already been recited in books i.e., the Purāṇas and other religious treatises. He, therefore, chose

27 वामनचरित्र or a part of अष्टमस्कंध; 28. विवेकवणझारो; 29. भ्रमरपच्चीशी; 30. सप्तमस्कन्ध or प्रह्लादाख्यान; 31. रुक्मिणीहरण; 32. दशमस्कन्ध; 33. द्वादशमास. (34) नासिकेतोपाख्यान, (35) व्रजवेल, (36) विष्णु सहस्रनाम.

To these some add (1) बभ्रुवाहनाख्यान, (2) डांगवाख्यान, (3) सुरेखाहरण, (4) लवकुशाख्यान, (5) ज्ञानगीता, (6) वल्लभझघडो, (7) रेवाख्यान, (8) भीष्मचरित्र, (9) कर्णचरित्राख्यान, (10) जयदेवाख्यान, (11) रामायण. (12) महाभारत, (13) अश्वमेध, (14) रघुवंश, (15) हरिवंश, (16) कपिलगीता or तृतीय स्कंध, (17) नरकासुराख्यान, (18) द्रौपदीवस्त्रहरण and (19) पांडवोनी भांजगड. (20) His first attempt at Daśam, a mss. of which is in the Gujarati Press of Bombay.*

* This list is kindly arranged by Mr. Natvarlāl Ichhārām Desai, B. A.

A list of Premānand's works, published, unpublished and seen by Mr. Ambālāl Jāni, will be found at pp. 110-116 of Subhadrāharaṇ, Premānand Jivankalā, by A. B. Jāni B. A. (1924).

1. An interesting notice of the hostile attitude of such rival reciters will be found at pp. 83-86 of Premānand Jivankalā in Subhadrāharaṇ, by A. B. Jāni.

some of the most outstanding incidents in the life of Narsinh Mehtā, the great devotee of Krishṇa, and by the magic of his genius treated them in such an intensely popular vein, that to this day not a single individual, man or woman, who claims to be a native of Gujarāt, will be found unacquainted with either of his poems on those subjects. The delineation of the characters, the descriptions of the various situations, and the simple language, coupled with the smooth run of the verses appeal to all, and from one year's end to another itinerant beggars and charity-seeking Brāhmins contribute and testify to his popularity by singing them in street after street of the towns and villages of Gujarāt, even today.

Poems connected with Narsinh Mehtā

Two auspicious occasions in the lives of Narsinh Mehtā's two children furnish the subject matter of his poems: शामळदासनो विवाह and कुंवरबाईनुं मामेरुं. These were the marriage of his son Sāmaldās and the day when it was announced to him that his daughter Kunvarbāi was to become a mother–a very great event in the life of a Hindu woman–when in consequence thereof in order to to show his pleasure at the event he was called upon to make presents to all her relatives-at-law. The incident of his having drawn a Hundi (bill of exchange) on his Master Krishṇa at Dwarka and the performance of his deceased father's Śraddha (funeral obsequies) are told in verse. Narsinh Mehtā's poverty is proverbial, and so is the richness of his faith in his Lord Krishṇa. The ill-feeling of his relatives and their readiness to pour ridicule on him, when, on account of his poverty, he was found to be materially embarrassed, as for example, at the time of his son's marriage, as well as the readiness with which Krishṇa delivered him from his troubles, form the themes of his poems. The picture he has drawn of the manners and customs of those times (we have not changed at all since then, and it is true today as it was then) is so vivid, the quiet humour pervading his narration when e.g., a sister-in-law or a mother-in-law asserts her authority over the daughter-in-law, the extremely amusing way in which the ladies of the caste bantered Narsinh Mehtā and his strange party of Sādhus, who, contrary to all practice, accompany him on such an auspicious though worldly occasion, the ramshackle house of the poor devotee, and his still more ramshackle conveyance, yoked to old and worn-out bullocks in which he drives from Junāgadh to his daughter's husband's place–Una–the genius displayed in all these is so wonderful that no translation into English of these verses can convey any idea of the original. An intimate knowledge of the manners and customs of the natives of Gujarat is necessary to appreciate these poems and no outsider would, therefore, be able, even if he understood the language, to appreciate the full beauty of the composition and its accuracy. A few extracts are, however, given below.

In Kunvarbāi's Māmerun, he thus describes the abject poverty of her father, Narsinh Mehtā:

Description of Narsinh Mehtā's house

"After his marriage, Mehtā lived with his wife. In his home he would worship Dāmodar, with a necklace, and sectarial marks and seal-impressions on his fore-head and body. His associates were Sādhus, Vaishnavas and ash-besmeared ascetics, and in his house would be heard the blowing of conches, the beating of Kartāls and the ringing of bells. In the open space in the middle of the house, there were clusters of the Tulsi plant (sacred to Vishnu) and night and day there was singing. No tilling of the soil, no business, no commerce were carried on. The devotee of Hari was absorbed in the contemplation of God. Any Vaishnav who came to his house was welcome to dinner, and Mehtā passed his days in singing the praises of

God. The Lord of the Universe supplied the food and Mehtā had an abiding faith in Him."[1]

The conveyance in which Mehtā and his party travelled is thus described:

"The vehicle was old and the yoke was crooked. The **सांगी** had its sticks broken. The **तळावा** and the **पींजणीs**–the parts of the vehicle which prevent the wheels from slipping off the axle-tree–belonged to different individuals. The pair of bullocks was borrowed......A sack was tied to the rear of the vehicle, in which were a number of musical instruments. There was a bag full of holy white or yellow clay **(गोपीचंदन)** and the sacred Tulsi wood. How could the bullocks who were wanting in physical strength go forward? The party of Vaishnavas (consequently) pushed the vehicle from behind. They shouted and encouraged the beasts (by pushing the cart) to go forward when the road was uphill and (when they

1. महेते मांड्यो गृहस्थाश्रम, पतिव्रता घेर नारी परम,
दामोदरनी सेवा करे, माळा तिलक ने मुद्रा धरे.
साधु वेरागी वैष्णव संग, शंख ताळ ने वागे चंग,
चोक माहीं तुलसीनां वन, अहर्निश थाय कीर्तन,
नहि खेती, उद्यम वेपार, हरि भगत महेतो तदाकार,
जे आवे ते वैष्णव जमे, गुण गाईने दहाडा निर्गमे.
विश्वंभर पूरुं पाडे अन्न, विश्वास घणो महेताने मन.
बे संतान आप्यां गोपाळ, एक पुत्री ने एक ज बाळ.

मांमेरूं, कडवुं ३, कडी १ थी ४.

had climbed up) cried out, 'Victory, Victory to the Lord of Vaikuntha.' When one bullock refused to move, out of sheer exhaustion, and sat down, the other dragged (the vehicle) on. The one that had fallen down was made to get up by twisting his tail; a thousand (such) strange scenes occurred. The joints of the vehicle had parted company. The **सांगी** made a grating sound, the wheels creaked dreadfully. They got into (the vehicle) and alighted (from it) and again got into it with the names of Rāma and Krishṇa on their lips. (Thus) Narsinh Mehtā came up (at last) at noon and the whole village of Unā turned out to have a look at the spectacle."[1]

1. जूनी व्हेल ने धुसरी वांकी, सांगी सोटा भांगीजी,
कोना तळावा ने कोनी पींजणियो, बळद आण्या बे मागीजी.
× × × ×
व्हेलनी पूंठे कोथळो बांध्यो, मांहि भर्यां वाजिंत्रजी,
गांठडी एक गोपीचंदननी, तु[illegible]सी काष्ट पवित्रजी.
× × × ×
बळहीणा बळ्दो शुं हींडि, ठेले वैष्णव साथजी,
सोर पाडे ने ढाळ चढावे, 'जे जे वैकुंठनाथजी.'
एक बळ्द गळीओ थई बेसे, आखलो ताणी जाय जी,
पड्याने पुंछ ग्रही उठाडे, कौतुक कोटी थाय जी.
सालेसाल जूजवां दीसे, रथ तणां बहु वक्रजी,
सांगीनो बहु शब्द ज ऊठे, चूचवे छे बहु चक्रजी.
चडे बेसे ने वळी ऊतरे, ले रामकृष्णनुं नामजी,
मध्याह्ने महेताजी आव्या, जोवा मळ्यूं उना गामजी.

मामेरूं, कडवुं, ४ कडी ५ थी १३.

Description of Krishṇa as a Baniā

In the "Hundi" the description of Sri Krishṇa turning up in the bazar at Dwārkā, in the guise of a Baniā Shroff to take up and honour the Hundi drawn on him by Narsinh Mehtā, is so lifelike and characteristic of persons of that community in every little detail, that he who reads it, at once recognises on it the stamp of the genus Baniā.[1] The simper of the Baniā and the stutter in his speech, his badly folded turban and bedecked figure rise up before the reader as a living image.[2]

Periodical recitation of his poems

Some of his poems have made such a deep impression on the people of Gujarāt, that they are sung both in public and private, all through the year.

1. वेश पूरो आण्यो मारे व्हाले रे, नाथ चौटानी चाले चाले रे;
छे अवळा आंटानी पाघडी रे, व्हालाजीने केम बांधतां आवडी रे.
दीसे वाणीओ भीने वान रे, एक लेखण खोसी कान रे.
त्रिकमजी वणिकने तोले रे, नाथ उतावळुं ने बोबडुं बोले रे.
सोनानी सांकळी ने कंठे दोरो रे, केडे पाटीवाळो कंदोरो रे.
सेलुं बांध्युं केडे बेवडुं रे........
करे हिंडतां हाथना लटका रे, सादी दोरीना केडे पटका रे.
ओढ्वने खांधे कोथळी रे, ते तो पारसी बोले तोतडी रे.

हुंडी, कडवुं ६ ठुं, कडी २ थी १२

Compare also, with this the description of a cloth-merchant which form Krishṇa had assumed in मामेरुं: कडवुं १३, कडी ७ थी १०.

2. See pp. 51-52 Premānand Jivankalā, Subhadrā Haraṇ by Ambālāl B. Jāni for other similar instances of चित्रालेखन by Premānand, in his other works.

Some people make it a point to read Sudāmā Charitra every Saturday, and the Māmerun or Hundi every Sunday. The former is always requisitioned when Gujarāti women are busy with preparations for the observance of the first pregnacy ceremony of a relative.[1] In the month of Chaitra sounds of the recitations of his Okhā Haraṇ fall on the ear, in almost every town and village if not in every home, and the Śraddha is sung at every annual ritual bearing that name. In the monsoon, villagers are very fond of hearing his Dasama Skandha read, in addition to the Nalākhyān and the OkhāHaraṇ.

His mastery over poetic aesthetics, and poetics

Premanand was a master of the रसशास्त्र, poetic aesthetics and अलंकारशास्त्र, poetics as understood in Sanskrit, and in his works, we find everywhere illustrations of all the nine रसs. It is said that the Okhā Haraṇ was written with the purpose of illustrating the शृंगाररस (the sentiment of love), the Raṇayajna the वीररस (the sentiment of heroism), the Māmerun the हास्यरस (comic sentiment) and the SudāmāCharitra the शान्तरस (the sentiment of quietism). But truly speaking, Premanand is the master of all the रसs and in one and the same poem, we come

1. The occasions on which Premānand's poems are still being sung with zeal and animation are fully set out at p. 47 of Premānand Jivankalā Subhadrā Haraṇ, by Ambālāl B. Jāni.

across, numerous illustrations of all of them each one being the best of its kind. Who can say that in the OkhāHaraṇ the description of the battle between Okhā's husband, and her father's army fails in any way short of similar descriptions in the Abhimanyu Akhyān or Sudhanvākhyān, or that the tragic scenes in the Nalākhyān are inferior to such scenes in the Daśama Skandha? Can it be said that the quiet humour and latent satire, which are the prevailing features of the scene where Nāgar ladies banter the wife of Narsinh Mehtā for the lateness of the Śraddha dinner, are a whit worse than those disclosed in a parallel scene in the Māmerun where these very gentle souls are anxiously scanning the situation, and Narsinh Mehtā is called upon to distribute presents to them? It is true, that the motif, the leading purpose of writing a particular poem is the illustration of a particular रस, because the subject matter of the poem exemplifies or typifies it. The OkhāHaraṇ is meant to exemplify the love of a young girl for her swain, the Sudāmā-Charitra, the affection of one friend for another, but it must be said that Premanand could handle all in one and the same poem with the same conspicuous ability.

It would occupy too much space to notice each poem of Premānand's even in the most cursory manner. It must suffice to give an outline of some of his most celebrated works.

Some poems noticed

The Daśama Skandh (Tenth Chapter of the Bhāgwat), the Nalākhyān, the Okhā-Haraṇ, the Raṇayajna and the Sudāmacharitra, are among them, though the Vāman Kathā and Sudhanvākhyān are also equally worthy of our study.

Daśama Skandha

The first part of the Dasama Skandha is taken up entirely with the childhood and boyhood of Krishna. The various incidents in his life, the different allegorical situations in it, his love for and his mischief with the Gopis, his affetion for cows, his life at Gokul and Brindāban, his killing his maternal-uncle Kaṇsa and liberating his real father and mother, his final separation from his adoptive parents, Nanda and Jasodā, these have furnished Premanand with themes and his interesting genius has made his creations realities to the people of Gujarāt. Krishṇa had gone down to recover a ball which had accidentally fallen into the waters of the Jamnā while playing hockey with his fellow cowherdboys. The river was inhabited by a fierce sérpent-demon called Kāliya-Nága, the black serpent, so fierce that the intensity of his black coloured poison had made even the waters of the river dark, and made it most dangerous for birds even to fly over it. On Jasodā being informed of this untoward event, she burst into a long and feeling lament, and Premānand's description of this incident is a lyric of unique beauty. The pathos is such that few readers can resist shedding tears at the bitterness of the mother's grief revealed therein. The following is but a feeble version of a part of it, the concluding six lines:

Jasodā's lament

"With rings in his ears, and flute in his mouth, he used to return home (from the forests) in the evening. He would point at his stomach with his finger to say that he was hungry, addressing me as mother. His scarf was yellow and he would tuck his Dhotar up between his legs and ask for the churning rope, knowing that I, his old mother was exhausted. Now that he is gone who will help me to churn the milk? He was lord of the Gopis, how will they now live without him? How will his little companions fare? The cows will die mutely sorrowing. Why has my darling turned his face from me? What can have enticed him?"[1]

1. मारुं माणेकडुं रीसाव्युं रे सामळीआ,
तारा मनमां आ शुं आव्युं ? रे सामळीआ
हुं अपराधण माताने मूकी शामाटे झंपलाव्युं रे ? रे सामळीआ
संतान रूपीयुं मोटुं धन ते करमे लीधुं लूंटी.
में नव जाण्युं जतन करीने, रतन पड्युं केम छूटी ? रे सा०

The passages describing Krishṇa's determination forever to leave Gokul for Mathurā, and how on the news being communicated to Nanda and his wife Jasodā that the child whom they had so lovingly brought up was not really their own, but the son of Vāsudev and Devaki, they refused to believe it and declined to allow Krishṇa to live on at Mathura are of great excellence, very pathetic, and touching in their very simplicity. Jasodā refused to believe that her son could be the Lord of the Universe. She says: "I am the mother of my child Krishṇa, and shall weep and weep, and weep for him and shall never believe that my child is God." The situation pictured is so human that even a rustic appreciates it the moment it is described.

Nalākhyān

The Nalākhyan is another masterpiece of Premanand. King Nala was introduced to his future wife Damayanti by a

पुत्र पामी हुं छेल्ले आश्रमे, उछेर्यो प्रतिपाळी,
नीपनो रस ढळी गयो, हुं विजोग अंगे बाळी. रे सा०
काने कुंडळ मुखमां मोरली, सांजे गोकुळ आवे,
भूख्यो छउं कही पेट देखाडे, मा कही मुजने बोलावे. रे सा०
पीत पछेडी काछ कछे, मुज कने नेतरूं मागे,
हुं घरडी माने थाकी जाणी कोण वलोववा लागे? रे सा०
तुं प्राणेश्वर, तुं गोपेश्वर, गोपी देह केम धरशे?
बाळ सखानी कोण वले? आ गायो हीसी हीसी मरशे. रे सा०

दशम, कडवुं ५६: पा. २७२ पदबंध भाग.

royal swan. At the assemblage of her wooers)स्वयंवर) in spite of the gods being desirous of her hand, she chose Nala, and that set one of them, Kali, the presiding genius of this evil age, against him, especially as he was a candidate for her hand, but had arrived too late. Kali induced him to gamble. He lost his kingdom in the game, and went out to the forests with Damayanti, where, through the wiles of Kali, he deserted her. Alone and helpless she wandered, till after various vicissitudes she reached her father's palace. Nala too in the meanwhile had been passing through great ordeals. He was stung by a cobra and had lost his original form, becoming much distorted and very ugly. All the same, Damayanti was able to find out where he was, and under pretence of holding another (स्वयंवर) gathering of those who would seek her hand, she managed to get him back to her father's. On recognising each other, they ask mutual forgiveness, and the married life, commenced in such an inauspicious manner leads eventually to great happiness. Some of the passages of this poem have become famous in Gujarāti literature. The description of the charms of Damayanti, when she prepares for the great gathering at which she was to choose her husband is simply inimitable. Then the bitterness of her grief when she comes to realise that her husband had deserted her in the dead of night, for no apparent fault of hers, which finds expression in the magnificint lines beginning with "The daughter of the king of Vidarbha wandered about in the forest bewildered and perplexed in the dark night,"[1] wherein she interrogates each tree, shrub, beast and bird of the forest, if it has seen her husband, is a capital instance of how Premanand was able to lay bare the most delicate as well as the most sorrowful feelings of the human heart, in a striking way. The mother, the father, the husband and the wife, their joys and sorrows, are painted on the canvas of this poem by a master hand. This much one can say, without fear of contradiction.

OkhāHaraṇ

The OkhāHaraṇ[2] is a much simpler poem, where there is neither complexity of situation nor of sentiment. Okhā is the daughter of a powerful King Bāṇāsur blessed with a thousand hands, and protected against death by the blessings of Śiva, save it be from the hands of his son-in-law. Bāṇāsur, therefore kept his daughter confined in a solitary tower, access to which was prohibited to all except a female companion called Chitralehā

1. वैदरभी वनमां वल्वले, अंधारी रात, भामिनी भय पामी घणुं, एकलडी ए जात.

2. Really speaking it ought to be AniruddhaHaraṇ as it was he who was taken away from his bed-room in Dwārkā by Chitralehā clandestinely in the dead of night to Ushā's (Okhā's) bed-chamber in Shonitpur.

who was an incarnation of Destiny. Okhā happened, as she grew up, to see in a dream her future Lord who was the grandson of Krishṇa. She importuned Chitralehā to bring him to her and she did so by means of her magical power. The lover and his beloved were detected and a fight ensued in which Bāṇāsur was defeated. Then bowing to the inevitable, he bestowed the hand of his daughter on the person of her choice, and thus every one was reconciled. The flights of fancy indulged in by the poet in this romantic episode, are so many and so affecting that now one passage and now another is found on the tongue of almost every woman in Gujarāt. Parents teach it to their children, the educated to the uneducated, and even those who cannot read but know it by heart teach it to their companions. For instance, the lines beginning with "Okhā says, listen to me, my friend! bring me my husband as soon as you can,"[1] can any day be heard from the lips of a Hindu lady, who with the singing of these beautiful lines whiles away the tedium of her work.

Battle-śacrifice

The late Mr. Tripāthi says: "The poet's works are full of episodes in which the gentler sex exerts her benign, softening and even pious influence over the heart

1. ओखा कहे सुण साहेली! लाव्य नाथने वहेली वहेली.

of man, and he hedges her about with a halo of divinity which makes rough man not only love, but respect her." One of his poems is entitled the Battle-sacrifice (रणयज्ञ), and its subject is the war by Rāma against Rāvaṇ, the Paris of the Indian Iliad. This Paris has kept Helen, Sitā, in a solitary garden for years in his capital city (लंका), and he daily visits her on the mission of love, but always returns baffled by his own heart. And why? A ferocious monarch and voluptuous lover as he was, he might force Sitā laying violent hands upon her honour. What makes him desist? Sitā's husband is at the gates of his capital with a powerful army. Rāvaṇ therefore has the option of restoring Sitā to him or of forcing his Helen to yield to his wishes; but he can do neither, and is in a quandary. His haughty spirit disdains to yield in humiliation to an enemy; on the other hand, he can do nothing with Sitā. Always calling on Sitā with what the great English poet would call 'Tarquin's ravishing strides,' he is baffled in her presence by his own feeling that she resembles his mother, and he always returns to his post as did Lady Macbeth saying of King Duncan, "Had he not resembled my father as he slept I had done it." Some orientalists have sat in criticism upon Vālmiki, the author of the Rāmāyaṇ, and found fault with the high improbability of this part of human nature in Rāvaṇ. The Gujarāti poet as we have seen above, furnishes a strong reply to that criticism. Rāvaṇ, moreover, has his own wife whom he loves and respects, and though he has kicked and driven away his brother (बिभीषण) for telling him that he has wronged Rāma, and must beg his pardon and restore Sitā, Rāvaṇ cannot treat his wife in the same way, when she gives the same advice, and follows it up with a virtuous dissertation. "Mad woman!" replies the Lord of Lankā to her, "dost thou think I am mad? I was the first to philosophise on this matter: see why I have done this. I have tasted the highest sweetness of worldly blessing, victory in war, and all that royalty and triumph can shower on a king. Now I am tired of it all, and my aspirations turn in another direction. I no longer care for this pomp and glory. My heart is set upon a glorious end to my career—glorious death on the battlefield at the hand of the Divine Rāma." He longs, in fact for a glorious death to crown a glorious life. When all was lost Rāvaṇ played one of his trump cards by sending his brother Kumbhakarṇa against Rāma. This extremely virile giant was blessed with the sleep of Rip Van Winkle. When once asleep he used to snore on for months together, and it was a problem how to wake him. Rāvaṇ tried various devices, ran horses over his body, had big kettle drums and tambourines beaten aloud at his ears, and serpents sent though his nostrils but all in vain. Then his wife came to the rescue and said that he was a worshipper of Śiva and only music and dancing would wake him. Rāvaṇ tried this and was successful. He was much wroth at his sleep being interrupted, and asked Rāvaṇ the cause of his being wakened up prematurely. Rāvaṇ told him the reason and he was greatly exasperated at hearing of his misconduct. Rubbing his hands, and shaking his head, Kumbhakarṇa exclaimed: "You have ruined yourself by displeasing the Lord of the Universe. You have to fight with a powerful person. Brother! why did you make Raghunāth (Rāma) angry? While lifting the Tryambak (bow at the स्वयंवर of Sitā) you got your twenty arms crushed (underneath it), Rāghav set you free and still, O Lord of Lankā! you have proved an ingrate. He it is who bridged the waters of the ocean, he it is who caused stones to float like flowers, he it is who pierçed the clouds without difficulty. Still, my brother! you have not learnt reason. You have got millions of women in your house, whom the gods desire to look at. Why, then, have you brought Sitā? It seems your bad habits nave not left you although you have become old. You have conquered the whole world, but have not yet conquered lust (passion) and anger. Your dark hair has turned grey, still your mind has remained dark. Like a night without a moon, like a house without light, does our city of Lankā appear (deserted) without our brother Vibhishaṇa [who has gone over to Rāma as you did not listen to his advice]. The wife of another is like a flame of fire, a snake, a poisonous creeper. She will take the lives of yourself and your family, so you had better go and bow down your head before Rāma's feet. I am not afraid of death, but you had better take warning in time. If you do not follow my advice, you will go to the door of Yama (death) with your family. If you merely wanted to keep her separate in a garden, why did you bring Jānaki here? If you cannot conquer Sitā, how will you conquer Rāma?" Rāvaṇ then said to him, "O Kumbhakarṇa! hear this tale of woe. Whenever I look at Sati (chaste) Sitā, it seems as if I were looking upon our mother. If I were to take my heart away from Sitā, it will burn with my dead body (I shall die). How can I now bend my knee to my foe Ramā? It will blacken my face, (i.e., I would die of shame)." Rāvaṇ failed to take the advice of Kumbhakarṇa, and fierce fighting ensued wherein both sides having performed prodigies of valour, he lost the battle and was killed.[1]

1. कर घसी कुंभकर्ण बोल्यो, धूणी पोतानुं शीश,
घर घाल्युं भाई वेलडा! तें दुभव्या श्री जगदीश, वीरा!
बळीआ साथे बाथ, वीरा! कां दुभ्या रघुनाथ वीरा?

Story of Sudāmā

One of the most admirable traits in the character of Krishṇa and the happiest episode of his life was the right hand of fellowship and help which he extended to his poverty-stricken school-friend Sudāmā. After passing their early schooldays at the Āshrama (house) of Sandi-

त्रंबक लेतां ताहरा रे, चपाणा वीश हाथ,
काढी मूक्यो तने राघवजीए, थयो कृतघ्नी लंकानाथ! वीरा! बळीआ० कां दुभ्या०
सायरजळ जेणे बांधीयुं रे, शल्या तारी पुष्प समान,
मेघाडंबर सहेजे छेदियुं रे, तोय तुंने न आवी सान. वीरा! बळीआ० कां दुभ्या०
लक्ष घरुणी घेर ताहरे, जेनां दर्शन इच्छे देव,
तो सीताने शुं लावीओ रे? थयो वृद्ध न गई कुटेव. वीरा! बळीआ० कां दुभ्या०
जगत जिती तें जेर कीधुं, पण न जित्या क्रोध ने काम,
शाम केश उज्ज्वळ थया रे, तोए मन रह्युं तारूं श्याम. वीरा! बळीआ० कां दुभ्या०
चन्द्र विना जेवी जामनी रे, दीप विना जेम धाम,
त्यम विभीषण बांधव विना, दिसे उज्जड लंका गाम. वीरा! बळीआ० कां दुभ्या०
परनारी जेवी पावकज्वाळा, सापण, विखनी वेल,
जीव लेशे तारो कुटुंब साथे, जई रामचरण शीश मेल. वीरा! बळीआ० कां दुभ्या०
हुं मर्ण थकी बीहीतो नथी, पण तुं वेळासर चेत,
नहि माने शीख माहरी, जाशे जमपुर स्वजनसमेत. वीरा! बळीआ० कां दुभ्या०
जो वाडीमां बेसाडी जानकी, तो लई आव्यो कोण काम?
तुंथी सीता जिताती नथी तो केम जिताशे राम? वीरा! बळीआ० कां दुभ्या०
रावण कहे कुंभकर्णने रे, सांभळ दुःखनी वात,
ज्यारे देखुं सती जानकी, जाणे होय आपणी मात. वीरा! बळीआ० कां दुभ्या०
जो त्याग करूं चित्त सीताथी, तो ते वळशे शबने संग,
हवे केम नमुं रिपु रामने, मुख लागे काळो रंग. वीरा! बळीआ० कां दुभ्या०

रणयज्ञः कडवुं १० मुं, कडीः १-११

pani Rishi in Avanti, where Sudama acted as head monitor and Krishṇa and his brother Balaram were pupils, Sudāmā started life as a poor and humble Brāhmin, and became the father of ten children, the whole family living in utter poverty and misery. Krishṇa on the other hand became the ruler of Dwarkā. Sudāma's principles were very high and philosophic. He, though a Brāhmin stricken with abject poverty, never begged.[1] A time came when he and his wife and children had to go hungry for two days and the very clever and worldly wife of Sudāmā, who till then had by various shifts and means been carrying on her household, lost patience and called upon Sudama to go and see his rich friend; he would surely find out the reason of his coming and help him, without Sudāma having to beg. To this request Sudāma gave a flat denial. He said that even to go there in the garb of humility was tantamount to begging, and that he would never do. Then ensues a fine and spirited discussion between the husband and wife, the latter ridiculing a philosophy which takes no account of food, family and children; and the former, by various arguments, trying to enjoin contentment and patience upon her. The mother in her very characteristically appealing tone speaks with tears in

1. His determined vow to which he stuck to the last was: it was better to die than ever to beg of any body.

याचवाथी रूडुं मरण, माम न मूकीए रे.

her eyes. She says: "O Chief of Rishis! my mind has become dull, I beseech you. I do not like this philosophy (lit., knowledge) of yours. O Chief of Rishis! the children are weeping; get us food, I beseech you. Even the great Yogis and Bhaktas (devotees) cannot do without food. O Chief of Rishis! without food you cannot think of offering prayers. The whole world lives on food. The religion and spirit itself will not stand without food."[1] Her practical philosophy at last prevailed and Sudāmā went to Krishṇa, with a little parched rice (**पहुंआ**) as a present to his friend's children. This measure of rice has now passed into a proverb in Gujarāti, to typify a humble but affectionate tribute from a poor to his rich friend (**सुदामाना तांदुल**). Krishṇa's reception of him far exceeded his expectations and the parched

1. आंख भरी अबळा कहे, ऋषिरायजी रे,
मारूं जड थयुं छे मन्न, लागुं पायजी रे.
ए तो ज्ञान मने गमतुं नथी, ऋषिरायजी रे,
रुवे बाळक लावो अन्न, लागुं पायजी रे.
अन्न विना चाले नहि, ऋषिरायजी रे,
मोटा जोगेश्वर हरिभक्त, लागुं पायजी रे.
अन्न विण भजन सुझे नहि, ऋषिरायजी रे,
जीवे अन्ने आखुं जगत, लागुं पायजी रे.
धर्म प्राण अन्न विना नही, ऋषिरायजी रे.
उभो अन्ने सकल संसार, लागुं पायजी रे.

सुदामाचरित, कडवुं ४, कडी १५ थी २२

rice which he had taken with him was heartily eaten by Krishṇa and his family. Krishṇa divined the purpose for which he had come. Before Sudāmā dared to open his lips, Krishṇa's will had worked a miraculous transformation in the home of his penurious friend. His hovel had become a palace, his shrunken and starved wife had become a woman of perfect beauty, full of accomplishments (Padmini), and his pock marked children looked like cherubs. Thus when Sudāmā returned apparently empty-handed and disappointed–for Krishṇa gave him no presents in return for his measure of rice–cursing his wife for having made him break his vow, he little dreamt of what had happened at home in his absence. He could not recognise his home, nor his wife who came out to greet him as he was slinking away with excuses, thinking he had made a mistake and was in the neighbourhood of the house of some opulent person. A humorous scene ensued. Mutual explanations soon made him aware of the change wrought in his circumstances, and he felt the faith in his friend justified.

Narsinh Mehtā's story of Sudāmā inferior

Narsinh Mehtā also has written a poem on this subject but his treatment of it is very different. Narsinh's verses are a simple matter-of-fact narrative of the movements and pathetic feelings of an earnest devotee like himself, while Premānand has vitalised them all, and painted an animated picture in which both devotion and humour play an equal part. His verses manifest the life and movement of a human being living in the midst of the world with its limitations. This sense of reality is lacking in Narsinh.

Fault-finding by critics in Premānand's verse

Fault has been found with Premānand's poems, in that they are not written in छन्द्s but merely in देशीs (particular and popular forms of composition, not bound by the classical rules of Prosody). It is true he has not chosen the former mode of versification for a large bulk of his compositions, but it would be wrong, therefrom, to conclude that such an erudite scholar of Sanskrit was ignorant of the science of Prosody. We find in many places his poems interspersed with छंद्s, द्रौपदीहरण (Kidnapping of Draupadi), अष्टावक्राख्यान (Ākhyān of Aśtāvakra–a Riśi crooked in eight parts of his body), and ऋष्यशृंगाख्यान (Ākhyān of Riśi Śrungi) which are attributed to him are largely composed in the regular recognised छंद्s, and also many crude छंद्s (छंदनी चाल) are found in his well-known poems.

and description

His descriptions of men and women are replete with अलंकार्s. They are studded with similies and metaphors. In fact, at times he loses control over himself under the inspiration of his subject, and goes on piling metaphor on metaphor and simile on simile, till the reader, out of sheer exhaustion from following and analysing them, stands aghast. Fastidious critics have, therefore, found a flaw in his otherwise perfect poetry. They say, a style simple and homely, such as is employed by him, cannot stand the strain of difficult subjects. In the treatment of such it loses its simplicity.[1]

A picture of his times

A charge is laid by some of the modern critics against Kavi Premānand, that his poetry does not reflect the state of the country, nor of the society of the times during which he lived, nor of his mind. But a minute examination of his various Akhyanas will reveal the state of his mind, as also of the customs of the society of his time. With regard to the political state and upheavals of those times, one must say that the masses did not care even to know (except in recitals in deeds of sale, mortgage etc.,) as to who ruled over them, so long as they were allowed to carry on their trade, earn their livelihood, observe

1. The series of metaphors and similes, in the description of Damayanti's beauty and charms put into the mouth of the swan before King Nala, beginning with वेल जाणे हेमनी, अवेव फुले फुली, चकित मन थयुं माहरूं, गयो दूतत्व हुं भूली is stupendous, and makes one pause for breath at every two or three lines. For this beautiful passage refer to his Nalākhyān, कडवुं १५, कडी १–१६.

unhindered their various religious customs and celebrate their social functions. It mattered little to them whether the ruling power at Ahmedābād was a Mohammaden Viceroy from Delhi or an agent of the Marāthās or Peshwās from Poona. Such was the state of society in Premānand's time. Although he ordinarily does not refer to events in his life, Premānand has,

An important event in his life

at least for once, not neglected to refer to an outstanding event in his life, viz., the famine of V. S. 1729. He has given a very realistic picture of that famine in Gujarāt, in one of his masterpieces, the Riśyaśrungākhyān (ऋष्यशृंगाख्यान). Special mention should be made of its fourth and the fifth cantos: a few selected passages from the poem are given below.[1] The last canto depicts the state of his mind, rather

1. The whole description of the ravages of this famine of V. S. 1729 being very long (covering two cantos) only a few typical lines are given here.

ताप बळे खेय, त्राह्य त्राह्य करे जे तेय,
निशवासरनो भूली भेद, खेंचवा मांडयुं (काळे) मनुष्यनुं मेद. ९
केळगर्भ समां संतान, लेई नासती शीळे स्थान,
दवे अग्नि लाग्यो चोपास, बळ्या राजमहेल आवास. १२
वांढा काळने नारी केवी, लढी शर्वरीने नव सेवी,
पोता जेवो दिवसने कीध, छती स्त्रीए रंडापो दीध. १५
न जुए कुमारिका वृद्ध, सर्वभक्षीनी पेठे करे बद्ध,
पुत्र पण मर्यादा मूकी, नहि निर्लज्जने लाज ढुंकी. १९
राय जोई प्रजाने दुःखी, पाळो भमी भटकी करे सुखी. २५
हस्ती पायक ने हय खास, छोड्या राजाए थई निराश. २७

the struggle, as to why he came to depict the ravages of famine. Just as, in modern times, some are of opinion that when a war, or a famine, or some other natural calamity, is raging in the country, it is shameful for a poet to sing any other theme except the woes and the dreadful ravages of the war, or the famine, or the flood;[1] similarly the question

वेदपाठी घनपाठी धाय, शूद्रनुं अन्न झुंटी खाय. ३३
सती मूकती सत्य ने नेम, अन्नकाज करे नीचशुं प्रेम. ३४
गया वणज अने वेपार, उद्यम एक रह्यो अविधार,
चोरी लेवुं ने खावुं अन्न, पीवुं पाणी पूछ्या विण जन्न. ३५
कडवुं ४ थुं

दीसे अस्थिना ओघे ओघ रे, प्राणी मात्र ते भूखना भोग रे.
उदवस्त नगरने नीरखी रे, तरुहीणां खंडेरो परखी रे. १४
क्षुधातुर थयां प्राणी मात्र रे, भक्षे अन्योन्यनां गात्र रे. १९
ज्यम शूनी जणे संतान रे, क्षुधाए भक्षे तेनां वान रे,
त्यम माता पुत्रने खाती रे, स्वामीभक्षी न त्यां लजाती रे. २०
वृद्ध माता पिताने मारी रे, पुत्र मांस रुधिर ले उतारी रे,
पाणी काजे उष्ट्रने चीरे रे, रहित जीवन मरे धीरे धीरे रे. २१
कंठे काचकी ने पग घसता र, दीसे पाणी काजे कांइ धसता रे.
कडवुं ५ मुं.

The above passage is not translated into English, as being too long, but it is cited here to show how vividly he could describe famine conditions.

1. See Jhaverchand Meghāni's complaint against modern poets: "त्यारे हाय रे हाय कवि! तुंने सागरतीर केरां शेणे गान गमे? When the country is suffering from calamities, O Poet! how can you sing songs on such subjects as the shores of the sea?" etc., quoted by Mr. K. M. Munshi in his Presidential address (p. 20) at the Thirteenth Session of the Gujarāti Sāhitya Parishad at Karachi, 1937-38.

was perturbing the mind of the poet whether he should write any poem or ākhyāna when people were undergoing the severe hardships of a famine. What would people say of him if he wrote poems in time of famine? The question seems to have disturbed his mind very much, but at last, after much brooding, instinct found a solution of the problem. He chose such a subject for his ākhyān that no one could dare say a word against him. There is a strong belief among religiously minded Hindus that a Yajna (sacrifice) performed in the name of the famous Riśi Śrungi, would bring down rain even when there is a drought. Therefore, as it was the time of famine, the poet chose for his theme the story of Śrungi Riśi from the Rāmāyaṇ and made use of all his powers in making the ākhyān such as would depict the actual state of Gujarāt in the famine year (V. S. 1729). In this very year, the poet suffered the loss of his wife. The pathos was thus heightened. He was doubly interested in writing the ākhyān.[1] It at once raised

1. सुखी थईए नाम सूणतां सूणो श्रोताजन्न रे,
कहेवा मात्र प्रेमानंद हुं हरि-वियोगे तन्न रे. १९ कडवुं बीजुं.

"O hearers! listen to what I say. By merely hearing the name of Śrungi, we become happy. But I, who am called Premānand ('Love combined with joy' i.e., Satchidānand, God) am only so in name; for my body is full of grief on account of separation from (caused by the death of) Hari (a name of God as also the name of his wife who died at that time.)" Tradition says her name

young Premānand greatly in the opinion of his readers and hearers, and the fear of being called a heartless man for writing a poem in famine times was removed thereby,[1] so much so that people began to make copies of it for themselves and also give away copies in charity to be recited by Brahmin story-tellers.[2]

was Harkore or Haribehen. (See notes by Messrs Kāntāvālā and Śaśtri., प्रा. का. त्रि. वर्ष ४, अं. २ p. 10.)

The poet has, here, used his own name as well as the name of God in a double sense. Such 'Vyangas' (implied meanings) are found in many of his poems.

1. तेमां काळ पडेलो कूडो, धन्यभाग नहि महाकाळ रे;
तदपि ओगणत्रीसो सूणतां कम्पे धावणां बाळ रे. २२
ते सत्तरसें ओगणत्रीसे काव्य करी शुं कीजे रे?
जातिस्वभाव मटे नहि भाई! काव्य कथी मन रीझे रे. २३
कडवुं २५ मुं.

"To add to the difficulties, there occurred a severe famine at this time; thank God, that it was not the worst; still on hearing the word "Twenty-nine", children at the breast shudder. In that year-v. s. 1729—what is the use of writing poems ? But, O, my brethren ! the nature of a poet cannot be changed; his mind can only be pleased by writing poems."

2. आ लखी लखावी पुस्तक अर्पे वक्ताना करमांय रे,
के भणे सूणे वांचे विधिए परिया पावन थाय रे. १७
पर्वणीए जो कोई वांचे तो ते ब्रह्मलोके भळी जाय रे,
सूणनारानी सात पेढी तो स्वर्गमध्ये मकलाय रे. १८
कडवुं २५ मुं

It was at one time customary in Gujarat to read this akhyan every year in the month of Jeth or Ashada (i.e., June or July) before the advent of the rainy season so that it may rain plentifully and the fear of famine averted. This poem was at one time very popular in Gujarāt as it treated of the art of Love (Kāma-Śastra).[1] There are in it also some observations about his life-long tussel with the Purānis, even in the year 1729.[2]

"He who copies it out or gets it copied out and then gives it away to a reciter or himself learns or reads it according to Shāstric rules will have his ancestors absolved from sins. If some one reads this poem on an auspicious day, his soul will find a place in the abode of God and seven generations of the hearers will be delighted in Heaven."

This shows the great reverence in which the poet was held in his times. His works came to be considered as sacred as those of Vyās and Vālmiki.

1. See specially the eighteenth and twenty-first cantos.

2. बनीया पुराणी बुल्बुला सुस्वरे भाखे ज्ञान
उपपुराण ने पुराणनुं मेळवे बहु मान.
कडवुं १२ मुं.

Here there is an implied (caustic) remark direcied at his opponents, the Purānis. A ll animals and birds living in the abode of Śrungi Riśi were learned and celibates. The poet says: "Even the bulbuls nightingales became Purānis by singing minor and major Purāṇas sweetly and by imparting knowledge, they used to receive respect in society." Premānand here compares his opponents who sing Purāṇas without understanding a word of it to birds.

The story of Śrungi Riśi as found in the Ramayaṇ is shortly as follows. In the reign of King Lompāda of Magadha, a friend of Dasharatha, father of Rāma, there occurred a terrible famine in Bihar. It was felt that if Srungi Riśi could be induced to come to his capital Champāpuri, and perform the rain-sacrifice the earth would receive plenty of water. But Srungi Riśi was living in a forest under the strict supervision of his father Vibhandaka, pledged to celibacy, so much so that he never saw the face of a woman. He did not know what were the distinguishing features of a male and a female. King Lomapada sent Mohalekha, a dancing-girl of exceptionally high merit in her art, to entice and bring Srungi Risi to his capital. This she did skilfully, in the absence of his father, by saying to the young Riśi that she would teach him कामशास्त्र (the art of love) which his father had not taught him, if he went with her. The Riśi enchanted by her beauty and artfulness followed her to the capital of Magadha. As soon as he set his foot on the soil of Magadha, famine disappeared and plenty of rain came down. Mohalekhā who was a celestial nymph cursed by Indra, returned to heaven and King Lompada married his daughter Śanta to the Riśi. He after begetting one male child, retired to the forest and obtained salvation. Śrungi means a man with a horn.

Autobiographical element in poems

Premānand's poems have a sort of autobiographical interest also. Almost all of them give the year, day of the week, month and date of their composition, together with the place where they were composed: Surat, Barodā or Nandarbār. They sometimes also give the number of lines and verses in each. In many of them he gives the purpose too with which they were written. For instance, he wrote Devi-Charitra to show to his detractors, who ridiculed him as a mere versifier of simple Purānic subjects, that he was equally at home in the rather foreign subject of Śakti-worship. It shows how he took up the challenge and produced a work which handles goddess worship-the worship of nature in its feminine aspect-in as popular a manner as his other works.

To persons so inclined, the dates of his works would greatly help in tracing the development and evolution of his genius, though, to an ordinary reader, there does not seem to be much or even any difference between his first and last productions.[1]

1. In Mr. K. M. Munshi's opinion Premānand was "A Prince of Plagiarists"-see his Gujarāt and Its Literature, p. 188. This is rather a strong expression to use for one benefiting by materials found in the works of one's predecessors. See pp. 244-45 of Dr. Thoothi's "The Vaishanavas of Gujarāt" for Premānand's leaning towards the Vaishanava Sampradāya.

Premānand's plays

The Editors of the Prāchin Kāvya Mālā (Reprints of Old Poetical Literature), the late Rāo Bahādur Hurgovandās D. Kantāvālā, the late Nāthāshauker P. Śāstri, and the late Chhotālāl Narbherām Bhatt, declare that Premānand wrote eleven plays, and that they had been able to find only three of them.[1] They have also mentioned by name, one drama, Duśtā–Bhāryākhyān (दुष्टभार्याख्यान), based on the story of बहुला the quarrelsome wife of Rājā Uttānpad of Mārkandeya Puraṇ[2] and another drama Māruti–Vijaya, by his son Vallabh, of which only the introduction and first scene were published in one of the issues of the "Sāhitya," (January A. D.

1 See their report-प्राचीन काव्यमाळानो वृत्तान्त–of 1893, page 19, where it is stated that: "तेनां सघळां नाटकोनां नाम सांभळवामां आव्यां छे, पण तेथी कांई विशेष जाणवामां आव्युं नथी, पण कहेवाय छे तेम तेणे बधां मळीने अगीआर बार नाटको रच्यां हतां." Again the Editors of that series had carried on correspondence with the Gujarāt Vernācular Society of Ahmedābād in 1894–6 for handing over to it their manuscripts. A list of 56 works from that correspondence is printed in the Buddhiprakāsh (January A. D. 1911), wherein all the names of Premānand's and Vallabha's plays and other works are published with details of their size (ग्रंथपूर), number of pages etc. For further particulars see A. B. Jani's PremānandJivanKalā, pp. 114–115.

2 See their report प्रा. का.–वृत्तान्त–of 1891–92, page 9, on मार्कंडेय पुराण भाग ४ थो: "एवुं ज बीजुं आख्यान बहुलानी कथानुं छे......ते उपर प्रेमानन्दे एक 'दुष्टभार्या' नाटक पण लख्युं छे." The story here referred to forms part of मार्कंडेय पुराण, cantos 69–73.

1919)[1] The three plays of Premanand are published as under:

I. Rośdarśika Satyābhama Akhyan (1891-2).

II. Pānchali Prasanna Akhyān. „

III. Tapatyakhyan (1893).

As their very names testify they (except the last) are concerned with popular subjects connected with Krishṇa and the Pāndavas. Their language strikes one as very modern and up-to-date, and the use of such phrases as "killing two birds with one stone," has led many to suspect that they could not have been written by Premanand. In fact, a miniature Bacon-Shakespere controversy (with the exception that in the Gujarāti controversy there is no corresponding Gujarāti Bacon) has been raging for several years past between those who maintain that they were written by Premanand and those who maintain that they are a later production. The former are headed by Divān Bahadur K. H. Dhruva,[2] the late Mr. Matu-

and controversy about their authorship

1 This portion of the play is reprinted as a (fourth) schedule, (pp. 149-163) in a book called प्रेमानन्दनां ज नाटको-a reprint of 13 articles in the वसन्त and 2 in the बुद्धिप्रकाश by ज्ञ-Mr. Matubhāi H. Kāntawālā, M. A., Editor of the monthly साहित्य now defunct, with an able and critical introduction by the late Chhotālāl N. Bhatt.

2 Divān Bahādur K. H. Dhruva has already published रोषदर्शिका सत्यभामाख्यान of प्रेमानन्द with conjectural emendations, in different Gujarāti Monthlies.

bhai H. Kāntāvālā and others. The latter are headed by that well-known Gujarāti scholar, the late Narsinhrão Bholānāth Divatiā, B. A., who has written a number of papers on the subject (since 1909 A. D.), and who, because of the inexplicable silence of those who were in a position to prove by means of the manuscripts which they allege to have found and published, and the furnishing of other convincing data about the genuineness of their finds, seems to hold the field to himself. So far, he has not been effectively answered, nor in spite of a prize of Rs. 500 offered by the Editor of the weekly paper "The Gujarāti," the late Ichharam S. Desai in 1910, has any one come forward to produce any old or original manuscript or copy of the plays.[1]

The pride and the hope of Premānand, however, in his mother-tongue, can all the same be summed up in a passage of great effectiveness,-from the word

1. Attempts have, however, been made, to show that most of the phrases and idioms which are alleged to be modern, are as well found in other productions which are admittedly acknowledged to be Premānand's.

Divān Bahādur K. H. Dhruva, the late Mr. Chhotālāl Narbherām Bhatt and Rão Bahādur H. D. Kāntāvālā have also answered some of the arguments of Mr. N. B. Divatiā, and tried their utmost to show that the plays were the composition of Premānand.

Mr. Ambālāl B. Jāni has also taken up the question and discussed it at pp. 99-101 of Premānand Jivankalā, Subhadrā Hāraṇ, as also in the monthly Samālochak 1914-5. Prof. Dolarrai R. Mānkad, M. A.,

of blessing (भरतवाक्य) uttered by Shree Krishṇa in the Satyabhāmā[1] play:–"May the Gujarāti language abound in delightful व्यंग्य[2] or implied satire with all its divisions and subdivisions. May every phrase of it be full of elegance and expressive. May it be figurative or embellished like a woman adorned with

Premānand's hope for his mother-tongue

of Karāchi, another student of Gujarāti literature, thinks that they were not written by Premānand but by his son Vallabh:

हवे आज हुं एक बाजुथी कहुं छुं के नाटको प्रेमानन्द जेटला जूना काळनां होय ए ज संभवे छे, त्यारे बीजी बाजुथी एम कहुं छुं के ते प्रेमानन्दनां नहीं, पण वल्लभनां छे." (See p. 42; Bhavnagar Sāhitya Parishad Report–विभाग ७ मो, 1924).

Mr. Vishnuprasād C. Jāni, Śastri Keshavrām Kāshirām, and others think that they were written by the late Chhotālal Narbherām Bhatt, in spite of his denial at the Fourth Session of the Gujarāti Sāhitya Parishad, Barodā, 1911. There are others also who think them to be written by Śastri Nāthāśankar Pujāśankar; but nothing has been definitely and conclusively proved: a shadow of doubt has been cast on the authourship of the plays attributed to Premānand, and interest in the matter has now waned somewhat.

1. सांगोपांग सुरंग व्यंग्य अतिशे, धारो गिरा गुर्जरी,
पादेपाद रसाळ भूषणवती, थाओ सखी ऊपरी.
जे गिर्वाण गिरा गणाय गणतां, ते स्थान ए ल्यो वरी,
थाये श्रेष्ठ सहु सखीजन थकी, ए आश पूरो हरि.

2. A word has three powers or significations: 1. वाच्य primary or expressed meaning, 2. लक्ष्य secondary or indicated meaning, and 3. व्यंग्य implied meaning, sense suggested by indirect allusion or implication. Words in the last sense are used in poetry only and never where scientific subjects such as logic and metaphysics are treated.

ornaments on her feet, excelling all its sister languages, and attaining to the high position assigned to classical Sanskrit. (In short) May God realize our hope to see it rise superior to all its sisters."

Sāmal Bhatt

Sāmal Bhatt,[1] possibly the rival and contemporary of Premānand's son, Vallabh, was born somewhere before A. D. 1700 and died after A. D. 1765 (V. S. 1821-22). He was a Srigod Mālvi Brāhmin by caste, and an inhabitant of Venganpur (now called Gomtipur), a suburb of Ahmedābād. His father's name was Vireśwar and

1. Divān Bahādur Keshavlāl H. Dhruva, B. A., ventures, in a private communication, to express the opinion that Sāmal must be a contemporary of Vallabh, and junior to Premānand. This opinion is based on the dates of some of the works of Sāmal: e.g., his Śiva Purāṇ (really speaking ब्रह्मोत्तरखंड of Skand Purāṇ) was written in A. D. 1748 (Samvat year 1804), and Padmāvati in A. D. 1718 (Samvat year 1774). In a manuscript copy of the Angad-viśti seen by him, the year of composition is given as A. D. 1752 (Samvat year 1808). Rākhidas had got a copy made of Sāmal's "Thirty-two Stories of Sinhāsan" for the special use of his courtier, Gamān Bārot. Divān Bahādur Dhruva has with him this copy, (Mr. A. B. Jāni used it for editing सिंहासनबत्रीसी. See First Fifteen Stories: Preface, p. 6), and the year of its transcription is given as 1740 A. D. (1796 Samvat year). All this leads him to think that a man who composed poems in Samvat year 1808 could not have been born prior to 1700. See also p. 197 of गुर्जर साक्षरजयंतीओ published by Jivanlāl Amarshi Mehtā (1921) where Divān Bahādur Keshavlāl states that Sāmal and Vallabh were rivals, and not Sāmal and Premānand.

mother's Anandibai, son's Purushottam and his teacher's or Guru's Nānābhatt.[1] He had also a pupil by name Ghelā Vyās. He was well versed in Sanskrit and Hindustāni or Vraj, as all educated people of that period were. He seems to have known Persian too, which was nothing unusual for a member of one of the highest castes since that was the court language, Ahmedābād being then under the sway of the Moguls. For the first time in Gujarāti literature, we find in his works a large admixture of Persian words.[2] He had a son called Purushottam, who was like his right-hand and who always accompanied him wherever he went to recite his poems. He had another son, who as his rivals described him was squint-eyed and ugly and possessed

His education

1 Sāmal himself has given these details at the end of the story recited by the Thirty Second Putali in सिंहासन बत्रीशी or बत्रीस पुतळीनी वार्ता (vide a ms. possessed by Mr. A. B. Jāni), as also the names of his other works and his object in undertaking them. Years of the composition of his poems given by Sāmal himself help greatly in ascertaining the time when he was alive.

पद्मावती (V. S. 1774), अभराम कुलीनो शलोको or पवाडो (V. S. 1781), नंदबत्रीशी (V. S. 1796-1802), पंदरमी विद्या or भोजभानुमती (V S. 1795), अगदविष्टि (V. S. 1799 or 1808), शिवपुराण really speaking-ब्रह्मोत्तरखंड (V. S. 1804), काशीखंड (V. S. 1806), रेवाखंड-नर्मदामाहात्म्य (V. S. 1808), सूडाबहोतेरी (V. S. 1821), सिंहासनबत्रीशी (V. S. 1777--1785 and 1796).

2. Though the admixture had begun much earlier. See foot-note, ante p. 62.

of no intelligence, who would "go to one place (Dhāmandwād) when asked to go to another (Gatrād)."[1] Sāmal must have been well acquainted with the stories and प्रबंधs written by Jain writers, as his own stories like नंदबत्रीशी, पंचदंड, विद्याविलासिनी show distinct traces of such study.

and Chhappās

Sāmal also studied Vraj Prosody and wrote his poems in accordance therewith, but the classical छन्दs not being so much in vogue amongst the people of Gujarāt, he had to write mostly in such easy modes as दोहरा, चोपाई, छप्पा (two and four and six lined stanzas), and the last kind, viz., छप्पाs has immortalised him: he is considered the best of the old writers of Chappās. He has also written some poems in झुलणा, सवैया and कवित.

Prejudice against non-religious works in Sāmal's time

The late Kavi Dalapatrām says[2] that in Gujarāt, when Sāmal flourished, all the poets had to take the themes of their verses from the Śāstras and Purāṇas. A writer of works which were the creation of his own fancy or imagination was tabooed, and for this reason Sāmal, who is considered the prince of story-tellers, had to put into his performance a flavouring of ancient Sanskrit or religious lore.

1 सामळभटनो दीकरो वाडो ने वतराड, धामणवाडे मोकल्यो, जई पहोंचे गतराड.

2. गुजराती भाषाना कविओनो इतिहास, बुद्धिप्रकाश, अं. ४ मास एप्रिल, १८६२.

Sāmal also a reciter of Puranic Stories

It is said that, like Premānand, Sāmal in the beginning of his career was also a reciter of Purānic stories adapted from the original Sanskrit. He went from one village to another to recite them, and everywhere he was disappointed: the vested interest of some reciter (पुराणी) always came in his way. This made him resolve on the composition of stories of homely life in the vernacular to oust the Sanskrit bards, and one thing assisted him. Sanskrit poems when recited to listeners who did not know the language sent them to sleep, but Sāmal's Gujarāti verses rivetted the attention of the audience, who followed his stories eagerly.

Sāmal's vow

A story is current that Sāmal had sworn to himself that he would never wait with his poems upon any one, unless expressly sent for, and he had to wait till he was thirty–four years of age to get one who could appreciate his work.[1]

and the patronage of Rakhidās

His stories penetrated so far inland as to attract the attention of a Leuā Kunbi Patel, Rakhidās by name, of the village of Sunj, in the Mātar Tālukā

1. See p. 3 of सिंहासनबत्रीशी, part II, by A. B. Jāni (1926) as to how Rakhidās through Gamān(ji) Bārot hearing his fame came to send for him.

of the Kairā District. Rakhidās, although of the agricultural or Pātidār class, was a lover of letters, and a bard or reciter of heroic poems, by name, Gamānji, whose company went far to encourage and develop his taste for poetry, formed one of his retinue. On hearing of his fame as a story-teller from Gamānji Sāmal was sent for by Rakhidās who not only kept him as an honoured guest, but invited him to stay with him permanently and compose and sing stories, settling some lands on him for his maintenance. For this princely gift,[1] help and appreciation, Sāmal has perpetuated the name of Rakhidās and put him on a level with Bhoj, the renowned King of ancient India, who by his royal liberality encouraged Kalidās and other poets.

Works of Sāmal

Sāmal has composed about twenty four works.[2] Although he has no school of followers like Premānand, still he had

1. Divān Bahādur Keshavlāl H. Dhruva has noted having seen the actual deed of gift; he has also secured a genealogical tree of Rakhidās. See special Jubilee Issue of Gujarāt Shālā Patra, page 62 (1911).

2. (1) Thirty two books or stories called बत्रीसपुतळी, including the twenty five books or stories of वैताळपचीशी which work took him ten years (A. D. 1740 to 1750) to write, (2) Seventy two books or stories called सूडाबहोतेरी, (3) शिवपुराण-ब्रह्मोत्तरखंड, (4) रेवाखंड, (5) रणछोडजीनो शलोको or बोडाणाख्यान, (6) अंगदविष्टि (A. D. 1752), (7) पद्मावती (A. D. 1718), (8) नंदबत्रीशी, (9) रावणमंदोदरीसंवाद, (Poems

one disciple, by name, Ghelā Vyās, a Travādi Mevādā by caste, whose grandson (daughter's son), Ichhāśankar, was alive in A. D. 1862. He had piously preserved the works of Sāmal Bhatt and specimens of his handwriting.[1]

Sāmal had no followers

Sāmal's works fall broadly into two divisions, narrative and didactic. His longest and best poems are narrative, though not entirely free from didactic vein. The story of MadanMohanā, one of his best narrative poems is a good sample of the

Nature of Sāmal's work

of the same name were written by Shridhar, Mâdaṇ, Narpati and Lâvaṇya Samaya, much earlier, say between V. S. 1565 and 1578 A. D. 1503-1522: Hari Lilâ Shodash Kalâ, by Ambâlâl B. Jâni, Introduction p. 12.) (10) उद्यमकर्मसंवाद, (11) सामळरत्नमाळा, (12) विनेचटनी वार्ता, (13) अभराम कूलीना शलोको or रुस्तम बहादूरनो पवाडो (A. D. 1725), (14) बरास कस्तुरी, (15) चन्द्रचन्द्रावती, (16) काळीमाहात्म्य, (17) शुकदेव आख्यान, (18) सुन्दर कामदार, (19) द्रौपदीवस्त्राहरण, (Its authorship is doubtful, as Sāmal generally did not write on such Purânic subjects), (20) भोजकथा, (21) पंदरमी विद्या, (22) रखिदासचरित्र (perhaps in this is included लेउवा कणबीनी उत्पत्ति) (A. D. 1715), (23) विश्वेश्वराख्यान, and (24) मदनमोहना.

The first seven were composed under the direct auspices of Rakhidās.

1 Junun (old) Narmagadya, p. 469 (Gujarāti Printing Press Edition, 1912).

former, while Sāmal RatnaMāla is an example of the latter. It consists of a string of poetical passages, setting out the merits and demerits of various classes of individuals, of both the sexes, especially the fair sex, describing the several virtues and exhorting people to beware of the pitfalls of youth, to be prepared for death, to be ready to keep their promises, to profit by learning and so on. Many of his verses on these subjects have become highly popular and are often quoted.

Specimen of his didactic verse

"It is the stomach for which one has to labour, it is for the stomach that one has to work as a bondsman. It is for the stomach that one has to carry burdens and it is for the stomach that one has to praise (flatter) others. It is for the stomach that one has to wander in foreign lands, and it is for the stomach that one is responsible for one's sins. It is for the stomach that women make a profession of evil and it is the stomach that makes one travel away from truth. Many are the tricks resorted to for its sake. People (are prepared to) go to hell to fill their stomachs. Sāmal says, Believe this to be true that it is the stomach (hunger) which makes men wicked."[1]

1. पेट करावे वेठ, पेट वाजां वजडावे;
पेट उपडावे भार, पेट गुण सौना गावे;

Sāmal's estimate of woman

He has seen woman in two aspects: good and bad. When pointing out evils wrought by her in public and in private life, he is unrestrained in his condemnation of the fair sex.

bad

"Some women have murdered their husbands and some have abandoned them. Some have left noble husbands to marry menials. Some have left their home and families and gone to others, some have even left kings and indulged their passions with slaves. Some have killed their sisters-in-law and mothers-in-law and also their fathers and mothers; woman belongs to the tribe of demonesses. She has taken away the strength of the strong."[1]

"She is so very faithless that one moment she

पेट भमे परदेश, पेटथी पाप करे छे;
पेट करे छे जार, पेटथी सत्य हरे छे;
वळी संच प्रपंच अधिक करे, पेट काज नरके पडे;
सामळ कहे साचुं मानजो, पेट पाप नरने नडे.

1. कैंके मार्या कंथ, कैंके परण्या परहरिया,
कैंके उंच अमीर तजी, किंकर वर करिया;
कैंक कुटुंब परिवार, तजी चित्त बीजे चाली;
कैं महिपतिने मेली, माननी गमते महाली.
कैंके सासु नणंद संहारियां मातपिता मर्दन कर्यां,
ए जीवती जात छे जक्षणी, जोर जोरावरनां हर्यां.

will call a man her brother and the next make him lover (husband)."[1]

and good

On the other hand, he is not blind to the healthy influences that woman is always capable of exerting, he has but praised or condemned them as occasion demanded.

Sāmal's woman a minister of pleasure

To Sāmal woman appears more as a minister of pleasure than as the tender mother devoting herself to the tender care of her offspring. He looks upon her as one whose business is to chase away care and in old age to soften the miseries of her husband's declining years.

"In youth, she gives pleasure and the happiness of her company. She comforts the body. She talks to you with affection and steals away the sorrows of your heart. She shares equally (your) happiness and unhappiness. She sings of your virtues with a sweet voice. She is accomplished, steals your heart from you and takes pride in it. In old age she tends you, her very sight is enough to remove pain from your heart. Even in death she does not leave you, but ascends the funeral pyre by your corpse."[2]

1. घडी एकमां कहे वीर, कंथ घडीमां करी थापे.

2. जोबनमां दे रंग, संग सुख, टाढक तननी;
व्हालपणे करी वात, मटाडे पीडा मननी;

In the closing lines of the stanza the poet says, "Wicked women are rare."[1] Perhaps this was Samal's real opinion, and his abuse of the sex merely the traditional masculine view of woman.

Story of MadanMohanā, a type of his narrative poems

The story of MadanMohanā, which in its main features, more or less resembles all other stories of Sāmal is the story of love at first sight. Mohanā, a young princess, has for her tutor a man. In order to avoid any mischief, she is being taught with a Purdah between the pupil and the master. Once, while she was at her lessons the son of her father's minister, Madan, happened to come to the teacher, and was a witness to a literary contest between them. This contest, which is a common feature of many of Sāmal's works, consists in the propounding of several riddles in verse by one and their solution by the other.[2] A dispute arose as to

सुखदुःखमां समभाग, राग रूडे गुण गाती;
चतुरा चित्त हरनार, सार उरमां मदमाती;
वळी वृद्धपणे सेवा करे, देख्याथी दिल दुःख टळे,
ए अन्तकाळे अळगी नहि, बहु स्नेह साथे वळे.

1. छे नीच कोई ज नारियो, स्वभावे सहु नही सरखी.

2 For instance:

Question—He is born with horns but loses them in his youth; when youth goes and old age appears, the horns reappear, who is he?

the correctness of a certain reply given by the princess, and the minister's son acted as arbiter and declared both to be in the right. The princess was a spirited lady and she drew away the Purdah and beheld an individual, godlike in beauty. She, a Rajput princess, insisted on being married to him, then and there. His intelligence and his beauty had done their work on her, and in spite of the protests of the Pandit and Madan, the former was compelled to tie the nupital knot, under threat of the princess committing suicide. Madan pointed out to her the imprudence of the step she was taking in such reckless haste. He said he was a Baniā, and, as such, far inferior to her in status, that his father was a servant and not a prince, that he was unworthy of her in many respects: "he was a goat, she an elephant; he was a fox, and she a lion; he was a snail and she a cobra; he was like a well (lit., sink) and she the ocean." He illustrated the indiscretion of her proposal by many stories, wherein those who had acted in such matters recklessly and hurriedly had come to grief.

Reply—The lady says I like your question. It is the crescent moon that is born with horns.

प्रश्न–र्शींग सहित जे जनमीओ, जोबनमां शींग जाय;
जोबन फीटी वृद्ध थयो, शींग फरीने थाय.
उत्तर–वात गमी वनिता कहे, अगन (? अश्व) तणो तुं इन्द्र;
शींग सहिते जनमीओ, चतुर बीजनो चन्द्र.

Tales within tales like the Hitopadeśa, the Arabian Nights, and the Decameron are characteristic of Sāmal. These stories are told by so many characters and are so numerous, that the main plot forms but a very small portion of the whole narrative. This packing, or to be more accurate, padding, partakes again of all the usual characteristics of the main story, in delineation and in telling, being interspersed with short homilies, preached in the vein of the moralist..[1] She replied to his position by telling counter stories, where the faithfulness of the fair had saved the

Story within story, characteristic of Sāmal

1. For instance, moralising on the evil consequences of recklessness Madan says:

He who is reckless, one day gets his head cut.
He who is reckless, loses his respect and honour.
He who is reckless, loses his wealth in no time.
He who is reckless, is never happy.

Again, he who is reckless is overcome by a number (lit., conflagration) of calamities.

Sāmal says, he who is reckless in his actions, has at last to repent.

सहसा काम करनार, कोई दिन शीश कटावे;
सहसा काम करनार, मान मरजाद मटावे;
सहसा काम करनार, जर जोतामां खोए;
सहसा काम करनार, सुख तेने नव होए;
वळी सहसा काम करनारने, दुःख दावानल आवी अडे,
सामळ कहे सहसा काम कर्याथकी, विमासण पिंडमां पडे.

situation, and she swore by all that was holy to remain faithful to him. The young man had his evil presentiments, but he was powerless before the persistent attitude of the princess, and at last they were joined in wedlock by the Pandit. Immediately after, the teacher resigned and wished to go away, reporting that her education was finished. The king, her father, then thought of finding out a husband for his daughter. While consultations were going on between the daughter and her parents, as to the best mode of selection, she confessed to her mother that she was secretly married to Madan. When the king came to know of it, the blow fell as Madan had anticipated. The least punishment the king could be persuaded to inflict on the delinquents, was banishment. The king wanted to kill all the three, but he was told by his minister, that the Śāstras enjoined that a Brāhmin should never be beheaded, and that, in spite of a thousand crimes on the part of a woman, humanity enjoined that she too should never be killed. The Divān said that really hls son was at fault: he should not have yielded to a situation which was foreign to all the traditions of his caste, community and family; and that, therefore, he should be impaled.[1] The king

1. Avoid a Baniā, who utters unpleasent words,
Avoid a Baniā, who makes his secrets public,

was pleased at this disinterested piece of advice, and commuted the death-sentence to one of deportation. Accordingly, the Brāhmin left at once, and the minister's son prepared to depart also, but the princess insisted on accompanying him. After a great deal of discussion in which the wife supported her contentions by various arguments and illustrations, it was settled that she should go with him, dressed as a man, to avoid such incoveniences as were inevitable in the case of a woman travelling under such difficult circumstances. The rest of the tale is a series of peripatetic adventures which befell them. Although both of them travelled in male garb and passed as brothers, yet the keen eyes of women never failed to discern the real state of things wherever they went, and at one place it chanced that they fell in with a courtesan (गुणका) whose evil intentions seperated them, and it was with great difficulty that the princess Mohanā was able to escape from her wicked clutches. Each, being thus separated from the other, travelled alone

Avoid a Baniā, who dces things in a hurry,
Avoid a Baniā, who cheats a woman.

वरजो तेह वणिक, जेह अकारुं बोले;
वरजो तेह वणिक, जेह पेटपेटांतर खोले.
वरजो तेह वणिक, जेह उतावळो थाये;
वरजो तेह वणिक, जेह वनिता वाहे.

and Mohanā being able to rescue a cobra from a burning jungle became the fortunate recipient of a present from the cobra in the shape of a jewel (मणि), which possessed great curative properties. To one bitten by a snake, to one suffering from leprosy in its most loathsome forms, to one deprived of his eyesight and to one unblessed with progeny, the charm gave relief. Armed with this specific, she visited city after city, and cured sufferers of their complaints. Curiously they all happened to be related to kings, and as she was taken to be a man, the reward invariably given to her was the hand of their daughters. She was thus able to marry about five or six princesses, but was careful to leave the city as soon after the celebration of the happy event as possible on various pretexts, such as a vow for pilgrimage, in order to guard her secret. But from the last place of her stay, Mohanā found it impossible to escape and, therefore, she prayed for a period to be allowed to her, before being called upon to live with the princess as her husband. During this period she laid anxious plans for discovering Madan, and one of them was that she caused a picture to be painted containing exact imitations of herself, Madan, the Pandit, and Madan's father. She filled in the most suggestive details herself, and placed it in a newly erected temple in the principal square of the town. She at the same time ordered free doles of food to be given to all ascetics, Sādhus and other strangers, coming there from all parts of the country, with instructions to those who had partaken of them, who were going out to foreign lands, to publish the news far and wide, and send in as many more applicants as possible. Her object indeed was that if Madan ever came that way, he would at once understand the import of the whole affair and they would be reunited; just when the time was expiring, and when she was preparing to sacrifice herself rather than reveal her identity, Madan appeared. He had met with a curious adventure after he was separated from her. While wandering disconsolately he had reached a place called Rupāvati. The daughter of the king of the place was under a curious vow, namely, to marry only the man who could give satisfactory solutions to her enigmatic questions, be he a pauper or a prince. Madan was an adept at this work and consequently he had to marry her. But he too delayed consummating his nupitals, till, as he said, he had made a certain pilgrimage. Excusing, therefore, his absence on this score, he once more set out in quest of Mohanā, and came to the place where the picture adorned the temple. He fainted at the very sight of the picture, which had a deep significance for him, and on the news being conveyed to Mohanā of the incident she came running to the spot. They recognised one another, and with feelings of indescribable delight, repaired to Mohanā's palace. An exchange of confidences took place, of course, and as a result of that, they resolved to keep up appearances till they reached their own native place. It may be mentioned that they had till then lived merely as brother and sister, and had sworn not to enter upon a connubial life till they were taken back by their parents into their respective families. Mohanā gave her father-in-law to understand that she had to go on an expedition for collecting certain arrears of revenue, and she started on it accompanied by her newly married wife with great pomp and circumstance. On her way she collected all her other wives, as did Madan, his. By the time they reached their home, their retinue had swelled into a large army, and the king was naturally alarmed at what he thought was an invasion by an unknown foe. But anticipating this difficulty, they had secretly made known to Madan's father who they were, and he came out on behalf of the king to parley with them. In the end, the whole story was laid bare, and those ladies who had married Mohanā had, of course, to transfer their affections to Madan, and he had the satisfaction of showing to his father and the king that he had been able to win not one, but more than half a dozen of princesses, king's daughters, though they thought him unworthy of Mohanā's hand. They both admitted their fault, and blessed the couple who, of course, lived thereafter in complete joy and happiness, and became the parents of five sons. Nor did they forget the Pandit, in their hour of joy, but sent for him and made him a present of thirty villages in commemoration of his having tied the nupital knot.

Sāmal's opinion of his own work

The poet gives his own opinion of the poem at the end. He says, "every verse is full of interest," "only a Pandit can appreciate this tale of good manners (विवेक)." "It contains simple language, simple verses (couplets), simple stories of good manners. He only who can teach in simple language is the true poet. Such a poem as retails the life story of men and women, describing their ingenuity, courage, wisdom, adventures, holy and auspicions deeds will teach wisdom and amuse the minds of the people. A description of human nature is always sure to be appreciated."[1]

1. It is also towards the close of the poem that Sāmal Bhatt indulges in his fling at Premānand as some critics suggest. He says:—

भण्यो न कोई पुराण हुं, भण्यो नथी कोई वेद,
रसालंकार न आवडे, मन न पामे खेद.
घर घर राग ताणुं नहि, पुत्र न मुज गुण गाय,
राजदरबारे रझळवुं, मेळवी नथी पसाय.

Introduction of riddles in poetry, Sāmal's main characteristic

Sāmal's besetting sin, no doubt, was the introduction into his peoms, in season and out of season, of those riddles, which at times degenerated into mere idle questions requirng no effort for their solution. They are a sort of mental gymnastics which, according to modern ideas need have no place in poetry, and this branch of verse-making fortunately created no imitators worthy of the name but practically began and ended with Sāmal.[1]

भाट ब्राह्मण ने भांडवा, लांबी मूके पोक,
रीझी भला भला कहे, तेथी थाये शोक.

"I have not learnt any Purāṇ (Premānand's poems were founded on the Purāṇas), I have not studied any Veda. I do not know figures of speech nor do I regret it. I do not go to house after house and sing there, nor have I got a son to sing my praises [Premānand's son, Vallabh, did so]. I do not wander from one court to another, and get presents. It is only the Bhāt (bards), the Brāhmins and the buffoons who bawl out loudly; the audience get pleased and praise them, but such a thing makes me sorrowful."

Doubt is cast on the authenticity of this passage. Divān Bahādur Keshavlāl H. Dhruva says that it is not found in many editions or manuscript copies of मदनमोहना. It appears only in Vol. V of the Brihat Kāvya Dohana of the Gujarāti Printing Press. See p. 13 of 'Premānand', an essay by Divān Bahādur Keshavlāl H. Dhruva (1905). No proof has till now been obtained of this passage having been included in any authentic copy of this story, which makes the authenticity still more doubtful.

1. It should be noted here that the system of introducing riddles was in vogue before Sāmal, and is found in Jain and non-

His delineations of male and female beauty are much inferior to those of Premānand. He is at his best in setting out the beauties of Madan and Mohanā, but they read more like a catalogue of points of beauty to be found in text books on the subject, rather than a natural description of human form and beauty as seen by a poet's eye. One might as well refer to a text book on horses and horsemanship to find out from it the points of beauty and gracefulness in a horse. The descriptions are, therefore, dull and without animation. They are too long to be quoted here but the curious reader would have no difficulty in looking them up.[1]

Sāmal's delineation of beauty inferior to Premānand's

The late Mr. Tripāthi sees in Sāmal traits of character transcending those of a pleasing story-teller. He says: "He wrote a large number of poems, all fictions, in which he constructed for his audience a new world of men and women who soared above the narrow minded and blasting social institutions of his countrymen, and he revelled in pointing out and picturing to them, modes of living which made

Jain Rāsa's and stories. There was a faint imitation of this kind after him. Dalpatrām was one who wrote in this strain. But it took no strong hold of any other poet.

1. See page, 371, Vol. V. of the Brihat Kāvya Dohana, for Mohanā and page 385 for Madan.

his characters, parents and children, men and women, meet each other upon terms of independence and toleration, which could have no place under the social prejudices and practice of his countrymen."

Tripāthi's opinion of Samāl examined

What he means by this is, that Sāmal's conception of social reform was much in advance of his times. Indeed it seems to be much in advance of even the present times. It is not his hero of a hundred stories, King Vikram, who like Haroun-al-Rashid flits unobserved from place to place and pays visits incognito with the help of his supernatural aide-de-camp, Vaitāl, who is the representative of this conception of social reform. But it is the female characters, his princesses, who seem to have caught Mr. Tripāthi's fancy. "The men and women whom he creates marry without any distinction of caste. Brāhmans, Kshatriyas and Vaiśyas [he might add Śudras, for one of his heroes once married the daughter of an oil-woman (घांचण)], intermarry in this world of the poet. And they marry by fancy, or charm or true love, and often in defiance of parental wishes." Then he develops a situation, where a young Baniā girl, who does not want to marry a husband chosen by her father, vows to remain a spinster all her life rather than marry him. Now, of course, this idea is foreign to Hindu religion and custom, and at the most can be taken merely as a threat on the part of the girl rather than that the poet wished to see this bold and original innovation introduced into Hindu society. The inter-marriages are there no doubt and marriages in defiance of parental wishes are also there. But then it is also to be remembered that Sāmal drew his inspiration from Sanskrit works and from legends current in his time, and in them it is not uncommon to find contretemps of this sort. Okhā married her husband, in definace of parental wishes and such inter-marriages as delineated above were not unusual in olden times. It would seem that he was rather recording old customs than seeking innovations.[1]

Part played by dancing women in Sāmal's stories

Dancing women (वारांगनाs) play a considerable part in the narratives of Sāmal. They were women like the famous Aspasia, well educated at a time when their sex was ignorant. They are assigned the task of helping heroes and heroines in distress by their ingenuity and skill.[2]

The great question of Fate and Freewill inspir-

1 As said before, he must have studied Jain works written by Jains and also Sanskrit and Prākrit works.

2. Amongst the five means prescribed for male accomplishment one was association with dancing girls to learn from them चातुरी (cleverness). They were not prostitutes by profession and association with them did not lead to anything evil.

ed Sāmal to write a poem.[1] By means of a large number of illustrative stories, he shows the fatuity of relying upon one of them only. He considers that they are both inseparable, they are one and the same. "Human Effort is the pivot upon which Fate or Destiny turns."

Dialogue between Human Effort and Fate

Sāmal's women throw his men into shade. They fill a very large and prominent part of his canvas. They are not the helpless, illiterate, limp, invertebrate creatures whom we see round about us even today. They are daring, educated, refined, resourceful, full of grace and beauty ever ready for adventures and mostly, be it said to their credit, chaste. They can sing, play. dance and ride. Indeed one wonders at times that the poet who delineated these characters should be the same as the author of those poems aforementioned in which he dwells on the vices of the sex; but as stated before he had to do so as the occasion demanded it.[2]

Sāmal's heroines

1. उद्यमकर्मसंवाद, a dialogue between Human Effort and Fate.

2. In this connection see pp. 12-13 of Preface to Sinhāsan Batrishi, Part I, by A. B. Jāni, where he quotes in Samal's own words, the object the poet had in view in writing the story of सूडाबहोतेरी: That it was a pure work (निर्मळ ग्रंथ) and that, the reader would profit from it according to his lights: the sinner would find in it a stone, the pious (हरिजन) a diamond.

Thus does Sāmal sing. He is a poet, bold and refined, and appears to have the whole field to himself as the foremost story teller of his time. Yet actually in the light of further research, he cannot be said to stand quite alone.[1]

Sāmal had predecessors and successors

Like Premānand, he was an accomplished Hindi scholar, and some of his peoms are interspersed with Hindi verses. His use of Persian words is also more frequent than that of any of his contemporaries.

Sāmal knew both Hindi and Persian

In closing his review of the seventeenth century Mr. Tripathi sums up thus: "Akho, Premānand and Sāmal are thus the three leading stars of Gujarāti poetry, and as will appear from the history of subsequent centuries, they are the only poets who throughout the whole history of Gujarāti literature, wrote pure and genuine poetry without any substantial subservience to religion." They were (लोककवि) poets of the people. They

Poems of Akho, Premānand and Sāmal not subservient to religion

1. There were a large number of story tellers in verse who preceded Sāmal, like the authors of Hansāvati, VikramaCharitra and several Jain authors. Among these Sāmal comes almost last chronologically. He has had a number of imitators too. On this point see p. 10 of Preface to HariLilā Śodash Kalā by Ambalāl B. Jāni.

influenced the people not only of their own days, but those who came after: indeed even now they have not lost their influence.

Minor poets of the century

The group of minor poets belonging to this century is too large to be passed over without notice. They are smaller stars, with varying magnitudes, with Vallabh, the son of Premānand at the top and versifiers like Dwārkādās at the bottom.

Mukund

Mukund came from Dwārkā and was a Gugli Brāhmin by caste. His best known work, the BhaktaMāl (a rosary of Saints or Devotees) was written in Samvat year 1708 (A. D. 1665). His lives of Kabir, who is admired both by Hindus and Mahomedans, and Gorakh are indeed well-written and full of information. The poet declares that "when Kabir expired all creation wept, men, animals and plants alike. Both Hindus and Mahomedans began to fight amongst themselves; one said Kabir belonged to the Hindus, and that they would burn him on a pyre; the other said, he belonged to the Mahomedans, and they would bury

his Kabir-Charitra

him in a grave. Seeing them thus fighting, the saint took pity on them and came back to the earth and tried to pacify both. To the Hindus he said, "Brothers! I should be burnt," and to the Mahomedans, "Why do you quarrel? I am born of dust and will return to dust (shall be buried)." He then divided his body into two, and gave one-half each to the Hindus and the Yavanas."[1]

Mode of ascertaining dates of minor poets

It is not possible, nor from our present point of view very material to ascertain the dates of the birth and death of most of the minor poets. The only means of ascertaining the time during which they lived and wrote are the dates and years of composition generally-almost invariably-given by all of them, in the closing lines of their poems. This has enabled the following poets to be assigned to this century.

1. Mukund was a Hindi scholar and the closing lines of his KabirCharitra summarised above are composed in Hindi.

(कवित)

बस्ती बनस्पति रोई, दुनी ओर बनकी,
हिन्दु ही मुसल्मीन, ल्ढे दोऊ मील मील,
कबीर हे तेरा मेरा, चिता घोर करंगे.
× × ×
महादयालु हे संत, स्वधामसे पीछे आये,
दोनुको समज दीनो, भाई हम जरंगे.
मुसल्मीनकु कहा कहाको फिसाद करो,
भाई हम जाय भूमि, मांही सोई परंगे.
वेसा उच्चारन करी देहके दो भाग करी,
हिन्दु यवनको दीने, संत दयावान जो.

Devidās, and his Rukmiṇiharaṇ

Devidās was a Gāndharva by caste, and lived at Sojitrā in the Petlād district. He wrote his Rukmiṇiharaṇ in Samvat year 1660 (A. D. 1604). It describes the marriage of Krishṇa with Rukmiṇi, whom he abducted at her own request while she was going to worship the goddess Ambikā in a temple. She was the daughter of Bhimak, the king of Vidarbha. She did not like Śiśupāl whom her brother Rukmaiyā wanted her to marry, and so wrote in secret to Krishṇa to come and take her away. Krishṇa did so. This sort of abduction was in vogue then, and was not considered disgraceful, as it was allowed by the then Shāstras. Directly Rukmaiyā came to know of this violence, he pursued with a large army the chariot in which the eloping couple were driving away. But Krishṇa was able to defeat him and his army and was at last going to kill him with a powerful arrow, when in a passage of some pathos his wife began to solicit him to spare him:[1] "Rukmiṇi began to entreat, O Yādavaji ! listen to what I say, O my dear lord ! The

1. रुक्मिणी विनती विनवे, यादवजी जी;
तमो सांभळो श्री महाराज ! कहुं प्रीतमजी जी.
ए खोड वेसे अमने, यादवजी जी;
ए मूको मारो वीर, कहुं प्रीतमजी जी.
में माततात सहु मूकीआं, यादवजी जी;
हुं तो आवी तमारे साथ, कहुं प्रीतमजी जी.
में तातभुवन सहु ताज कीधां, यादवजी जी;
मारे तन मन धन तमो आप, कहुं प्रीतमजी जी.
मारो भाई मारवो नन्न घटे, यादवजी जी;'
दुःख धरी एम बोल्यां वाण, कहुं प्रीतमजी जी.

disgrace of this deed of yours would rest on my head, O Yādavaji! therefore spare my brother, O my dear lord! I have left my mother, father and all, O Yādavaji! and have come with you, O my dear lord! I have left the palace of my parents, O Yādavaji! you are my all in all and you are my sole support, O my dear lord! It does not behove you to slay my brother, O Yādavaji! She spoke as above and said, O my lord!"

Description of wedding then, good even today

Krishṇa was unable to resist her entreaty and spared him. On reaching Dwārkā he celebrated a marriage with her in accordance with the usual rites and ceremonies, and from the description given by the poet of this celebration, it appears that we, in Gujarāt, have not changed in the least during the last three centuries in our marriage-rites. Some of the songs,[1] sung at the marriage of Krishṇa and Rukmiṇi are still used at weddings in Gujarāt.

1. For instance the song beginning with

ब्रह्माए दीधी दश गांठ, छबीला ! दोरडो क्यम छूटशे ?
तारो वसुदेव तात तेडाव, छबीला ! दोरडो क्यम छूटशे ?
वळी देवकी मात बोलाव, छबीला ! दोरडो क्यम छूटशे ?

Appropriate changes in the name of the bride-groom's father, mother, etc., are, of course, made.

Śivdās

Sivdās belonged to Cambay, at one time a very important city of Gujarāt. He was a Nāgar Brāhmin by caste and he is the writer of DraupadiSwayamvara, Dāngav-Ākhyān, Ekādasi Māhātmya, Kāmāvati-ni Vārtā, and other miscellaneous verses. The subject-matter of the first is taken from the Mahābhārat, and of the others from Purānic mythology. There is nothing striking in his work. He wrote the Swayamvara in Samvat year 1673 at Bijāpur in the Deccan. It is curious how many old poets of Gujarāt have lived in the Deccan and written their works there, even in times when communication between the north and the south was not so easy as it is now. Premānand did much of his work at Nandarbār, and this poet did his at Bijāpur still further south, while Virji, a pupil of Premānand wrote at Burhānpur and Ratanji at Bāglāṇ. (Virji, by the way, had migrated from Burhānpur, which was his native place, to Barodā).

Curious fact that some Gujarāti poets lived in the Deccan

Vishnudās, the forerunner of Premānand

Vishnudās, a co-pupil of Sivdās, also lived at Cambay and was a Nāgar Brāhmin by caste:[1] It is not known when he was born or died, but the

1. See Brihat KāvyaDohana Vol. VIII, Preface p. 29, as to the trend of poetry then.

dates of his works, about seven in number, range from A. D. 1578 to A. D. 1657 and he is therefore supposed to have lived to a very great age. He has versified many Parvas (Chapters) of the Mahābhārat and almost all the Kāndas (sections) of the Rāmāyaṇ, in addition to writing several Ākhyāns. Some of his other works, such as Kunvarbāinun Mosālun, LakśmaṇāHaraṇ and Sudāmā-Charitra, are now supposed to have furnished the originals on which Premānand worked. Vishnudās himself has quoted, in the Mosālun, Narsinh Mehtā's own verses on the subject, thus the fact, that Narsinh Mehtā had written a poem on this miraculous incident in his life, which till recently was in dispute is now proved, and Narsinh Mehtā's successors, like Vishnudās, Vishavanāth Jāni, and Premānand merely worked on the materials left by him. Premānand in his LakśmaṇāHaraṇ alludes to a work of Vishnudās bearing the same name, thus showing that he took advantage of the work of his predecessor. Vishnudās' poems, though they are very simple, still shew that he was able at times to infuse the narrative with force and feeling as occasion required it. He wrote one poem called the Dhruvākhyān, under the name of Haridās.[1]

1. Besides this one there was another poet of this name. He was one of the two sons of Bhālaṇ, whose names were Uddhav and Vishnudās. They too had composed the Rāmāyaṇ in verse; the

Viśwanath Jāni, the poet from whom Premānand borrowed

Viśwanāth Jāni, a Nāgar Brahmin by caste, belonged to Pātaṇ, and in A. D. 1652 wrote a poem called the Life of Narsinh Mehtā (नरसिंह मेहेताहं चरित्र). It comprises all the well-known incidents in his life, where Krishṇa helped him out of his difficulties. Parts of this poem, have been utilised by Premānand in his two most popular poems, the Māmerun and the Hundi, and in places there is such a close resemblance between the verses of the two, that it would appear as if the more famous but junior poet had "lifted" them out of the work of his contemporary, without acknowledging his indebtedness to him. He has written also the Hār-Charitra otherwise called the Hārmālā, and it is suspected that the work of that name attributed to Premānand was partially written by Jāni. "The fight of Ganim" is a historical poem said to be written by him.[1]

date given in the closing lines of one of its Chāpters is A. D. 1519. A short but informative and critical biography of Vishnudās with a list of his poems, is given in the Eighth Volume of the BrihatKāvya Dohana, from which I have summarised. The writer is Mr. Natvarlāl I. Desai, B. A., who has worked on this branch of literature under the guidance of his father, the late Mr. Ichhārām S. Desāi.

1. Very interesting notes bearing on this subject are to be found in the Eighth Volume of the Brihat Kāvya Dohana. This poem (गनीमनो पवाडो) is printed, though found incomplete, in the बुद्धिप्रकाश, May and September 1913.

Of Murāri, nothing is known beyond his works.

Murāri

His IśwarVivāh describes in a humourous way the difficulty that Siva (Mahādev) had in marrying the daughter of Menā and Himālaya. Śiva presented himself at the gates of the mother-in-law in all the glory of his clothelessness, riding a bullock with quite an army of Bhuts (spirits) following him. Menā was keenly disappointed, and cursed Nārada, a Rishi wellknown for his mischief-making nature. He had given quite a glowing account of the bride-groom which at close quarters turned out to be false. In the end explanations followed, and she was convinced of the mightiness of her son-in-law, and allowed the marriage to take place.

Śridhar Swāmi and his GauriCharitra

Śridhar Swāmi has also written a poem, called GauriCharitra, in which a celebrated incident in the life of Mahādev is described. While the god was undergoing austerities (तपस्) in a forest, his wife Pārvati undertook to divert his attention from it and she did so by transforming herself into a beautiful Bhil or forest-woman, and dancing before him. Her beauty and dance were enough to distract him and he offered to take her home. For a god like Mahādev, to fall from his high estate and offer to marry a Sudra woman was a great fall, but so enamoured was he of her that he ignored the disgrace. After a time an explanation was given and everything ended happily.

Narhari and his Gitā

Narhari a co-pupil of Akhā, wrote his Bhagvad-Gitā in Samvat year 1677.[1] This is all that is known of him. So far as we have been able to ascertain, this is the first poetical version or rather translation of the entire BhagavadGitā into Gujarati.[2] A perusal of it shows the poet to be a fine Sanskrit scholar, who has been able to render some of the difficult passages of the Lord's Song into smooth-running and simple Gujarāti. One does not feel as if one were reading the Gujarāti translation of a highly philosophical Sanskrit work; the expression of the sentiment and the translation of the thoughts are so natural that the whole poem appears to be an original work. Premānand during this period also produced another translation of the

1. He has also written ज्ञानगीता and वसिष्ठसार a Ms. copy of which is to be found in the collection of the Forbes Gujarāti Sabhā, Bombay. Both of them have been printed and published.

2. There is also the Gitā by RāmKrishṇa, but it is impossible to say when it was written. Various versions of the Gitā in prose and poetry are found in Gujarāti from the earliest times, it being a religious work.

same work, basing it on the Sanskrit commentary of Sridhar Swami.[1]

Vallabh:

Of the pupils of Premānand, Vallabh,[2] his son, stands at the top. Premānand is said to have assigned to some of them the lines on which they were to work, and his son, Vallabh, was advised to write poetry which would flatter no prince or possible patron. This advice was a bold innovation, as the custom was to overload poems with the praises of individuals from whom authors hoped to get help. Vallabh carried out the behest so far that he praised none save his own father, and that too with a vengeance. The great Hindi poet Chand, called Chand Baradāyi, he handles so severely as compared with his treatment of Premānand, that we feel contempt for one

his partiality for his father

1 It is published in पद्बंध भागवत, 3rd edition (1916), by the Gujarāti Printing Press.

2. There are many scholars who have cast doubt on Vallabh's authorship of poems attributed to him. As observed before, Mr. Mānkad considers that Premānand's Nātaks might have been written by Vallabh. As no Mss. copies of Vallabh's poetic compositions are forthcoming Mr. Rāmnārāyaṇ V. Pāthak considers them to be of doubtful authenticity. These are after all but mere conjectures. None of the above writers, who have raised doubts about the authenticity of some of the works of ancient poets, have been able to prove conclusively whose works they are, if not of the original poets.

so blind to the merits of others, that he could see no ability or good in any one else save his own father, whose fame was local, as compared with that of Chand. Excepting a few stray incidents illustrating his want of control over his temper, and roughness of manners and expression, at times bordering on boorishness, there is not much to learn about his life. These characteristics lie so much on the surface of his works that it is unnecessary to call special attention to them. His father's advice to him, never to praise a living individual, is said to have been the cause of his destroying a poem, written by him in praise of Premānand's friend, Mādhav Sheth, and it was for the same reason that he had to abandon his ambition of becoming a court-poet, as that at least would have compelled him to eulogise the reigning prince.

and impetuous temper

Allusion has already been made to the part taken by Vallabh in disparaging Sāmal.[1] The point at issue is said to have been whether the function of poetry was story-telling like that of Sāmal, the stories being founded on imaginary subjects; or whether it was the clothing of subjects with poetic figures and ideas, those subjects being taken from the Purāṇas. Vallabh, of course, upheld his father's

Vallabh's abuse of Sāmal

1. See page 94 footnote (1).

method, and spared no words in condemning Sāmal and his sons. It is said his Vallabh-Jhaghado[1] -the quarrel of Vallabh- is full of pitiless personal allusions. Sāmal's son was squint-eyed, and Vallabh spitefully referred to this defect in his abuse. His idea was that the sons of Premānand, himself and his brother Jivaṇrām, were there to defend their father as against the squint-eyed son of Sāmal.

Virji and his Surekhāharaṇ

Virji, one of Premānand's pupils seems to have been assigned the function of writing stories and he wrote the Surekhāharaṇ (V. S. 1720). In merit it did not stand high, and that gave a handle to Vallabh to banter even Virji. He called him a woman, an effeminate being, making a pun on the last syllable of his name-ji-which would bring out the meaning mother. The publishers of the Prāchin KāvyaMālā have said that as a counterblast to Sāmal's poem AngadVishti, where the great representative of the monkey tribe goes to Rāvaṇ, to see if he could negotiate a peace, Vallabh wrote KrishṇaVishti,[2] where

1. By some the authorship of it is attributed to Premānand. But really speaking this work has not seen the light of day.

2. It is the opinion of some that if it was ever written, it should have been written by Vallabh. But as AngadVishti was written in V. S. 1799 or 1808 by Sāmal, the fact that KrishṇaVishti was written as a counterblast to Sāmal's poem is entirely doubtful. No work of Vallabh written after V. S. 1781 has come to light as yet

Krishṇa goes as a messenger of peace to the Kauravas on behalf of the Pāṇḍavas. In doing so, he flings a word of abuse at a poet who could conceive of no other emissary than a monkey, when a far superior individual was at hand. Not one of his disciples to whom he had assigned special lines of work, was able to satisfy Premānand with his work. Virji, we have already seen, had failed, and so had Ratneśwar, who was directed to write verses like those of the well-known Marāthi poets, Moropant and Vāman. Vallabh was directed to follow the spirit of Hindi poetry and he did his work so well in his KrishṇaVishti, that Premānand was more than satisfied and called upon him to ask for whatever boon he liked. Vallabh said: "The vow you have taken not to put on your turban till there was literature worth the name in Gujarāti is now fulfilled. I too have taken a vow not to put on my turban till I have successfully carried out your behests. You say, I have done so now. Therefore, put on your turban." Premānand could not resist the appeal, and put on his turban. He did so for the nonce only as he felt that his vow had not been fulfilled in its entirety.[1]

Vallabh's Krishṇa-Vishti

and Premānand's satisfaction

1 माग माग मारा सुत ! मुख माग्युं आपुं तुने,
कवीश्वरे एवी घडी एक वार आणी'ती;

Vallabh nicknamed mad

Inheritance of Premānand's literary works

Premānand used to call him, Vallabh the mad, because he always found him like a mad man, running full tilt against some one or another. After his father's death Vallabh asked his brother Jivaṇrām to give no other share, to him out of the patrimony, than his father's works in their entirety. He cited by way of contrast the instance of Ratneśwar, whose sons divided his works, instead of one of them taking possession of all of them. The division led to their being lost to the world, as one brother got one portion of a poem, and the other, another. Jivaṇrām acceded to his request, but late in life Vallabh felt the pinch of poverty, as the works brought him no wealth.

His PremānandKathā unpublished

He is said to have written a life of his father, his last work, called Premānand-Kathā, in which to please his father's fancy, he has made use

द्विज अग्निकाष्ट माग्यां मृग लेई गयो जेह.
पाघ दं'रावी कविए, कविता बखाणी'ती.
यक्षे कह्युं ए तो में ज परीक्षा जोवाने ह्यर्यां,
पिताए कर्युं'तुं एम सुत रीत जाणी'ती.
... ...
वीरजीए पाघ आपी प्रेमथी प्रमाणी'ती.

यक्षप्रश्नोत्तर० ५२१

This and other statements will be found in the different volumes of the Prāchina KāvyaMālā relating to the different poets.

only of pure Gujarāti words. This work, however, has not seen the light of day.

Vallabh's ambition

His ambition was to write poems illustrating all the nine Rasas,-Tragic, Comic, Heroic, Terrific, Erotic, Wrathful, etc.

and his works

His works are the Duhśāsana-rudhira-pānākhyān (A. D. 1724), Kunti-prasānnākhyān (A. D. 1721), YakśaPraśnottar (A. D. 1725), KrishṇaVishti,[1] Vallabh-Jhaghado,[2] Premānand Katha,[3] MitraDharmākhyān (A. D. 1704), Yudhiśthira-Vakrodarākhyān (A. D. 1715) and many others. He is credited with having written some dramas[4] also.

Duhśāsana Rudhirapan

The insult offered by Duhśāsana to Draupadi, as told in the Mahābharat, is the subject of the DuhśāsanaRudhirapān. When Yudhiśthira staked her as his last stake, she was in her periods, and secluded as is the custom at such times. A message was sent to her to come to the Council. When she refused to attend Duhśāsana rushed to her chamber, and dragg-

1, 2, 3. These works having not yet been given to the public. their dates are not given.

4 Only a part of one of his dramas मारुतीविजय is published in a work, called प्रेमानन्दनां ज नाटको, by the late Matubhāi H. Kāntāvālā, M. A. For the names of his other dramas see the Buddhiprakāsh, January 1911.

-ed her in her *deshabille*, ignoring her protests, into the Council of elders. Bhima, unable to witness the indignity, silently vowed vengeance on him, and took an oath that he would not rest content till he had drunk the blood of the individual who had laid desecrating hands on his wife. The whole poem is in the heroic vein. Bhima is the hero with Krishṇa as his squire, his antagonist being Duhśāsana. Where the poet depicts the courage of Karṇa, he gives a picture of what courage in a Kśatriya means. The poem is conceived in a very admirable manner.

Yakśa Praśnottar

The YakśaPraśnottar, in which all the Pāṇdavas excepting Yudhiśthira are killed for failing to answer the questions set to them by the guardian jinn of a tree growing near a lake before being allowed to quench their thirst from it, and are brought back to life as the latter gave satisfactory answers, is couched in the tragic vein.

KuntiPrasannākhyān

The KuntiPrasannākhyān is an example of how he describes the preternatural or marvellous (अद्भुत रस). The mansion built by Maya Dānav –the architect of the gods– for the Pāṇdavas was a beautiful and marvellous piece of workmanship. Its description in the Mahābhārat is worth perusal. He was able to give to water the appearance of glass and vice versa; the delusion was so complete that people actually tried to walk on the water and removed their shoes while nearing the surface of glass for fear of wetting them. On this surface did the mother of the Pāṇdavas (Kunti) see the reflection of the seven-trunked elephant of Indra called Airāvat, and so life-like was the representation that she asked her sons to get the animal for her. For this purpose, Bhima and Arjuna had to go to the region of the gods-Swarga-in the heavens, on a bridge constructed of arrows. After a strenuous fight with the divine guardians of the elephant, they were able to bring him to earth and present him to their mother.

Attack on poet Chand

The opening portion of this Ākhyān consists of a bitter attack on the poet Chand. He says: "Chand has written one work only (Rāso) while Premānand has written two or three long poems (like Bhārata). Chand has praised a king of the earth (Prithirāj), while Premānand's poetry is like the sun. The Bhāts (the caste to which Chand belonged) are descended from the Brāhmins, while Brāhmins (the caste to which Premānand belonged) are descended from Brahma. Chand is thus inferior to the father of the poet (i. e., Vallabh)."[1] Towards the end of the poem,

1. भारत समुं प्रमाण, रासाना तमासा भाळो,
कर्यां भारत बे त्रण, भारत ऊवेखीए.

(according to one interpretation), he indulges in a mean attack on Sāmal in terms very thinly veiled.

and Sāmal

A Brāhmin, while gazing at the elephant which was brought down from heaven to earth, is made to write out impromptu verses, in which he says he would not accept as a reward for his poetry, gleanings from the harvest-floor of any one, alluding in sarcastic terms to the reward in kind that Sāmal had received from his Zemindar patron, Rakhidās.[1]

In this poem Vallabh is seen to be proud of his parentage and spiteful towards his rivals.

Mitra-dharmākhyān and abuse of Sāmal

The Mitra-dharmākhyān (V. S. 1760) relates the story of two friends, Indu and Mindu. In spite of the ungratefulness of one of them, who was

पृथ्वीश प्रशंसा कथी, मान शेनुं मोधुं तेमां,
प्रेमानंदनी कविता, सविताशी पेखीए.
ब्राह्मणथी भाट थया, वंशज विधिना आ तो,
कवीश्वरना पितार्थी चंद मंद देखीए.

कुन्तिप्रसन्नाख्यान, कवित १.

1. एवो जोग जोई एक, ब्राह्मण के भाट आव्यो,
गुण गावा लाग्यो झट, कविता नांखी करी.
शिवी सम दानेश्वरी, नृप अमे टेक रखी.-
दा कनेथी दान लेवुं, खळुं लेवुं ना जरी.

कुन्तिप्रसन्नाख्यान, कवित २०२.

on the point of murdering the other, that very friend rescues him from many dangerous and inconvenient situations. Even here, as some interpret it, Vallabh has not spared Sāmal, about whom he says that he is a disgrace to Gujarāt. "There are some (poets) who forget their duty as Brāhmins; they have chosen to inhabit Gujarāt, and therefore, bring disgrace on her. They solder without solder. (They solder disgrace to Gujarāt without solder)."[1]

Draupadi's wrath and rebuke to Yudhiśthira

In the dialogue between Bhima and his elder brother Yudhiśthira,[2] Vallabh has tried to delineate Wrathfulness. Bhima and Draupadi score here, and the wrath and anger depicted by the poet cannot be surpassed. The following extract shows how the poet makes Draupadi nag at her devoted husband: "If you wished to be merciful, why did you become a great king?.........If you wished to observe your

1. द्विजधर्म भूलनार, वास वस्या तेणे करी,
गुजरातने कलंक रेण विना रेवता.
मित्रधर्माख्यान.

There are some critics who, looking to the date (about V. S. 1785) when Sāmal went to the court of Rakhidās, are of opinion that this could not be an attack on Sāmal, but on that class of Brahmins, who go begging from door to door and thus bring disgrace on fellow Brāhmins, who were pursuing more creditable avocations, such as recitation of the Purāṇas.

2. Based on the किरातार्जुनीयम् of Bhāravi.

Dharma, then the instance of Kauśik who abandoned his kingdom was before you.........If your nature was gentle, then my lord, you should have rested satisfied with the one kingdom, Indraprastha, you had got.........Why did you perform the Rājasuya Yajna and incur sin ? You are born a Kshatriya and therefore you have to do these (evil) deeds. If you had been born an ascetic, then you would not have had to do anything bad. Draupadi glared while she spoke these words, with her head thrown back, and threatening with her uplifted hand."[1]

Vallabh and Premānand on the superiority of Gujarāti

Both Vallabh and his father were very proud of Gujarāti, which in their opinion was second only to Sanskrit. They could not brook hearing Hindi

1. दयाळु थवुं हतुं जो तो थया शें भूप मोटा ?
× × × × ×
धर्म ज्यारे धारवो'तो तो तज्युं कौशिके राज
× × × × ×
जो स्वभाव शांत हतो तो तो इन्द्रप्रस्थ एक
जे मळ्युं हतुं ते स्वामी ! लेई सुखी थावुं'तुं.
× × × × ×
राजसूय आरंभीने, पापमां शें जावुं'तुं ?
क्षत्रीकुळ धर्म धर्यो माटे कर्यां कूडां कष्ट,
थया होत तपसी जो, कूडुं क्यां त्यां गावुं'तुं ?
चक्षने चढावी करी, करांगुलीने हलावी,
शीर्षने धूणावी अति, वामा वदी वेण त्यां.
युधिष्ठिरवृकोदरः कवित ७८–८०

laying claims to that position and in the opening of this work, Vallabh narrates how his father tried conclusions with a Hindi, and by belabouring him with hard words proved, to his satisfaction the superiority of Gujarāti. The features of Gujarāti which struck them as the most remarkable are thus described by Vallabh: "In point of delicacy, it is more delicate than a lotus flower, and honey and nectar yield to it in sweetness. In no other language is such purity to be found, while in point of antiquity it is considered supreme.. It is the leader of the nine Rasas and it gives happiness. Only those who are not acquainted with it speak ill of it. Those who say that it is entirely lacking in spirit err, because they have not seen Gujarāti works dealing with heroic incidents."[1]

Vallabh vows that, if he be blessed with as long a life as his father, he will compose works which

1. कोमळता कमळथी अधिक देखाय जेमां,
मधु-सुधा मिष्टपणे हारी हारी जाय छे;
अमलता एना जेवी नथी कोई भाषा मध्य,
प्राचीनपणुं तो जेनुं मोटेरुं मनाय छे.
नव रसनी नायिका, सुखदायिका छे सिद्ध,
जाणे नहि तेह एना खोटा गुण गाय छे.
कईकणापणुं कहे छे नथी एना मांही रज,
वीर ग्रंथ भाळ्या नहीं, खता तेणे खाय छे.
युधिष्ठिर वृकोदरः कवित १६

will put the Divine language (Sanskrit), let alone Hindi, to shame.

Virji

Virji was an inhabitant of Burhānpur on the Tāpti. He came to Barodā and was welcomed by Premānand, who assigned to him the task of writing narrative poetry. Virji attempted it but with poor results and was always the butt of Vallábh's jokes. He was possessed of a good voice, and therefore Premānand called him to his help at times, and Virji sang his verses with success. His works comprise 1. Kámāvatini Kathā (A. D. 1669), 2. Balirājānun Ākhyān (A. D. 1675), 3. KākurājKathā, 4. SurekhāHaraṇ (A. D. 1664), 5. Daśavatār (A. D. 1686), and 6. VyāsKathā. Nos. 3 and 6 have not yet been published.

and his learning

Virji was vain, shallow and illiterate. He held out great promise but fell far short of it in actual performance. He boasts that as beautiful lines as he composed are not to be found in the Purāṇas, and that he was so painstaking that in order to write his BaliRājākhyān, he made a complete study of the Bhāgwat, the Bhārat and the Purāṇas, a stupendous task. He was also asked by Premānand to compose poetry on the lines of Persian and Urdu poets.

Ratneśwar, son of Meghaji, a Śrimāli Brāhmin

of Dabhoi, was a contemporary and a pupil of Premā-nand,[1] and had studied at Benares before he took to writing poetry. He had, like some other educated persons of his time, to fall back on the profession of reciting Purāṇas to earn his living, and thus had come into conflict with vested interests. Those older Purānis who had already been following the profession, could not brook this trespass on their preserves by a person of acknowledged superior intelligence, for he was educated at Benares, and the open insults and injuries, at times amounting to personal violence, offered to him, in order to drive him away from places frequented by them, were many and persistent. He was denounced, and insulted at caste dinners also, but he rose superior to these annoyances and at last triumphed over them. His work was appreciated by Premānand, who himself was no favourite of this orthodox Purāni tribe. He was led to leave Dabhoi, his birth place, because he feared that if he stayed there longer his life would be in danger. But on leaving home, he made a vow that he would compose a work that would be read in each and every home, that even old women at their spinning wheel would

Ratneśwar

His persecution by Purānis

1. His works were written between V. S. years 1739 and 1770. He was born in V. S. 1705 and died in 1775 as per opinion of Mr. A. B. Jāni, B. A.

recite it, and thus a death blow would be given to the business of the Purāṇ reciters.

Approbation of his work

He was a great favourite of the Vallabhāchāryā Mahārāj of the place, who called him the Vyās of the Kaliyuga, a very high compliment which added to the jealousy of his rivals. From Dabhoi he went to a place called Karṇat,[1] on the banks of the Narmadā and there wrote his Bhāgwat in twelve chapters (Dwādaśa-Skandha), which met with the approval of Premānand. With this composition he returned to Dabhoi, and his recitation of it won so much praise that all his townsmen made him a present of a house, which even now is known as "Ratneśwar's Rooms."

Unfortunate partition of his literary effects

Allusion has already been made to the division of Ratneśwar's literary effects amongst his sons after his death. They did not realise the value of their father's work and made a great mistake when they divided it up as they did. They squabbled over the Bhāgwat, a very substantial volume. In the

1 The poet himself says:

वसतो वाडव दर्भावती तज्युं नगर को कारण गति,
श्रीमाळी रत्नेश्वर नाम कर्णपुरीमां पाम्यो ठाम.

स्वर्गारोहण, अ. ८ क. ३८.

partition of the manuscript one secured the first and last three (1–3 and 10–12), and the other the remaining (4 to 9) chapters. The son to whom the first and last three parts were given was illiterate, and those who were jealous of Ratneśwar's reputation thought this a good opportunity for taking revenge on him even after his death. They told him that his father liked this work most, and hence he had better send it with him to heaven, by burning it on his funeral pyre. He agreed to this and was on the point of consigning it to the flames, when some old Brāhmins told him that it was usual to give libations of water to such departed souls and so he had better throw the leaves into water, or even if he dipped them into water, that would do. He did so, and in that way did the Purānis partially wreck their vengeance. They were thus lost. It is said that a Sādhu, Kālidās by name, has rewritten them.

His nature

Ratneśwar was a man of a long suffering nature, patient under calamities and of a dogged perseverance. In religion he was a Vaishnav, a devotee of Rādhā and Krishṇa. He was advised by Premānand to translate Sanskrit works into Gujarāti, as his knowledge of Sanskrit was scholarly, and, after Premānand, he was the next man to embellish Gujarāti with poetical translations of standard Sanskrit works. He was a master of versification (छंद composition.)

His works

Ratneśwar's works are: 1. The BhagwadGitā, 2. The MurkhaLakshṇāvali (signs of foolishness)[1] (A. D. 1714), 3. Sugṇāvali[2], 4. MahimanStotra, 5. ŚiśupālVadha, 6. Gangālahari, 7. The Bhāgwat,[3] all translations from Sanskrit, and 8. Kāmavilās, 9. RādhāKrishṇanā Mahinā, 10. Vairāgyalatā and several padas, his original compsitions, 11. Aśwamedh (V. S. 1743), 12. Laṇkākānda (Rāmāyaṇ), 13. ÁtmaVichār-Chandrodaya[4], 14. Swargārohaṇa (V. S. 1748).

1. See page 186.

2. Also a translation from Sanskrit, written perhaps to supplement the verses on foolishness. It is found incomplete.

3. Ratneśwar did not compose the chapters (स्कन्ध) of the Bhāgwat in their regular order as the first and tenth were written in v. s. 1740, eleventh in v. s. 1747, and second in v. s. 1749.

4. Through Mr. A. B. Jani's courtsey I have come across a copy of this poem published by one Kānji Vālāji at Bombay in A. D. 1869. In the preface he has given a curious legend, viz., that Ratneshwar's sister's young son, who was living in his house with his wife was so impressed with the lessons of Vairāgya (renunciation of the world) in it that he completely disregarded her. Once she was feeding a young calf. It became frisky and began to gambol. She addressed it and said "Don't do so, if you gambol about like that, my husband's uncle would breathe such a mantra into you, that you would renounce the world." Ratneśwar overheard this and, making inquiries, learnt the truth. He thereupon composed Kāma-Vilās (Kāmakalikā, a work on erotics) and gave it to him. He studied it and became the father of several children. Thereafter

In his Padās, he inculcates the Doctrine of Bhakti which according to him is indispensable to mankind. In various forms, at various stages in the development of the human race and in various countries, this yearning after Bhakti has manifested itself. In doing so, "some became devotees of the moon and the sun, some of the earth and some of the nine planets, Some of the clay, some of the dust, some of the gods inhabiting the river ghāts (bathing places), and some of the upright road-side stones. Some worshipped the tiger and some the elephant. Some would be found worshipping Shaikhs and some Hindu recluses (Gosāvi Sādhus); some worshipping man and some worshipping woman. There are a million kinds of devotee. What proofs shall I give you? Ratneśwar says, show your devotion to be earnest and you will enjoy the rare pleasure of salvation."[1]

Doctrine of Bhakti preached by him

Ratneshwar gave him the former book, he read it and became a sanyāsin. Only ten sections out of fourteen of this work are available. In the last four sections he had so vigorously set out the theme of each work that those who studied them, either renounced the world or became hopelessly steeped in the enjoyment of worldly pleasures. He therefore destroyed them by throwing them into water.

1. चंद्रना, सूर्यना सेवको को थया, भूमि ने नवग्रह तणा भक्त जाणो;
मृतकना, माटीना, घाटीना, भाथीना, हाथीना, व्याघ्रना मत्र आणो.

The Murkhāvali[1] catalogues the characteristics and doings of a fool, and is followed by a poem showing the characteristics of a wise man.

The Murkhāvali

The ĀtmaVichārChandrodaya (which includes Vairāgyalatā) is mainly taken up with philosophy and metaphysics.

His philosophical works

Haridās was a Visā Lād Baniā of Barodā, and was working as a steward or servant in Premānand's family. Association with the poet turned his attention towards learning and poetry and taking him as his Guru, he succeeded in obtaining some share of the good things of literature. He has composed about thirteen poetical works. He died during Premānand's lifetime, and he having been entrusted with the manage-

Haridās

Premānand's administration of his property

शेखना, भेखना, मरदना, मेरीना, भक्त लाखो दऊं शां प्रमाणो ?
रत्न कहे यलथी भक्तिने दाखवे, भाखवे भिन्न मुक्तिनी माणो.

पद ६, प्रा. का. माळा, १५ पा. १७

मेरी means a woman and not Virgin Mary, the mother of Christ, as one scholar of old Gujarāti interprets it, vide p. 77 Gujarātī Divāli Issue of 19th October 1930.

1 One Govind Bhatt had composed this work in Sanskrit in seventy shlokas. Ratneshwar based his own work on it and amplified it into eighty five; p. 28 रत्नेश्वरकृत कविता. Vol. XV. Prāchin KāvyaMālā. Mr. A. B. Jāni thinks that Govind Bhatt was a Bengali.

ment of his servant's property, gave rich caste dinners in his honour after his death and administered it to the complete satisfaction of his caste people.

His works

Some of his works are: SitāViraha (A. D. 1666), Marriage of Narsinh Mehtā's son—Śamalshāh (A. D. 1669–70), Śrāddha of Narsinh Mehta's father (A. D. 1671), and Bhāratsār (A. D. 1681). Needless to say that they are very ordinary, compared with the masterpieces of his Guru, but they are full of good descriptive passages.

Haridās gift of a poem to Ādhār Bhatt

The poem written by Haridās on the marriage of Sāmalshā, the son of Narsinh Mehtā, -called सामळशाहनो विवाह-appears from some of its editions, to be composed by Ādhar Bhatt,[1] a Khedāvāl Brāhmin of Broach. It has been conjectured that Haridās after writing it made a present of it to this Brāhmin, to enable him to earn his living by reciting it, the gift of the poem being considered a meritorious act.[2]

Dwarkādās

Dwārkādās belonged to the same caste as Haridās, and was a neighbour of Premānand. He had learned by heart many Bhajans in Gujarāti and Hindi, and once

1. By profession Ādhar Bhatt was a reciter of Ākhyāns. Some Ākhyān-poems are said to have been composed by him, but his authorship is open to doubt: there is no proof of it.

2. See p. 12. Preface to Volume VIII of the Brihat Kāvya Dohana.

Premānand suggested that he too should write some poetry. Vallabh, who happened to be near, in his usual way bantered him, by saying that one might as well expect old women or yokels to write poetry. Premānand took this remark of his son ill, and made up his mind to teach Dwārkādās how to compose poetry in a week, and by dint of perseverance, was able to get him to write quite presentable verses in a short time. He is said to have written about twenty five books, and several Padas including KrishṇaLilā.

-taught by Premānand

Gopāldās, a native of Surat, has written a work on Brahma-jnān, called GopālGita.[1] It is a treatise on Vedāntic philosophy in verse, according to the Saivaite school, written at Ahmedābād in A. D. 1650. He is the author of miscellaneous verses also on the same subject.[2]

Gopaldās

1. See ante p. 88, footnote.

2. Another poet of the same name flourished in A. D. 1570-75. He has written two poems, called the वल्लभाख्यान and the भक्तिपीयूष. He belonged to a village called Rupāl near Kadi, and was dumb from his birth. Gosāinji Vithalnāth, the son of the great Vallabhāchārya happening to see him at the house of a devotee of his-whose daughter was married to him-asked him who he was. On being told of the girl's and her husband's misfortune, the Gosāinji put a piece of betel-leaf chewed by him into the mouth of Gopāldās, and it is said that speech came to him. His poems, written at the bidding of the Mahārāj and also in recognition of this act of grace, are very popular with the Vaishnavas, and recited in their temples with appropriate music.

Dhandās

Dhandās said to be a native of Dhandhukā, has written two short poems, BhaktaGitā and ArjunaGitā, the latter of which is well known.

Ratanji

Ratanji, son of Haridās, lived in the Nāsik district at Bāglaṇ, and wrote a considerable poem based on an episode in the Mahābhārat, and called it the Ākhyān of Vibhramsi Rājā. He has versified another incident from the same work, relating to the removal of Draupadi's clothes in the presence of her elders in the Court of King Duryodhan of Hastināpur. The former was written in A. D. 1713, and, though long, is not without interest.

Jain writers

A list of about fourteen Jain writers who flourished during this period, is found in a paper contributed by the late Mansukhlāl Kiratchand to the second Gujārati Sāhitya Parishad (1907), but the works of only two are considered here.[1] One is Ānandaghan alias LābhVijayaji (Samvat year 1687), and the other is Nemivijaya (Samvat year 1700).

Ānandaghan and his Chovīśi

The ĀnandaghanaChoviśi (twenty-four poems of Ānandaghan), is a philosophical treatise, but the work of Nemivijaya is more

1 जैन गुर्जर कविओ, Parts I and II, by Mohanlāl Dalichad Desāi, have since then added many more to the number.

popular and interesting. His Śilavati Rāso (a story of a chaste lady by name Śilavati, which itself means chaste) is a treat in story-telling, and moreover, on account of the peculiar form of Gujarāti in which it is written, viz., a mixture of Apabhramśa, Māgadhi, Mārwādi, and Śaurseni words and terminations, it furnishes a rich mine for philologists to explore, who can see here very clearly the changes that Gujarāti has undergone midway between its origin from Sanskrit and its present form.[1]

Nemivijaya and his Śilavati Rāso

A Rāso means a story, and Rāsās are written, more or less, exclusively by Jains. The Brahmin writers used to style their poems as Ákhyan, Jain writers, Rāso. This is the chief diffence between them. They furnish very pleasant and instructive reading, and, above all, stir the emotions by their narration of the marvellous (अद्भुत). Attainment of one's desires by the recitation of Mantras, procuring of gold by alchemy, the wonderful qualities of gems and precious stones, the out-of-the-way doings of spirits and goblins, fiying through the air and such other marvellous things are the staple food of these Rāsā writers. Their purpose is always the inculcation of the

Meaning of Rāso

1 The book is prescribed as a text book for those University students who are reading Gujarāti for their M. A. Examination.

principles of Jain religion and morality; and usually end in meeting with a Jain anchorite (Sādhu) whose teaching makes the hero and the heroine renounce wordlly pleasures and turn themselves also sādhus; for instance, this very poem begins with the praise of chastity. "There is no mountain summit in the world as high as chastity. These are beautiful tales and verses about chaste and pure women."[1]

Summary of Śilavati Rāso

The heroine of the story is Śilavati and the hero is Chandragupta. He had taken offence at a remark of his wife before they were married, and soon after marriage, he left her. They remained separate for a very long time, during which Chandragupta met with various adventures, as a result of which he was able to subdue the elements, control spirits and do various other "uncanny" things, not possible for an ordinary human being to do. During the course of this voluntary exile, he happened to meet a beautiful woman, who opened his eyes to the fact that he had misjudged his wife and condemned her unheard. He felt the truth of her criticism and desired to go back to her. By a strange coincidence, a divine being took him to his wife for one night only on the back of an eagle, and the

1 शील समो संसारमां, शिखर न कोई थोक;
शीलवंत सतियो तणा, सुंदर कथा शलोक.

result of their union, which took place under the influence of a peculiar conjunction of heavenly bodies, was a boy who was endowed with the power of producing one gem from his mouth every day. He was taken away instantaneously by the same agency, fated as he was to continue his career of adventures for several years more. He was always successful and able to rescue several individuals from distress, and win the hand of many princesses. Śilavati, on the other hand, was condemned by her relatives on suspicion of having turned from the path of chastity, and various means were employed to do away with her, such as poison, snake-bite and lastly by leaving her as a prey for wild beasts. But she survived all these and fell into the hands of a prostitute, in whose house, she gave birth to a child. The prostitute, thinking the child would come in the way of the profession for which she had intended Śilavati on account of her beauty, gave him to a maid-servant with instructions to destroy him. The servant took him to a temple, and left him there, being unable to make up her mind to lay violent hands on such a beautiful child. The infant was rescued by a rich lady of the place, who brought him up as her foster-son, and on growing up, the boy was able to defeat an invading force of Bhils, the foes of the local ruler, and received a gift of several villages. Śilavati was told by the prostitute that cats had destroyed her child; horrified at this disaster she left the brothel and found shelter in the house of a Baniā.

On returning home, Chandragupta learnt of the plight of his wife, and once more set out to find her. On reaching the place where his son was honoured with Jāgirs, he was able to identify him by means of the gem coming out of his mouth, and on making further enquiries was able to find Śilavati too. She told him how she had been treated by the prostitute, and how the latter met with her deserts. Their happy reunion came to an end, by the renunciation of the world by both of them, under the advice of a pious saint, Gajadhar Muni.

In this brief outline of the story, the various marvellous incidents, where both the husband and the wife in their adventurous careers, had to grapple with spirits, witches, goblins and wild beasts, and from which by virtue of the chastity of the latter, they emerged triumphant, are not set out. The poet's delineations of human character where vice in the shape of prostitution and lust, avarice and dishonesty, stalks about are not dilated upon here, but in the original they afford a good illustration of the felicity of his style. His fine descriptions of forest scenery too, have not been referred to, while space forbids any lengthy allusion to his sincere solicitude for laying down and inculcating those principles of morality, which insist on truthful speech, and teach the cultivation of the virtues of self-restraint and purity of life. Compared to men like Premānand, Nemivijaya might appear to be a mediocre poet, but amongst those who rank below Premānand he surely holds a very high, if not the highest, place to which along with him Vallabh might very well aspire.

As a poet who makes story-telling his task Nemivijaya might not improperly stand as a rival of Sāmal and share the honours with him.

A Pārsi Poet

Reference has already been made to the part taken by Pārsis in the development of early Gujarāti literature.[1] It seems the ball set rolling so early as the fourteenth century continued to increase in motion steadily, and in the seventeenth century we meet with a poet,

1. Page 16, ante. In the Kārtik (Samvat year 1970) issue of "The Vasant," the late Mr. N. B. Divatiā quotes some instances of prose written by Pārsis in the fourteenth century. He quotes some more instances from later works (A. D. 1415); one of them is the Arda-Virāf Nāmeh, which was copied out by Behrām Lakhmidhar in Samvat year 1507, A. D. 1450. Its concluding passage is written as follows in incorrect Sanskrit:

अध्यारु बहिराम श्रुत अध्यारु लक्ष्मीधर लक्षतम्। संवत (१५०७) वर्षे मार्ग्रसर सितात द्वादशी तिथौ सोमदिने। अश्वनी नक्षत्रे वरैंआन जोग्य प्रवर्त्तमाने श्री.. नाग-सारनागस्कायां शुभं भवति।

cited at p. 23 of Preface to Zarthoshtnāmā, by Mrs. Meherbānoo and Mr. B. T. Anklesariā. Incidentally pp. 38–41 Ibid. give samples of

who instead of producing translations of religious books from Pehalavi or Zend into Sanskrit and from Sanskrit into the vernacular of the province, chose to write on an original theme. This poet was a Pārsi priest, by name Erwad Rustam Peshotan, born in A. D. 1619, a native of Surat. He belonged to a priestly family, as his immediate ancestors were either Mobeds or Erwads. Out of four works written by him, hardly one is concerned with a religious theme, pure and simple. They are all Nāmehs (i. e., chronicles or biographies). The Zarthosht Nāmeh (A. D. 1674), the Siyāvakśa Nāmeh (A. D. 1680), the Virāf Nāmeh (A. D. 1651) and the Aspandiyār Nāmeh, are narrations in verse of the incidents in the lives of the distinguished personages, whose names the poems bear. The second of these four has been edited (A. D. 1873) by a coreligionist of the poet, well known for his literary work, Erwad Tehmuras Dinshā Anklesariā. The work is based on that portion of the Shāh Nāmeh of the great Persian poet, Firdausi Tusi, which deals with the adventures of Prince Siyāvakśa, the son of Kai Kāvus. There is necessarily a mixture of fact and

Description of his work

Gujarāti prose written by Pārsis between A. D. 1626 and 1706. As a specimen of the prose prevalent then a couple of sentences are given here from a larger extract published by the late Mr. Divatiā.

१००० जोत सहसांमणनी। तेवन एक सहुस्र जोतनी समस्याणनी वगत समस्याण बलतूं हूइ ३ त्रन वेहेत भूम छांडीइ ताइ आतस लइनि जात किजइ.

fable in the Gujarāti poem just as there is in the Shāh Nāmeh. In fact, the charm of this poem lies in its romance, in its description of marvels and unusual events. One could trace in them a similarity to the poems of Sāmal in this respect. But still the work has an individuality of its own. Even at present, Pārsis speak and write Gujarāti, but they have managed to impress upon it a peculiarity of their own. Certain ideas, phrases, idioms, turns of language and of thought have almost made their Gujarāti into a special dialect of the language. The same thing is found in the Siyāvakśa Nāmeh. The poet is saturated with the religious and social ideas of his own community; the vehicle which he uses to convey them is no doubt Gujarāti, but it is Gujarāti clothed in an unfamiliar garb. Sanskrit and Gujarāti words form the groundwork, but the superstructure is composed of Zend, Pehalavi and Persian words and phrases which make it difficult for an ordinary Gujarāti to follow and appreciate the beauty of the verses. Indeed but for the lucid annotations of the editor, it would have been an uphill task for any one to understand the work fully.

His knowledge of several languages

The poet knew several languages, Persian, Avestā, Pehalavi, Sanskrit and Gujarāti. That he knew his own religion and literature very well goes without saying, but he seems to have studied Sanskrit literature and the manners and customs of his Hindu neighbours as well. His description of the beauty of the women of ancient Irān, and their ornaments, reads like one borrowed from a Sanskrit work,[1] and his description of a Persian banquet, is more like the description of a Gujarāti Hindu's dinner than of one partaken by a follower of Zarthosht in prehistoric Irān.[2] Besides these there are many passages where we find an assimilation of Hindu manners and

1. तम सीश फुल पुनम चंद ने अमाशी सूर ।
ए वेरान रांणमां एथी घणुं वरशे छे नूर ॥
तम नीडाळ टीक बुध वहेरेस्पत शुकर जडी ।
तम नाशका नथ ते सबचेराग कोणे घडी ॥
तम कान कुंडल जडेआ जाणे मांणक ने मोते ।
कोट अभरण पहेराविआं आप धणीए पोते ॥
कर चूड पोहोंची जाणे वीज चमक चमकीने जाए ।
पाए पेजण ते नेवरनो जह्मकारच थाए ॥

Your head-ornament is like the full moon and the bright sun on the Amāvāsyā day (the last day of the dark half of a month), and it rains a flood of light in this desert. Your Tik or Tili (a forehead ornament) is set with planets, like Mercury, Jupiter and Venus. Your nosering is like the fabulous gem, which gives light at night (Shabcherāg). Who could have made it? Your ear-ornaments (kundal) are set with rubies and pearls, and the ornaments on your throat seem to have been put on by the Lord himself. The bangles (Chud and Pohonchi) on your arms flash like lightning, and the ornaments on your feet tinkle.

2. खाजां लाडु जलेबी घेवर ज छे सार ।
मेवा मीठाई खुआन भरी भरी मेलेआं तेआर ॥

customs in the life of his heroes and heroines and other characters.

and of contemporary Hindu manners and customas

Altogether the work would, on a close perusal, be found interesting from several points of view: literary, in so far as it introduces into Gujarāti at a very early stage, the methods of Persian chronicles, thus creating a landmark in its history; philological, as it still retains several quaint forms of old Gujarāti words; and social, in so far as it records the imbibing by the Pārsi community of the manners, customs, superstitions and ideas of the Hindus among whom they lived.

Zarthosht Nāmeh

Zarthosht Nāmeh, a chronicle relating to the Irānian Prophet Zarthosht, is founded on a Persian work of the same name written by Zarthosht Behrām Pazdu in Persian (A. D. 1217), which in its turn was founded on a Pehalavi daftar. It sets out in the language current at the time, the stirring and miraculous incidents in the life of the Prophet and impressively traces his rise, his reception at the hands of monarchs, the trials and tribulations he had to undergo, chiefly brought about by ignorant unbelievers, the ultimate acceptance

एकशेट शारण तांहां बासेट हुआ पलेव।
माखण घीही तावेभां तांहां खाणमां ओशाइ जीणी शेव॥
शाल दाल परीशी तांहां उपर घीहीनी नालज दीधी।
जनशाजनशी अचार तेहनी एम वेवखज कीधी॥

of his message of sun–fire–worship and the conversion of kings. In majesty of description and simplicity of language it is a worthy precursor of the Siyāvakśa Nāmeh, with which it shares in common the traits noted above.[1]

1 Mrs. Meherbanoo and her husband Behrāmgor Temuras Anklesariā have edited this Nāmeh, and examined it from all possible points of view, such as research, philology, chronology, &c., in a scholarly preface. What the father began with the Śiyavakśa Nāmeh the son has supplemented by publication of poems written by Pārsi poets. Not only Pārsi but Hindu students of literature would find much to learn from the preface and the text. They would observe that in spite of a mixture of Sanskrit, Arabic, Persian, Pāzand and Gujarāti words, how smoothly the verse flows, and what a faithful picture it gives of the life of the old Irānians. The couple have done great service to Gujarāti literature.

They speak of another Pārsi poet, Noshirvān, a native of Navsāri, who has written verses on "five Gathas and six Gahambārs' (A. D. 1709), which in style, construction, language etc., resemble those of Ervad Rustam.

The following lines from the commecement of the Zarthosht Nāmeh furnish a good sample of the Prākrit written at the hands of Pārsi men of letters at that time.

पहेल परथम एक नाम अहुरमझदनुं लीधु,
ए जरतोशतनामूं अम परगट रोशंण कीधु.
ए आद परथम पहेलवी भाषा हती सही,
ते जरथुश्त बहेरामे पहेलवीथी फरुश परगट कीधु कही.
ते फरुशथी पराकरुत ते सरव भणीने जाणे,
धरंम पर धेभांन ते मंण हरख धरीने आहांणे.
ए सरव शूभ अखरे अखर वांची भणजो आम,
जे कोए मणशा सीखे शांभूले तेहेने बेहेशत रोशंण हूए ठांम.

CHAPTER VI

POETS OF THE EIGHTEENTH CENTURY

Eighteenth century

The next period (1700 to 1800 A.D.) saw the rise of the Marāthā power in Gujarāt, and what with the declining influence of the Moghuls, and the increasing predatoriness of the hordes from the Deccan, peace in that province was not to be. The rule of the Gāikwād at Barodā did not ensure quiet. In fact there was no central authority in the province to ensure peace, and it was not a rare sight to meet with tax-gatherers of three or four powers at a time, the Moghul's, the local Nawāb's or petty Chief's, the Gāikwad's and the Peshwā's swooping down upon the unhappy villagers and terrorising them into payment. Consequently, whatever education and learning the common people were acquiring suffered. They became depressed and dejected, and hence we miss the brightness in the literary production of this century which illumined the days of the three premier poets. The production is poor. Mr.

Output "imbecile" and sectarian

Tripāthi calls it "imbecile".[1] It certainly is, at any rate, sectarian, if one could use that term to denote work which came from the pen of the devotees of the different gods and goddesses, each in praise of his own patron or patroness, Vishnu or Krishna, Śiva or Ambā.

Goddess represents female element in nature

The goddess Ambā represents the female element, impersonates the might of God and as such is worshipped as the mother in nature. She is known and addressed by various names, but the central principle of the representation of motherhood in her person is never lost sight of. Her terrible aspect as the avenger, the killer of demons, as the rejoicer in carnage and blood, as one who would only be appeased by means of sacrifices, as the representative of nature "red in tooth and claw" is forgotten in the tenderer and kindlier feelings of a mother towards her children, and in invocations to her, we always find more prominence given to the humane side of her nature.

Vallabh Bhatt

The Garbās of Vallabh Bhatt (A, D. 1700), all of them addressed to her, have acquired more than an ephemeral

1 "Some twelve poets directly or indirectly attached to this new faith (of the Vallabhāchāryas) supply the country during this period with an imbecile kind of poetry, where we generally miss the vigour and philosophy of Narsinh as well as the gentle purity of Mirān." The Classical Poets of Gujarāt.

popularity. He himself was a very sincere devotee of the Mātā (mother, goddess), and even his name is perpetuated along with another devotee (said to be his brother), by name Dholā,[1] in the cry with which her followers greet one another in her temple, "Vallabh Dholā Ki Jai"–"Victory to Vallabh and Dholā." He lived mostly in Chunvāl, famous as the seat of the worship of Becharāji or Becharā Mātā. He came from Ahmedabād, and was a Bhatt Mevādā by caste and is therefore known as Vallabh Bhatt.

He diagonised the disease of the period as depression and disappointment. He grieved over the immorality of the age and poured out his lamentations before the Mātā (Mother). He wrote with great vigour and force[2] so as to open the eyes of his readers to the miseries of the times.

Seats of the goddess

In Gujarāt there are three celebrated seats of the goddess, the most famous being at Ārāsur (Ambā), the second in Chunvāl (Bahucharā or Becharā), and the third on the hill of Pāvāgadh near Chāmpāner (Kāli). All these seats have their own legends, and their special follow-

1 He had two other brothers; one of them was Hari Bhatt and his name too is coupled with that of Vallabh at the time of greeting: "Vallabh Hari Ki Jai". Dholā and Hari also essayed verses.

2 For an appreciation of his work see pp. 470-1 Junun (old) Narma-Gadya, Gujarāti Printing Press edition.

ers of both sexes. They are popular with the higher and middle as well as the lower classes, like the Bhils and Kolis; and the Garbās of Vallabh Bhatt include a descriptive chronicle of all these seats. The singer or reciter, admires the powers of the goddess, her beauty, her dress, her ornaments and winds up with solicitations for her favour. The curious reader will find an exact counter-part to this species of Gujarāti literature in Bengāl, where poet after poet of the early and middle era of the Bengāli verse literature, has sung of Kāli almost always as a mother and protector and very rarely as a destroyer. The first nine days of the month of Aświn are specially set apart for the worship of the goddess, and it is during this period that the singing of these Garbās is most indulged in, in Kāthiawad by men and in Gujarāt by women. It is a pretty sight to see the women moving in a circle beating time with rhythmic clapping of the hands, bending half down as they sing these Garbās late into the night, at places like Surat, Barodā, Ahmedābād and Bombay. These dances are more graceful than those of the men, who merely jump and skip and shout and yell, and clap their hands.

Nature of Garbā literature

Vallabh[1] has written of Krishṇa too, and he

1. A legend says that he was at first a Vaishanav but happening unconsciously to spit in a Vaishanav temple, was reproved by the

Vallabh's description of the present age

has written a Garbā[1] on the Kalīkāl (the iron age). He laments the signs which betoken this unhappy age, and invokes the help of the goddess to purge the world of it. He says, "Even before her age, a girl becomes a woman, O Bahuchari! and often bears children."[2] He describes the scarcity and famine of Samvat years 1787 and 1788 (A. D. 1731). "Grain had become very dear, and irreligion had increased beyond all bounds. How was one to judge of the actions of others when each man exceeded his neighbour in committing excesses. Those who were brought forth from their loins and womb, and who shared of the element of both (parents), had to be abandoned for the sake of the stomach, and children had to be sold away." "Send us, O mother! therefore (all) the rains we want, so that we may not lack bounteous crops. Pour only a drop of your

Hardships of famine

keeper. He said, children foul the laps of their parents. "A mother" he was told, "might tolerate it but not a father." To which he replied, "Very well. Then I will worship my Mother." He thus became a convert to goddess worship.

1. Just as Sāmal is known for his Duhās and Chhappās Vallabh is known for his Garbās.

2. See footnote 1, next page.

nectar, on us, your children, on the cattle and on our village.''[1]

and miseries of an ill-matched couple

His Garbo on "An ill-matched pair" (कजोडुं), a young or child-wife, and an old husband, with one foot in the grave is, however, a most enjoyable piece of poetry; nothing like it is met with in the early period of Gujarāti verse. Every line in it tells, and the miseries of a girl approaching womanhood married to an old man daily growing more decrepit, are so graphically described, that no apology is needed for making an extract from it to show that nearly three centuries ago the thoughtful men of the land were alive to the evils of such marriages. A young wife lays the whole blame of this uneven match on the goddess-mother (गोरमा) and prays to her never to repeat the mistake again.

1. वय विना वनिता वेषमां हो बहुचरी! गर्भ ज धरे अनेक.

× × × ×

अन्न अति मोघां हुवां हो बहुचरी! अधर्म व्याप्यो असाध्य,
को कोनी करणी जुवे, हो बहुचरी! एक थकी एक अगाध.

उदरथकी उपजावीआं, हो बहुचरी! उभय तणो जे अंश,
ते तन पेट तजावीआं, हो बहुचरी! विक्रय कीधो वंश.

× × × ×

म्हो मांग्या मेघ मोकलो, हो बहुचरी! खट रस नावे खोट,
आई अमि छांटो नांखीए, हो बहुचरी! छोरु ढोरु ने गाम.

"O mother ! you have given me an old husband and thereby ruined my whole life. How much should I blame you ? ... ... O mother ! I am but a child, and he is grown up and old. O mother ! his very sight terrifies me. He is a fool and an idiot. O mother ! my youth is blossoming and hence I look beautiful and my husband is like a mummy. O mother ! he is soft-headed, hideous and worn out. O mother ! I am exactly sixteen and he is eighty. O mother ! in appearance, he looks like a demon with all his senses gone. O mother ! on a winter night one likes to indulge in many pleasures, but O mother ! an old fool (like him) acts as if he were a dumb creature. O mother ! I want to enjoy myself at night and therefore anoint my eye with collyrium and he threatens me, stick in hand, with a beating. O mother ! every word he utters is a grumble, how is his nature to be changed ? O mother ! my husband is aged, how can he gratify my desires ? O mother ! the nine days sacred to goddess Mātāji are very plesant. O mother ! on the tenth or Daserā day every one is in holiday attire but my husband is so weak and ugly that I feel ashamed of him ... ... O mother ! while every one is enjoying the festive days of the Divāli, to me they are the flames of the Holi fire. I am unlucky, I have nothing to hope for ... ... O mother ! while my hair is black, his head has become grey. O mother ! I am in the bloom of youth but my whole life is blasted. He dribbles at the mouth, his eyes water ... ... When I bespread the bed with flowers he begins to weep ... ... O mother ! why was I not strangled at my birth ? why was I not poisoned ? ... ... O mother ! my husband is dying. I feel as if I would become a Sati ... ... O mother ! I entreat you with folded hands to give me in future a husband with the vigour of youth."[1]

1. गोरमा! घरडो के भरथार के मुजने आपीयो रे, लोल,
गोरमा! धिक्क कीधो अवतार के शुं कहुं तुजने रे, लोल.

× × × ×

गोरमा! हुं तो नानुं बाळ के, ए तो मोटो बुढीओ रे, लोल;
गोरमा! दीठेथी पडे फाळ के, मुरख मुढीओ रे, लोल.
गोरमा! मारुं थयुं जोबन के, पियु वरखो थयो रे, लोल;
गोरमा! घेलो कद्रुपवान के, जाते वही गयो रे, लोल.
गोरमा! सोळ मुने प्रत्यक्ष के, एने हेंसी थयां रे, लोल;
गोरमा! दीसंतो जाणे जक्ष, के बुध सघळी गई रे, लोल.
गोरमा! शियाळानी रात के, स्वाद होए घणा रे, लोल;
गोरमा! मुरख घरडी जात के, जेवो गुंगणो रे, लोल.
गोरमा! रजनी रमवा इच्छुं के, आंजुं आंखडी रे, लोल;
गोरमा! मारीश करतो बोले के, एक कर लाकडी रे, लोल.
गोरमा! गाळ नीसरती वाते के, स्वभाव केम फरे रे, लोल;
गोरमा! पीयुनी घरडी जात के, अर्थ क्यांथी सरे रे, लोल.
गोरमा! घरमां नवरात्रीना दिन के, बहु सोहामणा रे, लोल;
गोरमा! विजयाकेरो दिन के, सहु शणगारमां रे, लोल.
गोरमा! दुरबळ मारो कंथ के, घणो लजामणो रे, लोल;

× × × ×

From the opening line of the poem it appears that this unhappy child-wife belonged to the Nāgar Brāhmin caste, the most cultured and advanced community in Gujarāt and Kāthiawād.[1]

The unhappy wife of a Nāgar Brahmin

Dwārko (A. D. 1710) belonged to a village in Charotar called Bhālej though he passed his life in Dākore. His verses are not many and they concern the life of Krishṇa. Some of his didactic verses are however simple and effective. His poem called चेतवणी (A war-

Dwārko

गोरमा ! सहुने मन दीवाळी, के मारे मन हुताशनी रे, लोल;
गोरमा ! मारा करमना भोग, के हुं तो निराशणी रे, लोल.

× × × ×

गोरमा ! मारा काळा केश, के ए आखो पळ्यो रे, लोल;
गोरमा ! हुं थइ जोबन वेश, के जनमारो बळ्यो रे, लोल.
गोरमा ! म्होडेथी चुए लाल, के आंखे पाणी गळे रे, लोल.

× × × ×

गोरमा ! सेजे बीछावुं फुल, के ए देखीने रुवे रे, लोल;

× × × ×

गोरमा ! जणतां न दीधी फांसी, के वीख दइ मारती रे, लोल.

× × × ×

गोरमा ! पीउजी सुता मरवा, के जाणे थाउं सती रे, लोल;
गोरमा । कर जोडी लागुं पाय, के देजो समथ धणी रे, लोल.

1. (i) The Garbo beginning with आज मने आनंद वाध्यो अति घणो मा, and (ii) शणगारनो गरबो, (iii) धनुष्यधारीनो गरबो, (iv) चोसठ जोगणीनो गरबो as well as (v) बहुचराजीनो गरबो are also very popular.

ning V. S. 1800) is wellknown. He says: "Be warned, while there is time. When will there be another opportunity to receive a warning? Youth will flash past, age will come apace. Then your strength will flee, you will be a tottering old man. Māyā (delusion of the world) has blind-folded you and you do not see anything ... ... Dwarko therefore tells you to remember and to pray to Rāma, lest all be lost.[1]"

His didactic verses

Bhāṇdas has in his Hastāmalak (A. D. 1721) in the form of a dialogue between Śankarāchārya and a stupid looking Brahmin boy, Hastāmalak, discussed several questions of Vedāntism. Hastāmalak was really an avatār of Parabrahma, the Supreme Being, and he has explained to Śankar the principles of Adwaitism, Dwaitism (Monism, Dualism) &c.

Bhāṇdas

Kālidas, (about A. D. 1725–1730), a Nāgar Brahmin of Vasāvad in Kāthiāwad, is best known by his Pralhādākhyān though he has written other works called the Sitā-

Kālidas

1. चेती ले चेत्यानो अवसर फरी फरी क्यां मळशे रे?
जोबन जानां वार न लागे, जरा आवीने टळशे रे.
टळशे त्यांथी नहि रहे धारण, थर थर काया ध्रुजे रे;
मायानी अंधारी नांखी, तेमां कांई नव सुझे रे.
× × × ×
कहे द्वारको राम भजी लो, नहि तो जाशो हारी रे.

Swayaṁvar, the Dhruvākhyān, the IśwarVivāh, and also several poems in praise of Śakti (goddess)[1] whose follower he was. The story of Pralhād (V. S. 1817), the child-devotee of Vishnu is well-known. He was born in the family of a demon, HiraṇyaKaśipu (हिरण्यकशिपु) by name, a great foe of Vishnu. His brother was killed by the god and so he had vowed vergeance on him, but the god escaped him once by making himself invisible. Thereafter by severe austerity and penance, the demon made himself immortal by getting a boon from Brahmā, which rendered

and his Pralhādākhyān

him immune from destruction by anything created or born in the ordinary way, at morning, evening or night, and by any weapon whatsoever. He was, further protected from death either on the earth, or in the sky or at sea. Pralhād, his son, was a follower of Hari, and in spite of the sinister methods by which he tried to instil into him a hatred for Vishnu, he found the boy drifting more and more towards the worship of his foe. He tried to terrorise him into giving up this worship. Yet though he tortured and almost killed him, his son remained adamant. At last Hiraṇya gave Pralhād an ultimatum that unless he showed his god to his father he would be killed. So, one day, Hiraṇya stood over his son, dagger in hand,

1. चण्डिकाना त्रिभंगी छंदो.

and demanded a sight of Vishnu under pain of death. The boy was told to produce his cherished god from a near by pillar[1] and strange to say, on the boy invoking his presence, the pillar split with a loud crash and a strange figure, half-man half-lion, (Nara-sinh) presented itself to the eyes of the tyrant. Nothing daunted, he began to fight with him and had his stomach torn or ripped open by the claws of this man-beast. This happened at a time which was neither evening nor night, i.e., at twilight hour, and he was killed on a doorsill, which was neither earth nor sky nor water. Thus the boon was evaded and the tyrant killed. The narrative is full of vigour, and is told in simple language, which sustains very well the interest of the reader, thus making the poem popular.

Pralhādākhyān depicts the रौद्र (wrathful) and भयानक (terrible), Dhruvākhyān the करुण (tragic) and IśwarVivāh the शृंगार (erotic) रस (sentiment in poetics).

Trikamdās

Trikamdās, a Nāgar Brāhmin of Junāgadh (A. D. 1734-1769) was more a politician than a literary man. His poems on Dākorenāth and RukmiṇiVivāh which are in

1. This threat to the boy begins with the celebrated verses, "Boy ! show me, show me, your Lord of the heaven (Vishnu)."

बाळा ! देखाड देखाड तारो वैकुण्ठपति.

VrajBhāshā have been published. His life has been written by Kavi Revāshankar in sixty stanzas of the चंद्रावळा छंद. Trikamdās calls himself a descendant of Narsinh Mehtā from his uncle Parvat Mehta's side.[1]

Pritamdās

Pritamdās (A. D. 1778–1798) was a Bhāt of Bāvlā, who had migrated about A. D. 1761 to Sandeshar in the Kairā District and sometimes lived at Nadiād. As a rule the Bhāt community is illiterate, and although at one time considered to represent the poet-laureates of native courts, its members have now come down to the position of menials. The more is the credit due to this poet, in that being born in such a community and having very little intercourse with either learned men or learned languages, he has left behind him works, many of which are held to be popular today, and often sung by the masses. Of his domestic life, only this much is authentically known that his first wife, who was his senior by two years, had made his life miserable by her sharp temper, and that whenever storms disturbed his domestic tranquillity, he always used to employ himself till they blew over, in writing devotional songs to Krishṇa, instead

belonged to an illiterate class

1 'Trikamdās' Poems' have been published by Mr. Natvarlāl Ichhārām Desāi, B. A. and Nayansukhrai V. Majmudār B. A., LL. B. at the Gujarāti Printing Press-Bombay (1931). Trikamdās has also written परवतपचीशी and miscellaneous Padās.

of answering back. At times he used to leave the house to his wife and go away on a pilgrimage to Dākore, where he was always welcomed by the priests, who delighted in listening to his verses. His second wife was a better woman, but his last years were clouded with much unhappiness. He became blind and he lost his wife when he was seventy-two.[1] Even then he did not abandon his favourite pursuit, and oftentimes did his pupils, if they happened to be near, take down his verses as they fell impromptu from his mouth.

Good influence of his Guru

Pritamdās was a great believer in the good influence that comes to a man through his Guru. He ascribed all his good work to his Guru Govindrām,[2] whom he met at Nadiād, and great was

1. As a result of personal inquiries made by Bhikshu Akhandānand and his assistant, he asserts that Pritamdās was a lifelong bachelor. If this be so, then this highly interesting phase of his life turns out to be a myth. Bhikshuji's sources of information certainly were better than those of the late Mr. Ichhārām Desāi and till any other fresh material comes to light, we may accept Bhikshuji's conclusion. He also says that Pritamdās was born blind. 'Pritamdās-ni Vāni', published in A. D. 1925 with an exhaustive introduction on the life and works of the poet by Bhikshu Akhandānand with the help of Patel Chhotābhāi Umedbhāi is an excellent guide to the study of his poems.

2. Bāpuji and not Govindrām was his Guru: 'Pritamdās ni Vāni' Introduction, pp. 30–31.

his grief when he left him after eleven years of constant intercourse. A large portion of his poetry is founded on the text given in the footnote.[1]

Pritamdas' works

His works are: 1. The SārasGitā (A. D. 1774) an episode in the life of Krishṇa, (2). The JnānKakko (A. D. 1776) verses on religious knowledge each beginning with a letter of the alphabet, 3. GuruMahimā (greatness of Gurus) and 4. JnānMās (1781–83). Besides these he has written verses on the birth of Krishṇa, BhaktiPrakāś, JnānPrakāś, BhagavadGitā, AdhyātmaRāmayaṇ, JnānGitā, KrishṇaLilā and numerous Padas and Garbis.[2] The Padas of Pritamdās and the Garbis of Dayārām have attained equal popularity. **पद तो प्रीतमनां.** This is how they are spoken of.

On Śringār and Vairāgya

They are naturally divided into two parts, those relating to Śringār (love) and those relating to Vairāgya (freedom from worldly attachments) or Jnān (know-

1. सद्गुरुने शब्दे सउ तिरथ तेहने रे.

i.e., he who has got the word (direction or instruction) of a good Guru has got in himself all the places of pilgrimage. (The word of a virtuous teacher, is enough to win salvation which is attained by travelling to different holy places.)

2. There are some more. See p. 40 of the Introduction to 'Pritamdās ni Vāni.'

ledge). Both have secured a hold on the minds of the people of Gujarāt.

He says: "Your body will be of no use to you even though you try to preserve it in innumerable ways. Even if you cut the purest of gold and eat it, when the time comes, the body will perish in a moment."[1]

Extracts from his verses

"The way of God is the way for the brave, cowards are not wanted therein. You have first to sacrifice your head (dedicate your whole being) and then remember God. He who offers to him, his son, his wealth, his wife and his head, will be able to enjoy the sweets (of devotion)."[2]

"Know this that the happiness of the world is like a dew drop, it is a fact that it will disappear in a moment, therefore, remember God, O Pritam! and be purified."[3]

1. काया रे तारी काम न आवे, जो करे कोटी उपाय रे,
वणशी जातां वार नहि लागे, जो कुंदन कापीने खाय रे.

2. हरिनो मारग छे शूरानो, नहि कायरनुं काम जोने;
परथम पहेलुं मस्तक मूकी, वळती लेवुं नाम जोने,
सुत वित्त दारा शीश समर्पे ते पामे रस पीवा जोने.

3. जगतनुं सुख झाकळनुं छे पाणी रे, जाणी ले.
वणशी जातां वार नहि, सत वाणी रे, जाणी ले.
प्रीतम! प्रभुने भजीने, पावन थाजे रे, जाणी ले.

Out of a great number of Padas composed by him illustrating the adventures of Krishṇa in his childhood the under-noted five or six are very often on the lips of women.

(1) हे जसोदाजी ! आवडो लाडकवायो लाल न कीजे.

O Jasodā ! do not spoil your child so much.

(2) हे वांसलडी ! वेरण थई लागी रे व्रजनी नारने.

O flute ! you have become an enemy–a disturber of the peace–of the women of Vraj (when Krishna plays on you).

This whole poem so graphically expresses the feelings of the women of Vraj, envying the flute because it is pressed by the lips of Krishṇa, that it is quoted below in full.[1]

1. हे वांसलडी ! वेरण थई लागी रे व्रजनी नारने,
तुं शोर करे, जातलडी तारी रे, मन विचारने. हे वांसलडी !–१

तें एवडां कामण शां कीधां ?
श्यामलीए मुख चुंबन लीधां;
मन व्रजवासीनां हरी लीधां. हे वांसलडी !–२

तुने कोड करी कृष्णे झाली,
गौ नाद सुणी आवी चाली;
तुं विश्वंभरने बहु वहाली. हे वांसलडी !–३

पूरत तुं कांई नथी लावी,
उघाडे छोगे छे आवी,
भगवान तणे मन बहु भावी. हे वांसलडी !–४

(3) मन मोहनलाल ! मारगडो मूको तो मथुरां जाइए.

O thou ! who hast charmed our hearts, move out of the way, so that we may go to Mathurā.

(4) हरि भजनथकी छोटा होय ते सौथी मोटा थाये.

By the worship of (Hari) God, he who is lowest becomes highest.

(5) हरिभजन विना दुःखदरिया संसारनो पार न आवे.

Only prayer to Hari (God) can relieve one from the woes of the world.

(6) जीभलडी रे ! तुने हरिगुण गातां आवडुं आळस क्यांथी रे ?

My tongue ! why do you become so very idle when it comes to singing the praise of God.

तें व्रत व्रतादिक शुं कीधुं?
राधा थकी मान अधिक लीधुं.
तुने आलिंगन प्रभुए दीधुं. हे वांसलडी !–५

"O flute ! you have become an enemy of the women of Vraj. You are blustering, just consider your origin. (I)

What charms have you thrown on him that the Dark One (Krishṇa) kisses you with his lips ? You have captivated the hearts of the residents of Vraj, O flute ! (2)

Krishṇa has taken hold of you with love, the cows hearing your strains have come running. You are very dear to the Lord of the Universe, O flute ! (3)

You have brought no dowry with you, you have come boldly and publicly, yet Krishṇa has taken a great liking for you, O flute ! (4)

What fasts have you observed that you have taken a place higher than Rādhā ? God himself has taken you in his arms, O flute ! (5)

His कक्का and चेतामणी (a warning) are full of precept and wholesome advice.[1]

Ravidās, Prāgdās and his other contemporaries have written verses on Vedānt, JnānMārga &c.

Śivānand

Sivānand was a Nāgar Brāhmin of Surat, (A. D. 1600–1644). He confined himself exclusively to singing the praises of Siva or Mahādev. He became a Sannyāsi late in life and his Ārtis (songs) are chanted with zest, at the time the god is worshipped in the evening with a lamp waved before or in front of the idol to the accompaniment of the music of kettledrums and bells. All his poems are modelled on the style of the followers of Vishnu or Krishṇa, who have not left a single incident in the daily routine of the life of their god unsung, such as his bath, his dinner, his dress and his amours. Some of these poems are in Hindi or Vraj.[2]

and his Ārtis

1. Kavi Narmadāshankar calls his poetry full of sentiment giving delight both to the learned as well as to the common people. His language is pure, simple and full of metaphor. See p. 471 'Junun Narmagadya' of the Gujarāti Printing Press.

2. He was wellversed in the three शास्त्रs (sciences): मंत्र (spells and magic), धर्म (religion), न्याय (logic) and रागरागिणी (musical modes). He was known as a follower of Śiva. His verses have a remarkable jingle and tilt. He has marvellously well utilised the रसs (sentiments) and अलंकारs (figures of speech).

Narbherām

Narbherām who died at the great age of eighty-four (in Samvat year 1908, A. D. 1852) was born in A. D. 1768 and was a Modh Brāhmin of Pihij, a small village (very near to Nadiād) in the Petlād Tālukā of H. H. the Gāikwād's territory. His Guru was one Chhotālāl, who taught him to write such verses as could be sung on festive occasions, in praise of Krishṇa or RaṇchhodRāiji, the presiding deity of the famous temple at Dākore. He passed his whole life in worshipping Krishṇa either at Dākore or Dwārkā, and in writing poems in praise of him whom he adored. They amount to about twenty in number, and some of them describe autobiographical incidents. For instance, once while going to Dākore, he was robbed of all he possessed. He went to a village near, Panosarā by name, where the villagers were so moved by the losses of such a sincere devotee of Krishṇa, that they started

How faith helped him

The main feature of his poems is that he sees no distinction between Vishnu and Śiva. He calls them one and the same.

ए बे एक स्वरूप अंतर नव गणशो, (२)
भोळा भूधरने भजतां (२) भवसागर तरशो, जयदेव ! जयदेव !

They both are one in form, see no difference in them. By worshipping the simple hearted Mahādev, you can cross the ocean of the world. Hail god: Hail god.

He has written several eventide songs (Ârtis) in praise of Mātā (Goddess) also.

a subscription list and repaid him many times over what he had lost. Another time, while on a pilgrimage to Dwārkā, the officers on the bank of the Gomti asked him for the tax or toll which each pilgrim has to pay before being allowed to bathe in the sacred waters. He said, he was unable to pay and instead of the money presented the officers with a short poem, in which he told the deity that he had nothing to pay, "the oil seed had no oil in it", and that he should be allowed to go free. The officers were so pleased with it that they allowed him to bathe tax free.[1] Once when he was very dangerously

1. नाणुं आपे नरभो रे, वावरजो छोगाळा !
गांठ मारजो ताणी रे, धोळी धजावाळा !

कपटी केशव जाणत तो, शाने आवत पचाश जोजन ?
सांभळ्युं श्रवणे, साधुने छापे छे, माटे मळवा धर्युं मन,
दरशन धोने रे दूर करी पाळा. नाणुं०

भेख देखीने नजर नथी करता, छाप आपो छो हरि,
पाघडी भाळी छाप खावी छबीला ! परीक्षा तो एवी करी.
समश्या लेजो समजी रे, जे कही कानड काळा ! नाणुं०

हारो छो जनथी नथी हरवाता, माटे हरि हठ मेल,
कहे नरभो छोटालालप्रतापे, नथी ए तलमां तेल,
लेवानुं मुज पासे रे, हरि ! हरि ! जपमाळा. नाणुं०

(He says ironically) Narbho will pay you money Krishṇa ! and you may spend it. Tie the knot of your money bag firmly, you whose ensign is a white banner. If I knew Krishṇa to be deceitful, why should I have come so many miles ? I had heard that the

ill in his sixty-ninth year and was on his deathbed, he composed two poems narrating his faith in Krishṇa. The last one shows that he died at Gomtipur near Aḥmedābād.[1]

How the image of Krishṇa was carried away from Dwārkā to Dākore

The story as to how the god of Dwārkā was brought to Dākore in Gujarāt, is that an individual of a very humble origin Bodhāṇā and his wife found it very hard, as they were very poor, to travel every year to Dwārkā to pay their respects to Krishṇa. They therefore prayed to him to come to their place, and be installed there. They were so devoted to him that they grew the Tulsi (black basil) plant on the palm of their hands, and

Sādhus were given the seal impressions (of शंख, चक्र, गदा, पद्म), free, and hence my mind was made up to see you. Therefore, remove your guards and let me visit you. When you see a man dressed as an ascetic, you brand the seal on him without delay. But seeing me dressed in a turban, you prevent my receiving the stamp. Is this the way in which you discriminate between your devotees? O dark deity! understand the problem I have put before you. You are not defeated, you allow yourself to be defeated by your devotees. Therefore, Hari! leave aside your obstinacy. Narbho says, by the grace of Chhotālāl, that this oil-seed has no oil in it. All that can be taken from me is the rosary with the beads of which I repeat Hari! Hari!

1. The vigour of his verses forthwith appeals to the heart. Homely and everyday instances are skilfully woven into his verses. His words never miss their target.

thus propitiated him. With great caution, Krishṇa evaded the strict surveillance of his keepers at Dwārkā, who were naturally loth to allow their only source of income to fall into other hands. The distance from Dwārkā to Dākore was immense, and the only means of conveyance was a dilapidated cart with a famished team of bullocks, that could hardly cover a mile an hour. But Krishṇa was bent upon executing his plan and working a miracle: he managed to reach Dākore in a very short time. The local priests of Dwārkā, the Gugli Brāhmins, pursued him closely, and the image had to be thrown into the Gomti–a namesake of the river at Dwārkā–to avoid its falling again into the hands of the infuriated mob from Kāthiāwād. It was subsequently recovered from there as Krishṇa made a compromise with the Brāhmins, and it is now installed in the famous shrine at Dākore, which attracts at every full moon, tens of thousands of devotees from Gujarāt. In celebration of this persistent faith of Bodhāṇā and his wife, which secured for Gujarāt the residence of a deity worshipped over the whole of India, the poet has written several short Padas (about 600) which he calls "Verses of the moustaches of Bodhāṇā" (बोदाणानी मूछनां पदो), meaning that Bodhāṇā was able to twirl his moustaches like a triumphant hero, he

Celebration of the event in verse by Narbherām

having done a most patriotic deed–spiritually of course. In fact, he calls him the saviour of Gujarāt. He names him in the same breath with the spiritual celebrities of India, like Pundarik, Shuk, Bhagirath and Narsinh Mehtā. Pundarik kept the god at his house. Shuk recited the Bhāgwat in a way which was like nectar in its effect, Bhagirath brought the Ganges down from the heavens to the earth, and Narsinh Mehtā's power over Krishṇa is already known. In prowess he compares him to Balirājā, to Hariśchandra, to Brahmā, to Surya, to Indra. These Padas are worth perusal.[1]

Haridās

Haridās (A. D. 1774) was a Kśatriya by caste and born at Kuntalpur (Kutiāṇā) near Junāgadh. He was a protege of Divān Raṇchhodji who had given him employment. He has written the "ŚivaVivāh" and several Vedantic Padas and they are recited by Sādhus and ascetics near Kutiāṇā and Bardā. His language is provincial Gujarāti, full of Urdu words, the latter testifying to the Mahomedan influence at that time paramount in Sauraśtra.

Another poet of the same name has written 'Kālikā Mātā no Garbo', in which is described the

1. His padas comprise भीष्मस्तुति; जयविजयशाप; गजेन्द्रमोक्ष; रासलीला; नागदमन; परीक्षितगर्भरहस्य and वामनचरित्र. They describe incidents in the life of these devotees of Vishnu. His Garbis are virile productions.

legend of the goddess having destroyed PatāiRājā and his kingdom, for his having tried to violate her chastity.

Govindrām

Govindrām (A. D. 1781–1814) was an Audich Brāhmin of a small town called Āmod, near Broach. He has, like Vallabh Bhatt, written on the evils obtaining in this sinful age of Kali,[1] but his verses are more effective. Every line is effective. He first describes the evil practices of the Brāhmins, who had taken to drinking and, forgetting their exalted office, had elected to serve the inferior classes, selling their daughters in marriage and doing many other things that were improper. He, then, passes on to the Kśatriyas who also had abandoned their duty of protecting the cow, the Brāhmin and the Sādhu, having taken instead, to thieving, robbing and scandal-mongering. The Vaiś-yas had run away from their duties. Some of them killed their daughters in infancy, lacking the where-withal for their marriage. They kept false weights, in the name of Krishna committed fornication, and followed false Gurus. The Śudras also had forgone their duties. They had surprised every body by posing as Gurus. Some had begun to mutter incantations into the ears of others and claim money for that,

His verses deal with the evils of this age

1. संवत अढार त्रीसें गायो कलिजुगनो महिमायजी.

I sang the greatness of the Kaliyuga in Samvat year 1830.

while others had begun to lead immoral lives with their sisters, daughters and daughters-in-law. Wives of sons quarelled with their husband's mothers, and husbands took sides with their wives and abused their mothers. On the other hand, wives thrashed their husbands and favoured other men, while men allowed their wives to order them about. They even washed their clothes and cooked for them. Brothers quarelled with brothers over mere trifles. Krishṇa had anticipated this state of things in the Bhagwad Gitā, and told Arjuna that he would appear amongst them when such irreligion would prevail, to reform them."

There are other poems of his but they are all couched in the same style, satirizing the hypocrisy and vices of the times.

And the conversion of a Mahomedan to Vaishnavism

In a short piece he has described the rare event in the annals of modern Hinduism, of the conversion of a Mahomedan, Ali Khān by name, to the tenents of the Vallabh sect or Vaishnavism at the hands of Vallabhāchārya. The convert is one of the eighty four well-known followers of this sampradāya (cult).

Udayaratna

Udayaratna, a Jain poet of this period (Samvat year 1769, A. D. 1713) has been selected out of about twenty four or five Jain poets, to show what kind of poetry they wrote. He wrote at Cambay, Pātaṇ, and other

15

places, and his verses on the Nine Hedges of Virtue or continence on the part of males, (especially Jain Sādhus) are about the most popular in Gujarāti literature. Virtue according to him is to be protected from lapses, by nine hedges, in the shape of abstention from certain temptations. The first hedge is that a man who wishes to remain virtuous should not live in a place where women live. However careful a rat is, it is in danger if a cat be near. Similarly for one wishing to remain chaste, there is a chance of his fall, if he lives near women. The second hedge is the avoidance of even talk with women. Just as by seeing a lemon at a distance, the mouth begins to water, so a virtuous man (a Sādhu) might slip if he were even to exchange a word with the opposite sex. The third hedge is, not even to sit where women usually sit, that is, on cots, sofas, etc. The poet says if you mix pumpkin with moistened and kneaded flour the dough loses its flavour. Similarly if you enjoy sitting on soft couches and sofas (used by women) you are likely to endanger your virtue. The fourth is not to look at the fair sex. If you look long at the sun you injure your eyesight, so, if you look at women, you lose your strength of mind. The fifth hedge is to avoid the places where you can hear even the tinkling of their bangles, places like wells, and

a type of Jain writers

Nine hedges of Virtue

ponds (which women frequent for fetching water). If you enclose butter or wax in a pot and place it near fire, it is sure to melt; even so, the sound of women's voice would melt the virtue of a man. Sixthly, you must taboo even the remembrance of any good times you might have passed with them before you took the vow of chastity. If you place a bundle of hay over fire, it brightens up. So, remembrance of past pleasures stirs up similar thoughts. Seventhly, all exciting foods should be eschewed as they feed the passions. Eighthly, avoid over-eating, eat very sparingly. If in a pot which could hold one pound of grain only, you put two pounds, cover it and place it on fire, the cover is sure to fly off, on account of pressure from within. So, over-eating has the danger of removing the lid of continence. The ninth prohibition is against indulgence in fashionable dress, use of cosmetics etc. There is one last general behest conveyed in these words: "Do not travel alone with a woman, do not talk (with her) on the road, even two men should not sleep on one bed, nor should one easily be moved to use abusive language. A daughter aged six and a half, and a son aged seven, should not sleep with her father and his mother, in the same bed."

Ratno

Ratno, belonging to the humble class of dyers (भावसार) at Kāira, has written in Samvạt year 1795, A. D. 1739, on the laments of the Gopis at their bereavement from Krishṇa.[1]

Jivrām Bhatt and his allegorical poem

Jivrām Bhatt of Dholkā near Ahmedābād, has imitated the VivekVanjhārā of Premānand in his "Travels of Jivrāj Śeth." Jivrāj makes a voyage to dispose of his merchandise. The perils of the sea are described: at last his ship reaches the harbour. He begins his task of disposing of his goods. He seeks and obtains a wife Nivritti and she bears him a son and a daughter. His career closes. The poem is an allegory: Jivrāj is the soul and the poem describes his journey and anxieties in the search for bliss. The wife is meditation, the fruit of the union is Jnān, knowledge, and Bhakti, devotion. The successful issue of the venture is absorption into Śivraj, the divinity, the Brahma. These verses he wrote in Samvat year 1800, A. D. 1744.

Mādhavdās and his works

Mādhavdās, son of Sundardās (A. D. 1721), was a Vālmik Kāyastha of Surat. In simple language he has written the Dasām Skandha, the Rukmiṇi-Haraṇ, and the OkhāHaraṇ. The poems, are however, devoid of spirit.

1. The late Mr. Govardhanrām Tripāthi and Kavi Nānālāl Dalpatrām praise his Bār Mās (Twelve Months). Ratno was a real (Ratna) gem.

CHAPTER VII

POETS OF THE (FIRST HALF OF THE) NINETEENTH CENTURY

Prevailing note of the last period continued in this century

There are some poets born in the eighteenth century, the dates of whose works however overlap it and hence they are considered as belonging to the next century. The division is merely chronological as we do not find any sharp dividing lines; the first half of the nineteenth (A. D. 1800 to 1850) may be taken to be merely a continuation of the eighteenth century, so far as the prevailing note of the literature is concerned. It is proposed to treat only of the first half of the century here, because, towards the middle or rather end of that half, English education began to be imparted to the youth of the province, and a movement began which has revolutionised the literature of Gujarāt as it has done elsewhere in India. In the first half of the century

except in two particulars

then, the followers of Śiva, the worshippers of Vishnu, the devotees of the goddess, and the Sādhus of the Jains continued to write and chant their devotional songs, and an additional note was struck by a new order of ascetics, led by Sahajānand Swāmi, and a cluster of poetesses took up the thread where it was left by Mirān Bāi four hundred years before. These are the distinguishing features of this period, which continues till A. D. 1850.

Dhirā Bhagat

Amongst the half a dozen or more poets who are known by the appellation of Bhagat[1] (a devotee) Dhirā Bhagat (A. D. 1753–1825) holds no mean rank. He belonged to a place called Gothdā near Sāvli, in the Barodā district, and was a BrahmaBhāt by caste, a caste known proverbially for its arbitrary ways and sharp temper. He was a Vaishanavite at first and later though he became a Vairāgi he continued to attend Vaishanav temples on festival days. He had got Haribhakti (devoutness) and Ātma Jnān (self knowledge), in legacy so to speak. He studied under several Shāstris and thus acquired culture. His association with Sādhus made him a mystic also. His 'Awalvāṇi' is similar to Kabir, Sunderdās and Akhā's works. Though he had a dislike of becoming a Guru, he had to entertain a number of disciples. His wife was Jatanbā, a woman with a hot temper, and said to be

1. A Bhagat is one who is not attached to the world and its pursuits but devotes his life to meditation and walking in the ways of god. Even the words ascetic or hermit do not correctly interpret the term Bhagat, as used in Gujarāti.

his maternal uncle's widow whom he had remarried. He owned some ancestral fields, and acquired the privilege from the Thākore of Bhādarvā of charging at each marriage in his territory, a fee of eight annas on the part of the bridegroom, before allowing the nupitals to be celebrated. This marriage duty, called Toraṇaghodā, the receiving of the bridegroom's horse-ghodā-at the place of marriage adorned with festoons-Toraṇa-brought him some income to supplement the produce of his fields and on the whole he was well off. He was not well educated to start with, but while just entering upon his teens, he happened to fall in with a gifted Sannyāsi, whom he acknowledged as his Guru, and from whom he got instruction in that knowledge (Jnān) which he celebrated so well in his poetry. The functions of a Guru and his pupil are elaborately narrated by him in several songs, which are over-flowing with gratitude towards a teacher, who, as it were, took him out of darkness into light. He did not know Sanskrit, but knew a little Hindi. Still, as appears from even a cursory glance at his works, the absence of the knowledge of Sanskrit was no obstacle to his thorough understanding and exposition of the principles of Yoga and Jnān. He preferred Jnān to Yoga, and was as greatly attached to ĀtmaJnān (self-

Gratitude towards Guru

Work more popular than Akhā's

knowledge) as Akhā, while his poetry shows that he expounded it much more popularly and with greater felicity of language than he.

How he spread knowledge of his work

Dhirā had hit upon an original plan of spreading the knowledge of his work amongst the people and giving it publicity. Living near the shores of the Mahi river, he often used to go there for a bath, with pieces of paper on which were written out his latest compositions. He bottled them up either in hollow sticks of bamboo or small gourds, and tightly closed their open ends or mouths, thereafter letting them loose on the surface of the waters. They were thus carried away to different parts of the country, where on being picked up, they were sure to be read by strangers.

His pupils

Dhirā had many pupils, one of whom Bāpu Sāheb Gāikwād deserves the title of a poet.

Dhirā's Kāfis

The long compositions of Dhirā are eleven or twelve in number,[1] but he is best known for that work of his which is written in a form called Kāfi. He is master of that form and no other poet in Gujarāt has been

1. They are: रणयज्ञ; स्वरूपनी काफीओ; मतवादी; आत्मबोध; ज्ञानकक्को; योगमार्ग; प्रश्नोत्तरमालिका; अवळवाणी; छूटक पदो; गरबीओ; धोळ; अश्वमेध.

able to approach him.[1] In his work, called स्वरूपनी काफीओ, he has very instructively shown the correct duties of a Guru and a pupil, and how fleeting are the pleasures of youth, wealth, body, mind and worldly pursuits. The instinct of heredity–for all Bhāts or Bārots are descended from families of court–poets or singers–has lent great force to his poetry, and his style is virile. He uses the common vocabulary. He never employs hard or obscure words. He makes his meaning clear in simple language and so his Kāfis are more popular than the satires of Akhā.[2]

1. Dhirā was not the first to write Kāfis; Akhā and other Bhagats had written them, and written them well.

2. This is one of his well-known poems:

फूल्यो शुं फरे छे रे? भूल्यो भवकूपमां पडया;
मनुष देहरूपी रे खोयो मणि हाथे चढयो.
डाह्यो थई दुनियामां फरे छे तेणे शुं सर्युं तारूं काज?
तें न जाण्युं जे जावुं पलकमां, केम करी रहेशे लाज?
डहापण तारूं जाण्युं रे, ज्यारे जम हाथे चढयो. फूल्यो०

× × × × ×

मनमां ले शिखामण मारी, ममता मूकी परी;
कर स्मरण सरजनहारनुं, जनम सफळ ले करी;
दास धीरो कहे छे रे सौथी तुं सरस नीवडयो. फूल्यो०

Why do you gad about so elated? You have fallen into the well (pit) of the world, you have lost the gem of human birth after having acquired it. You walk about like a wise man of the world, but how will that benefit you? You do not know that in a moment

He tries to persuade. He does not use the lash and tear the skin like Akhā.

Nirānt Bhagat

Even more gentle and mild than Dhirā in his language, was Nirānt Bhagat (A. D. 1770–1846), a Pātidār of Dethāṇ near Barodā. Like the majority of people living round about Dākore, Nirānt too, was in the habit of going on a pilgrimage to the famous shrine, every full-moon day, growing the Tulsi plant in the palm of his hand. Once he fell in with a Mahomedan, by name Miyān Sāheb, a monotheist in belief and non-worshipper of images. He had a long talk with his Hindu fellow traveller, whom he ultimately convinced

you will have to leave it and then how will you look respectable (face your creator)? You will know how wise (ironical for unwise) you are when the myrmidons of Yama (death) carry you away.

Take my advice, leave off your attachment (to things mundane), Remember your creator, and reap the full fruit of your birth. If you do it, then your servant Dhiro says, that you would come out the best of all.

This is another:

गुरु विना ज्ञानी रे, ते तो नर अंध ठ्यों,
दीपक छे घटमां रे, जो तेपर छार ठ्यों.

× × × × ×

A man with knowledgs but without a Gûrû (who alone could have imparted it properly) is like a blind man. The light is there, inside the chatty (inside you), but there is a cover (of ignorance) over it (which only a Gûrû can remove).

His seareh after BrahmaJnān

that his God was always near him, and that it was, therefore, meaningless to go in search of Him, Tulsi in hand, every month. Nirānt felt the truth of the preaching and accepted him as a Gûrû. This story may be true or not, but it serves to show the transition of the poet from being a mere worshipper of the image of Krishṇa to a state of mind, where images are discarded, and where BrahmaJnān (knowledge of the Brahma) is held to be sufficient for salvation.. His poetry accordingly shows both phases of his belief.

His pupils

Nirānt had married two wives, and was father of about eight children, whose descendants still survive. He passed most of his time at Barodā. He left behind him about seventeen pupil followers, three of whom-Vanārashibāi, Girjābāi and Jamnābāi, were ladies. The most distinguished of his pupils was Bāpu Sāheb Gāikwād, who had come to him for spiritual guidance and instruction, after sitting for a time at the feet of Dhirā Bhagat.

His rival becomes his pupil

He had a rival at Vāghodiā, a Brāhmin, Manchhārām, to whom he has addressed a letter in verse (A. D. 1801) putting to him certain problems on the philosophy of Vedānt. The language of the letter is a reflection of the nature of the writer. It is full of humility—he calls himself the dust of the feet (पदरज) of the Brāhmin, who, he says, in the very nature of things is supposed to be more cultured and learned than a mere Pātidār. Manchhārām was unable to answer them, and ultimately joined the band of Nirānt's followers. The absence of all aggressiveness, the tranquillity, so to speak, breathed by his verses show his peaceful and quiet temper.

His language simple though mixed

There is a great admixture of Urdu words in the works of Nirānt; with that exception, his language is pure and simple.

Definition of Brahma

He thus defines Brahma: "That which has no form and no attribute, that which has no name, that which owns nothing and at the same time owns everything, that which is like the tree and the seed.[1]

Meaning of Nirānt

The very name 'Nirānt' signifies, peacefulness, absence of all anxiety.

Bāpu Sāheb Gāikwād

Bāpu Sāheb Gāikwād (A. D. 1779-1843) was a Marāthā Sirdār, belonging to a well-connected family at Barodā.

1. रूप नहि जेने, गुण नहि, ने नाम नहि छे एवुं:
कंईए नहि, ने सरवस तेनुं, वृक्ष बीज छे जेवुं.

He started life like the other scions of his family, and passed his time in acquiring the accomplishments proper to his station in society, riding, wrestling, sword exercise, lāthi play, etc., which had nothing to do either with religion or letters. But from his childhood he was fond of frequenting temples, and while there, used to question any Śadhu or ascetic who happened to drop in, about religious matters, and if he did not get a satisfactory reply, treated them with scant courtesy. He thus acquired a taste for spiritual matters early in life, which resulted in a full and rapid development later on at the hands of Dhirā and Nirānt Bhagat. He was sent by his father to look after his lands at Gothdā, where Dhirā lived, and it was thus that he was initiated by him, into matters spiritual till he acknowledged him as his Gûrû, and served him so loyally as to prepare his *hookāh* for him, a service generally attended to by menials.[1] After his return to Barodā he forsook the life of a Grahastha (householder), and became a Bhakta, i.e., passed his time in discoursing with saints and holy people, in chanting religious verses and writing sacred poetry. He continued for a time to serve the Gāikwād, but his heart was not in his work, and he was often found fault with, but always

renounces sport for religion and literature

1. He has narrated this incident in a poem.

escaped by going to His Highness direct, and reciting to him some of his own lines which pleased the Mahārāja so much, that he easily forgave him.

His passion for singing Bhajans

Bāpu Sāheb was as fond of reciting Bhajans[1] in company, as Narsinh Mehtā was, and like him, he was once invited by the Dheds of a certain locality in Barodā, to give them the benefit of his recitation. Bāpu Sāheb accepted the invitation unhesitatingly. His father, when he came to know about it, felt considerably scandalised at his son's conduct, and asked him to leave his house. Bāpu Sāheb cheerfully carried out the behest, and went to live in a separate house. His mother-in-law also rebuked him, and he in reply wrote out some verses, the purport of which was that he confessed he was spoiled, but that it was like the spoiling of a stone by the touch of the philosopher's stone, or like the spoiling of a pupil by the company of his Gûrû.[2] After a few years, his relatives took him back into the family house.

1. Hymns. Devotional songs.

2. अमे वगड्या, अमे बगड्या, लेजो जाणी रे,
भाई ! अमे बगड्या, अमे वगड्या, लेजो जाणी.
× × × × ×
पारससंगथकी पत्थर जोने बगड्यो,
थयो पारस ने जाणे कोक ज्ञानी रे. अमे०

Singing of dirges by women in public

In Gujarāt and Kāthiawād, after the bamboo bier on which a dead body is carried to the burning ground has left the house, it is usual for the females—of the house, of the caste and of friends–to form themselves into a circle or divide into pairs, and accompanied by the rhythmic movement of their hands which regularly move away from and fall back on their chests–commonly called beating the breast–recite a dirge (**राजीआ**), in which the virtues of the deceased are sung, exaggerated and extolled.[1] Bāpu Sāheb, while once passing by the way, happened to witness a party of such female mourners, chanting a Rājiā. He was struck with the emptiness of the subject–

तमे बगडो तो भाई! एवा बगडजो,
त्यारे तो मटे चोराशीनी ज घाणी रे. अमे०
सतगुरुना संगथकी सेवक जुओ बगड्यो,
जेणे सतनाम लीधुं छे छागी रे. अमे०

Compare Narsinh Mehtās following well known pada .

एवा रे अमो एवा रे वळी कहो छो तेवा रे,
भक्ति करतां जो भ्रष्ट कहेशो तो करशुं दामोदरनी सेवा रे.

1. It is called a Rājio, perhaps because the deceased is given as much importance as a Rājā (King) by the mourners, whose death means such a loss to the family as the death of a king to his subjects. Women, very shrewdly take this opportunity, under the garb of supplying materials for lament, of trotting out their own grievances. For instance, the mother or sister of the widow of the deceased–supposing he has left one–would enumerate all the inconveniences hes had been put to during his lifetime by his mother or sister.

matter of the song, and also with the ignorance of the reciters. He therefore composed a dirge called RāmaRājio, in which he descanted upon the six great enemies (षड्रिपु) of humanity, Passion, Anger, Avarice, Fascination, Pride and Envy. Nirānt Bhakta approved of it, and in many places this didactic dirge has been substituted for the ordinary one.

His poems written in correct Gujarāti

He has written no long or continuous poetic work, but many of his short poems have been preserved. In spite of his being a Marāthā by birth, with Marāthi as his mother tongue, he has written correct Gujarāti without betraying the slightest tinge of his foreign origin. Indeed, at times, he uses mannerisms or provincialisms as if he were one born to them.

Acknowledgment of debt to his gúrús

In numerous places, has he gratefully acknowledged the debt he owed to his two masters, Dhirā and Nirānt.

His advice to Hindus and Mahomedans not to quarrel

His intimate knowledge of the world and its ways is clearly reflected in his poems, but the one great service he tried to render to the people was his persistent preaching to Hindus and Mahomedans not to quarrel with one another, as in effect the God of the one was the God of the other. "That Rāma and Rehmān were one, O brothers! that

Krishṇa and Karim were one and the same, that between Vishnu and Allāh there was no difference; that Allāh and Alakh (the Invisible) were one."[1] He was said to be very independent in expressing his views, and equally independent in conduct, and surely it does require some freedom from prejudice to speak of Allāh and Alakh in one breath.

Premānand Swāmi

Premānand Swāmi (A. D. 1779–1845) lived at Gadhadā in Kāthiāwād, one of the three[2] principal seats venerated by the followers of Sahajānand Swāmi. He was well-versed in music, he sang and played well. He sings of Krishṇa Lilā as if he were a Gopi, "a sylvan maid" and Krishṇa her lover. He is hence called Premānand Sakhi.[3] His verses called "The bereavement (or death) of Sahajānand Swāmi," the founder of the

a follower of Sahajānand

Swāminārāyaṇ sect, with whom he seems to have resided, are said to have drawn tears from the eyes of his audience as he sang them. He has written

1. राम ने रहेमान तमे एक भाईओ जाणजो,
कृष्ण ने करीम एक कहीए,
विष्णु बिसमिल्लामां भेद नथी भाळ्यो,
अने अल्ला अलख एक लहीए रे.

2. Vadtāl, Ahmedābād and Gadhadā.

3. A female companion.

a poem–Thāl[1] –describing the dinner he would provide for his beloved Krishṇa, which gives a very good idea of the dainties and sweets which go to make up the banquet of a Gujarāti Lucullus.

Bhojā Bhagat

Bhojā alias Bhojal[2] Bhagat, was a native of Kāthiāwād. His family came originally from Gujarāt, and were Pātidars or Kunbi by caste. He was born (about A. D. 1785) in an illiterate family, and till the end of his life (1850 A. D.), he remained illiterate, in the sense that he never knew how to write. He recited his poems, and they were either taken down by his pupils or stored in his memory, to be communicated whenever required to his pupils and admirers. Many of them have thus passed from mouth to mouth, and are perpetuated by those itinerant singers who are met with every day in the streets of Gujarāt and Kāthiāwād towns and villages, and who pour them forth to the accompaniment of a stringed guitar, which is called a Tamboora (तंबुरो).

a remarkable personality though illiterate

1. A dish or plate (थाळी) full of different kinds of dainties meant for acceptance by the deity.

2. He likes to call himself Bhojal in his verses

(i)......एम बोल्या छे भोजल राम.
(ii)......भोजल भजतां पाम्या पार
हवे शुं करुं कक्कानो विस्तार ?

Bhojā's faith and its tests

Bhojā lived only on milk for the first twelve years of his life,[1] and thereafter came in contact with an ascetic who came to his village from the mountain forests of Girnār. He made a great impression on his youthful mind, and at his persuasion he began to partake of grain and other food. The ascetic taught him what devotion (Bhakti) meant, and Bhojal turned out such an apt pupil that in a short time his own village people and some outsiders began to adore him as a saint. Some time after he moved to a larger place, called Fatehpur, near Amreli. There he began to practise Tapa and passed whole days in counting the beads of his rosary and repeating सोऽहं सोऽहं or सोऽहं हंस:, which is known as *Ajapājāp*. This he did for twelve years, and at the end of the period was supposed to have acquired the power to work miracles. A Gāikwādi officer of the time Vithobā Divānji, who had then conquered a large part of Kāthiāwād and had his headquarters at the neigh-

1. He had not married and had renounced the world early in life, because he considered the other sex an encumbrance.

His brother's son Arjaṇ Bhagat and after Arjaṇ, his son Lakhmaṇ Bhagat succeeded to Bhojā's Gādi and Guruship.

Bhojā used to go to Virpur at the request of his pupil Jālā Bhagat. A room called Bhojā Bhagat's Gādi-Room (ओरडो) is still found at Fatehpur.

bouring town of Amreli, wishing to ascertain the truth of this fact, called him, and shut him up in a room, where he was supplied with food thrice in the day, but was kept under strict surveillance and not allowed to leave his place of confinement. Bhojā, undaunted by such strictness, quietly assumed his accustomed posture of sitting and began to tell the beads of the rosary. This continued for a fortnight, and by divine grace, it is said, all desire in him to answer any call of nature had vanished although he partook of hearty meals. The Divānji was convinced that Bhojā was no hollow saint, and he asked for instruction at his hands. Bhojā said, he was an ignorant villager (Kuṇbi), and dared not preach to officers, perhaps, his rough language might hurt their feelings. The Divānji said that he would forgive anything in such a Sādhu, and then it was that Bhojā composed those 150 Chābkhā (whips) which have made him famous. Some of them were addressed direct to the Divānji but he took them in good part.

His followers

His last days were passed at Virpur, where there is a temple dedicated to him and where his footprints are adored. Members of his family are still alive, and there is still a large following of his in Kāthiāwād, although he has not founded any separate sect or cult like Kabir or Sahajānand.

His Chābkhā a masterpiece

Just as Narsinh Mehtā is considered unique for his Prabhātiyān, Sāmal for his Chhappā, Dayārām for his Garbis, Pritam for his Padas, and Dhirā for his Kāfis, so Bhojā is considered a master of Chābkhā-poems in the nature of moral whips.

His Salaiyākhyān

Excepting for his Salaiyākhyān[1], he has written no continuous work. This little story is to the effect that the parents of one Salaiyā were in the habit of never taking their meals before they had satisfied the wants of at least one Sādhu. Once it rained incessantly for a week and they could get no Sādhu, and hence they had to remain hungry. At last one was found who was afflicted with leprosy and running sores, still they brought him home with great pleasure and after washing his feet, placed before him rich food. He said he was a cannibal and always ate one human being and would eat the cooked flesh of their son if offered without a single tear from their eyes. Nothing daunted by the difficulty, both husband and wife prepared themselves to kill their only child and cook his flesh to gratify the Sādhu. The boy cheerfully submitted to the ordeal, and was killed and cooked by his own mother. At last when every-

1. Chalaiyā or Salaiyā has furnished the subject matter of poems to poets from the time of Nākar.

thing was ready, the Sādhu objected that he could not dine at the inauspicious house of a childless couple. His hostess was equal to this difficulty too. She said she was five months pregnant and to convince her exacting guest of the fact, took up a knife to cut open her body to show him the unborn foetus. Here she was stopped, and the Sādhu revealed himself as Hari, who had been immensely pleased with their devotion which he rewarded by reviving their dead child.

His Horis

He has written some Horis[1] also, the most popular amongst them being "a request to Krishṇa" by a Gopi to assist her in her difficulty.[2]

Denunciation of hypocrisy in ascetics

He was pitiless in denouncing those hypocrites who cheat the world in the garb of Sādhus. Some of his Chābkhā (whips) are laid on with rigor. He says: "The Bāvā applying ashes to his body, starts to cheat the simple world. He gives threads and papers into which he says he has worked magi-

1. A Hori is a kind of song generally sung in the Vasant season (spring), depicting the joyful feelings of the heart at the advent of spring.

2. The first lines being

नाथ! मोरी अरज सुणो अविनाशी!
हुं तो जनम जनम तोरी दासी.—नाथ.

cal properties, and he distributes pills saying that they are unfailing in their effect. You will find that many of them are really Kuṇbis and low castes (Kolis) and to them come day after day shoals of women with a view to worshipping them. They—the Sādhus—address them as mother, but really their hearts are burning with carnal passion. They gather together male and female followers and enjoy with them a meal of bread, milk and sugar. Bhojā Bhagat says that these Sādhus have drowned their followers in the sea of the world (sins)."[1]

In yet another "whip" he sings: "Look at these so called Bāvās, who have assumed their garb to cheat the world. They daily frequent that place for a bath where women congregate to draw water. The Bāvā sits down to sing his songs before widows and females, when he finds that there are no males in the house. He takes an opportunity of fondling the children of others just in order to introduce

1. दुनिया भरमावा भोळी, रे चाल्यो बावो भभूती चोळी.
दोरा धागा ने चीठ्ठी करे बावो, आपे गुणकारी गोळी,
अनेक जातना एवा बने छे, कोई कणबी, कोई कोळी रे.–दुनिया०
नित्य नित्य दर्शन नियम धारीने, आवे तरिया तणी टोळी,
माई! माई! कही मान दिये पण, हैये कामनानी होळी रे.–दुनिया०
चेलाचेलीने भेळां करी बावो, खाय खीर खांड ने पोळी,
भोजो भगत कहे भवसागरमां, बावे मार्यां बोळी रे.–दुनिया०

himself to them and win their regard. When the wife of a good man is in the sulks, the Bāvā makes it his business to go to her and appease her. He behaves as if he were a saint and he imposes on the wise, but really he is as we have shown him. Although he is ash-besmeared, he lusts for women and wishes to live on deception. He burns incense and pretends to meditate but this he does to impose upon simple people. Bhojā Bhagat says that by worshipping him you are really going to the Kingdom of the Dead."[1]

The following "whip" is also widely known: "O my soul, adore the creator. This world is but a dream: wealth, riches, goods, treasures, sons and family (will be left behind). You will have to depart alone and be subjected to a beating by the god of death. Imposing houses and beautiful balconies,

1. जोई ल्यो जगतना बावा, धर्या भेख धूतीने खावा.
प्रेमदाओ घणी पाणी भरे त्यां, नित्य नित्य बावो जाय नहावा,
रांडी छांडी घेर नर ना होय तो बावोजी बेसे गावा रे.–जोई ल्यो.
लोकनां छोकरां तेडी रमाडे बावो, पराणे प्रीतडी थावा,
गृहस्थनी स्त्री ज्यारे रीसाय छे त्यारे, बावोजी जाय छे मनावा रे.–जोई ल्यो.
सिद्धाई देखाडी शाणा समजावे, पण हवाल छे हावा,
राखोडी चोळी पण रांडोना रसिया, खोळे हरामनुं खावा रे.–जोई ल्यो.
धूप धरी ध्यान धरे बावो, भोळाने भरमावा,
भोजो भगत कहे भावे सेवो एने, जमपुरीमां जावा रे.–जोई ल्यो.

endless terraces and palaces of billionaires and millionaires, all these they have left behind. You will be carefully tied up in a bamboo frame work (bier) on which flowers are thrown, and at the four corners of which four cocoanuts are hanging, and the mourners will follow you with loud cries. You could not sleep but on the softest of beds, you might pursue a hundred professions, but they will burn you all the same, carefully stoking the fire just as a blacksmith melts iron. On the cremation ground they will pile up firewood in a square heap on which they will deposit your body, covering it with still more wood. The mourners will set fire to the heap and surely enough the fire will throw out burning coals. After the burning is over, both the male and female mourners will take a bath and go back to their own houses, and Bhojā Bhagat says that after weeping for ten days, they will completely forget you."[1]

1. प्राणीआ ! भजी लेने किरतार, आ तो स्वपनुं छे संसार.

धन दोलत ने माल खजीना, पुत्र अने परिवार,
ए मेली जाईश तुं एकलो, पछे खाशे जमना मार रे.—प्राणीआ !
उंची मेडी ने अजब झरुखा, गोख तणो नहि पार,
कोटीध्वज ने लक्षपति तेनां बांध्यां रह्यां घरबार रे.— „
उपर फुलडां फरफरे, ने हेठे श्रीफळ चार,
ठीक करीने एने ठाठडीमां घाल्यो, पछे वांसे पडे पोकार रे.— „
सेज तळायुं विना सुतो नहि, जीव हुन्नर करतो हजार,
खोरी खोरीने खूब जळायो, जेम लोढुं गाळे लुवार रे. „

Every strand of his "whip" cuts like a lash and his repeated flagellations are couched in apposite language.

His style

Bhojā Bhagat's language is the very reverse of classical. He having never moved in cultured society, nor studied properly, it is neither refined nor smooth. It is rough and full of provincialisms; it comes from the heart, and without undergoing any process of tempering, strikes the imagination of the reader or hearer, with the force of the blow of a steamhammer. It is rough like that of a countryman's but none the less sincere.

Manohar Swāmi

Manohar Swāmi (A. D. 1788-1845) was a Nāgar Brāhmin of Junāgadh,[1] whence he migrated to Gogo near Bhāvnagar in A. D. 1828, in search of employment. Gogo was in the early part of the nineteenth century a strong-

स्मशान जई चेहे खडकी ने, माथे छे काष्टनो भार,
अग्नि मेली सौ उभां रह्यां, अने देहे झरे अंगार रे.—प्राणीआ
स्नान करीने चाली नीकळ्यां, नर ने वळी नार,
भोजो भगत कहे दश दि रोइने पछी मेल्यो विसार रे.— ,,

1. He was the maternal uncle (मामो) of Kālidās of Vasāvad, āhe au thorof Prahlādākhyan and Sitā Swayamvar. At the age of thirty five, being displeased with the behaviour of his wife he left home and went to Gogo. He also lost all his inheritance—a fur ther possible inducement to leaving home.

hold of Nāgar Brāhmins, who later on crossed over to Bhāvnagar and headed by the late Gaurishankar Udaishankar Ozā, C. S. I., did so much for the development of that state. Manohar was a clever calligraphist, and an expert in the imitation of handwriting.

an ascetic poet

He was once charged with forgery but acquitted in default of convincing testimony. He was a scholar in Sanskrit and Persian, and he studied the Upanishads through their Persian translations, made in the reign of Akbar. For generations before, Junāgadh had become the battlefield of the two rival creeds, Vaishṇavite and Śaivite, and as a result he had lost faith in and liking for both, and ultimately in A. D. 1838 took refuge in Sannyās (renunciation of the world). He lived as an ascetic too at Bhāvnagar in the Nilkaṇth Māhādev temple, assuming the name of Sachchidānand, and in that capacity was the guru of Gaurishankar. He has written commentaries on the BhagavadGitā, the RāmaGitā and a grammar of Gujarāti. He has also composed poems in Gujarāti and Sanskrit against the tenets of Vallabhāchārya. Like all true reformers, he hated those worshippers who went to temples for show. He also disliked idol worshippers, saw no good in pilgrimages and favoured only that salvation which comes from the discovery of

His dislike of mere show

the Swarup (one's own form or self). His verses are at times simple and at times hard and philosophical, but always free from provincialisms, and are plainly the product of a cultured, observant and practical mind. He asks how does one expect salvation without a good teacher, and, how can you get him, in a world "where some are full of lust, some of anger, some of avarice, where the really generous appear to be humble, where some are on pleasure bent, while others prefer retirement (from the world), where some are happy and some unhappy, where some are learned scholars (Paṇdits), and some are astrologers, where those who are deceivers wield power, where some are wealthy, and some poor, some sing, some dance, where some start false creeds and where some are worshipped as gods, where none can resolve the doubts of their pupils, but acquire wealth by knavery. They call this mere form of the body, real Brahma, and do not understand what the soul is. It is the case of a blind person following another blind person and both falling into a well. He who sits at the feet of a real Guru, having strong faith in him, his false arguments, his errors and his difficulties (of intellect) are sure to be removed. He would then know what is Sachchidānand.[1] He would

How salvation is attained

1. The Existent, Wise and Happy (state).

then disappear within himself. Manohar says, the fear of death and birth would (then) be gone and his doubts would also vanish."[1]

Girdhar, known as the writer of the only popular versified Rāmāyaṇ[2] in Gujarāti, (V. S. 1893) was the son of a petty village officer (Talāti) of a small village called Māsar in the Barodā district. He was a Dasā Lād Baniā by caste. He was born in A. D. 1787 and died in 1852, in tragic circumstances. His sister was mar-

Girdhar

1. कामी, क्रोधी, लोभी कोई दाता, दीन जणाय,
कंई रागी, कंई त्यागी, कोई सुखी दुखी देखाय.
कंई पंडित, कंई जाण्या जोशी, छळीआ बळीआ थाय,
कंई घरबारी, कंई भीखारी, कंई नाचे, कंई गाय.
कंई पाखंडे पंथ चलावे, प्रभु थईने पूजाय,
शिष्य तणो संशय नव टाळे, धूतीने धन खाय.
देहाकृतिने ब्रह्म ठरावे, चैतन नव ल्हेवाय,
अंध अंधनी पाछळ चाले उभय कुवामां जाय.
दृढ विश्वास धरीने जे कोई, सद्गुरुशरणे जाय,
तेना संशय, तर्क, विपर्यय ग्रन्थी सौ भेदाय,
मनोहर जन्ममरण भय भांगे, संशय दूर पळाय.

2. In writing his Rāmāyaṇ he has not relied on Vālmiki's Rāmāyaṇ only but has also borrowed from Hanumān Nātak, Agni Purāṇ, Padma Purāṇ and Tulsidās' Hindi version of it (Rāmāyaṇ). Similarly for KrishṇaCharitra he has utilised besides the Bhāgvat other well known works such as Hari Vamsh, Padma Purāṇ, Nārad–PanchRātra, Mahābhārat &c.

See p. 749 'Girdharkrit Rāmāyaṇ' published by the सस्तुं साहित्यवर्धक कार्यालय, Ahmedābād.

ried at Barodā, and she called him there and got him employment. While in Barodā he added to his rudimentary education in the vernacular, some knowledge of Sanskrit and Hindi from a Jain Gorji, Vallabhavijaya. Later, he came in contact with a Vaishnav Mahārāj Purshottamji,[1] under whose influence, he took to Bhaktimārga and began to write verses on Krishṇa Bhakti. He started on a pilgrimage with another Mahāraj Rangilāl by name. On their return, he wanted to visit the renowned seat of the Vallabhācharya Mahārāj at Shrināthji near Udeypore, but Rangilal[2] did not permit him to do so. He took the prohibition so much to heart that he retired to his tent, and shortly after passed away.

known for his Rāmāyaṇ

His works comprise the TulsiVivāh (A. D. 1815), a poem on the marriage of Krishṇa with the Tulsi plant, a symbolical function held every year on the night of the eleventh of Kārtik Sud, 2. The RājsuyaYajna (A. D. 1831), a poem describing the imperial sacrificial ceremony performed by the Pāndavas, and composed in a month, 3. The GokulLilā and 4. Twelve months of the bereavement of Rādhā, 5. The Rāmāyaṇ, 6. The

His other works

1. He taught him poetics.

2. He belonged to the RādhāVallabhi sect, which cares more for Rādhā than for Krishṇa, not so the Vallabhis.

Aśwa Medha. 7. The Mathurā Lilā alias Krishṇa-Lilā practically the whole of the Tenth Skandh of the Bhāgvat and several miscellaneous verses. His compositions are not of a distinguished order.

Ranchhod Bhakta

Ranchhod Bhakta, who was alive in A. D. 1804, was a Baniā of Tornā, near Kapadvanj in the Kairā district. His Rāmāyāṇ, RādhāVivāh, description of Rādhā becoming sulky with Krishṇa and Ranchhodji no Garbo, narrating how Krishṇa for the sake of his humble devotee Bodhāṇā quitted Dwārkā for Dākore, furnish a specimen of his style which is such as to appeal to and be understood by even the masses. In his miscellaneous verses is found a short poem, which is comic, describing the virtues of the God of Sustenance, अन्नदेव.

Ranchhodji Divān

Ranchhodji Divān (A. D. 1768 to 1841) has left his name engraved on the pages of the history of Kāthiāwād. In the earlier part of his life, he wielded the sword rather than the pen, and although a Nāgar Brāhmin by caste, he had mastered the profession of arms so well, that the states of Junāgadh, Jāmnagar and Cutch had at one time or another had to experience his singular martial prowess. It was in A. D. 1805 when Colonel Walker "settled" the somewhat anarchical state of the province by fixing the amount of "PeshKash" (subsidy) that Ranchhodji found the work for his sword gone, and took to the pen. Many allusions have been made to him by English writers like Sir John Malcolm and Mrs. Postans. In Blackwood's Edinburgh Magazine mention is made of his superb qualities. Mrs. Postans, who saw him reposing under a vine-clad bower surrounded by a number of amanuenses, sitting on Persian carpets, says that "his large black eyes lustrous as burning lamps, were illumined by the fire of intellect within, and he was an acknowledged patron of poets, men of science and literary genius." He assisted Government in putting down the practices of Sati and female infanticide. In Persian he has written the Tārikh-e-Sorath, a history of Sorath and also the Rukāt-e-Gûnāgûn (various letters). He has translated into Vraj, a great work called the Śivarahasya, besides a number of other works, while in Gujarāti, he has also written about a dozen works, chief among them being the ŚivaGitā and Chandipāth nā Garbā, the latter being a rhapsody, narrating the rather gruesome adventures of the goddess Śakti. Like some other natives of Junāgadh, he had contracted a dislike for the Vallabh form of Vaiśṇavism, and he went so far as not to name any member of his family with a name which would have even a remote tinge of that cult.

Opinions about him of English writers

His works

and dislike of Vaiśṇavism

Harirām

Harirām (A. D. 1824), a native of Surat and an Audich Brāhmin by caste, has in a simple style described the marriages-Swayamvaras-of several queens like Sitā and Rukmiṇi, besides writing verses on the bereavement of the Gopis.

Haribhatt

Haribhatt (A. D. 1829) lived at Barodā. He is said to have been the founder of a small sect of the name of Dātā Hari. An epitome of the life of Krishṇa, and a lullaby-like song, describing the sulky frolics the child Krishṇa indulged in with his mother Jaśodā, are his well-known works.[1]

Viravijay

Viravijay, a Jain Yati (ascetic) of Ahmedābād, who was alive in A. D. 1849, is famous in Gujarāti literature for

1. These are its opening lines:

हालरडुं

माता जशोदा बोलावे, जमवा लालने,
चालो लाडकवाया ! लागुं तमने पाय,
तेम तेम रीसाईने रंग रसियाजी आवे नहि,
पाछळ दोडे तेम तेम नटवर नासी जाय.
माता जशोदा बोलावे०

Mother Jaśodā was calling her darling for his dinner. My darling ! come along, I fall at your feet. But the dear little rogue would go into sulks more and more, and not respond to her. The more she would run after him, the faster he would run away.

17

some verses of his thirty-six couplets in all—full of moral and practical advice, such as these:

"Go (deal) not with depraved women, do not form friendship with or conceive love for the base. It results in disgrace, loss of home, wealth and life.

× × × ×

"Do not ridicule your teacher or a Sādhu, your king, or a learned man. Move away from a spot where you see elephants, tigers, serpents and men fighting......While eating your meals praise the food, do not run it down, do not dine in the sun, do not stay overnight with a sick man, do not drink water on an empty stomach."[1]

and his moral couplets

Quite a long list of miscellaneous poets, with nothing in them deserving of special mention, might be furnished here. They move in the same groove, some of them

Miscellaneous poets

1. वेश्या साथे वणज न करीए, नीचसुं नेह न करीएजी रे,
खांपण आवे, घर धन जावे, जीवितने परहरीए.–सुणजो सजनो रे.

× × × ×

गुरु, जोगी, राजा, पंडितने, हांसी करी नव हसीएजी रे,
हाथी, वाघ, सरप, नर वढतां, देखीने दूर खसीए.–सुणजो सजनो ! रे.

× × × ×

अन्न वखाणी, वखोडी न खावुं, तडके बेसी न जमवुंजी रे,
मांदा पासे रात तजीने, नरणां पाणी न पीवुं.–सुणजो सजनो रे.

show a little originality here or a flash of wit or genius there, but their performance does not rise above the commonplace.

Purushottam, a Rājput of Ikharvā near Jambusar and a disciple of Nirānt Bhakta; Mitho, a Dhādhi of Limbdi in Kāthiāwād; Mukund, a Praśnorā Brahmin of Kāthiāwād; Dayāl Ratandās,[1] Raghunandan, Hargovan (who died in A. D. 1841), a Bhatt Mevādā Brāhmin and a special devotee of Ambā Mātā,[2] Raghunāthdas,[3] Krishṇārām,[4] Dewā Sāheb, Dungar

1. The life of Salaiyā written by Ratandās which begins with,

शेठ सगाळशा साधुने सेवे वाणीओ पाळे व्रत

is well known.

2. His verses on the seat of the Mātā at Surat, will flatter any native of that place, in so far as he would be pleased to learn that outsiders attach so much importance and sanctity to some of its most ordinary temples.

3. Out of his many poems, long and short, the two following Garbis even now delight the ladies of Gujarāt:

(१) ओधवजी! संदेशो कहेजो श्यामने,
मारा सम जो, मूकी मननो मेल जो,
कानुडो कपटी रे, आवडो केम थयो?
छळ करीने छेतरीए नहि, छेल जो.—ओधवजी०
आटला दिवस रे, आवुं नव जाणती,
धरथी न जाण्या, धूताराना ढंग जो;
पाणीडां पीने रे, घर शुं पूछीए?
बाळपणामां कीधो, एशुं संग जो.—ओधवजी०

Bārot, Nāreo Rāmaiyo, Butio Bhakta, Shāntidās,[1] Bhavān Bhakta,[2] a Sādhu belonging to the Kānfaṭā

(२) तमे अजाण्या, हमे जाणीए रे,
मारो पालवडो नव ताणीए रे;
तमे समजी ल्यो मन मांही रे,
सामळीआ! वहाला! रहोनी वेगळारे.

4. The description of Kalikāl—the present or iron age–of this poet is both graphic and sarcastic. He ridicules almost all the present social customs of the Hindus; he does not like them to, squat on dirty roads for public dinners, nor does he approve of four members of a family going to a dinner on an individual invitation. That Hindus should greet one another by means of a salām instead of a Namaskāra, that they should sell their daughters, that those who call themselves Vaiśṇava should worship women, that girls aged ten and twelve should be with child, that women should bathe undressed, that five women should use only one water pot while answering a call of nature, that women should sing improper songs at time of marriage, that they should beat their chests uncovered in public and numerous other old corrupt customs and usages which are of daily observance in these days, are condemned by him outright.

1, His Garbis describing the amours of Krishṇa and the Gopis are popular with the female sex. One of them in which a Gopi invites Krishṇa to pass a night with her is often sung by them.

आवो मारे घेर माणवा, होजी राज!
आवो मारे घेर माणवा.

2. He has written about Krishna and Rāma. There is a fine dialogue between Rāvaṇ and his wife Mandodari in which she persuades Rāvaṇ to forego his animosity towards Rāma. It begins with

ओ राणाजी! रामनी साथे राग न राखीए.

(those who have their ears split–Gorakhi) Order of Sādhus, of Cambay, Rāvo Bhakta,[1] Nimānand, Potho, Durgādas, Nāthāswami of Dākore, Dānvijay, a Jain;[2] Ravidās, Mādhavdās, Jivaṇ, Raghurām,[3] Kuber, Lakhmidās, Revāshankar,[4] Devidās of Vasāvad, Rāmkrishṇa,

1. The famous lines—the only ones known of this obscure poet in which he supplicates the goddess Ambā to save his sinking ship is a fine allegory. It describes realistically the last moments of a ship and its battered condition. The ship is saved. The lines begin with

बेडो बाई ! बुडतो तारो रे, अंबे ! आई पार उतारो रे.

2. He has written a strange poem on eighteen cross relationships (अढार नातरां). A prostitute had twins, a girl and a boy. She did not like the bother of keeping them, so put them in a floating box, and cast them adrift on a river. Two men picked them up; one of them adopted the boy and the other the girl. When the twins grew up, they married. Eventually they came to know that they were brother and sister and repenting of the union, the husband left his wife, and went back to the place where his mother was following her infamous profession. Not knowing she was his mother, he lived with her, and a son was born to him by his own mother. When his sister-wife came to know where he had gone, she saw her mother who was also her mother-in-law, and told her of the incestuous union she had formed. The daughter then enumerated the strange result of the connexion, she was her mother, mother-in-law, brother's wife, co-wife and so on. Ultimately, all three took a vow to leave the world by way of penance for their wickedness.

3. He has a poem called "Narsinh Mehtā ni Hundi" just like Premānand's.

4. His चंद्रावळा (Chandrāvalās), a particular sort of metrical composition, are well known.

Rāje, Bhukhaṇ Bhakta, Thobhaṇdās, Abhivijay, Kumudchandra, Govinddās,[1] Jaśvijay, Vajio,[2] Krishṇadās,[3] Jivaṇdās,[4] Vāghji,[5] and Rājārām,[6] almost exhaust the list.

The sect founded by Sahajānand Swāmi, who came originally from Ayodhyā and assumed that name in V. S. 1857 in Gujarāt and Kāthiāwād, although not very old, has been successful in winning a

1. The quarrel between Krishṇa and his wife Satyabhāmā about the Pārijāt flower fomented by Nārad, is depicted by this poet, beginning with

हां रे नारद स्वर्गभुवन थकी आव्या,
एक पुष्प अनुपम लाव्या रे,
नारद स्वर्गभुवन थकी आव्या,

Its popularity amongst women is unmatched. It gives a most vivid description of what a woman's tongue can do when she sulks with her husband. Before her onslaught poor Krishṇa finds himself nowhere. She lost her temper with him, as Nārad had told her that Krishṇa had presented his co-wife Rukmiṇi, with the heavenly flower in preference to her.

2. He is one of the few poets who have written on the life of Rāma and Sitā. His "Message of Sitā to Rāma" is very touching.

3. His poem is called कर्मविपाक. Kavi Dalpatrām calls it कर्मकथा.

4. His poem is called JnānKakko.

5. His poem is called VāghVāni.

6. Author of RāmaKathā.

The Swāminarayaṇ sect: its wealth, its influence, and its tenets

very large number of adherents in both the provinces.[1] Its three principal seats, at Vadtāl and Ahmedābād in Gujarāt, and at Gadhaḍā in Kāthiāwād, wield enormous power over its adherents, and the special organisation of Sādhus created by the Swāmi, works with almost military precision and discipline in the carrying out of the objects of the Order, both spiritual and temporal. The seats are very rich, they own considerable immoveable properties and are believed to have large hoards of cash. Its working is most economical, and as it has been fortunate in attracting within its fold a large number of the artisan class, who have been taught that service rendered to the Order gratis is a step towards winning righteousness, it has to pay very little for its requirements. Sahajānand inculcated no doubt the Bhakti of Krishṇa or Hari, (Lakshminārāyaṇ Dev), but his methods were severely puritanical. The creed is a sort of protest against the epicurean and luxurious practices that have slipped into the Vallabhāchārya mode of worship.

1. The cult is generally known as the Swāminārāyaṇ Sampradāy, technically it is उद्धवी संप्रदाय. Its inspiration comes from Rāmānand recognised to be a second उद्धव who was a devotee of Krishṇa, and whom Krishṇa taught his doctrine of Prema Lakśaṇā Bhakti, before his departure to heaven. (See 29th Chapter of the 11th Skandh of the Bhāgvat.)

To render those who accepted asceticism or Sādhuship or even service in its temples immune against the temptations of the world and women, he enjoined as a first step abstention from contact with or company of women.[1] No Sādhu or temple servant (Pālā) is allowed to move out of the temple precincts alone. They have to do it always in pairs, even when going for a call of nature, so that one might act as a check on the other. His second injunction was that all varieties of cooked food that might be offered to them must first be mixed up,– bread, rice, pulse, vegetables and sweets–all must be made up into a hotchpotch, and then eaten, so that the sense of taste might be killed. The very simplicity of the cult seems to have acted as a magnet to the poorer classes, for whom it has indeed provided very good spiritual fare. In Kāthiāwād, it is no uncommon sight to see even Mahomedans (Khojās) who have accepted the Kanthi (necklace made of the beads of Tulsi wood) of Sahajānand. The creed of Sahajānand has brought great light and purity into their lives both by example and precept, and the

1. If even unconsciously a man of this sect brushes past or touches a woman he has to fast that day for penance. Men and women enter the godroom by seperate entrances. Women touch the feet of the wife of the Mahārāj, men those of the Mahārāj. Women have their darshan of the Mahārāj from a distance: he has to avoid their shadow even, lest he may have to fast.

credit of it is enhanced when we remember that some of the most turbulent and lawless tribes of Kāthiāwād have been tamed and humanised by the preachings of Sahajānand. The Sādhus of this Order were learned men and scholars, although some of them came from a very humble position in life. The poets of this Order naturally divide themselves into a separate group of which one Premānand Swāmi–sometimes called Premānand Sakhi has already been mentioned.[1] The others are Brahmānand, Muktānand, Niśkulānand, ManjuKeśānand and Devānand.[2]

Poets of this Order

Brahmānand,[3] who was of humble origin, a

1. Ante p. 241. His poems are published as प्रेमानन्द काव्य.

2. Mr. I. I. Maśruwala, B. A., who has written two articles in the "Gujarāti" Weekly (dated 21st and 28th July 1912), divides all the contemporaries of Sahajānand into four groups as under:

(1). Muktānand, Brahmānand, Premānand, Niśkulānand, Manju-Keśānand, Devānand and Âdhārānand.

(2). Achintyānand (Krishṇānand), Dayānand, Jnānānand, Bhumānand, Yagnānand, Sukhānand, Ayodhyāprasād.

(3). Nityānand, Vasudevānand, Śantānand and Achintyānand.

(4). Gopālānand, Muktānand and Nityānand.

Groups (3) and (4) have written Sanskrit works only. Group (2) he dismisses with the remark that they had written only miscellaneous verses and Bhajans.

3. A collected edition of his verses is published by the late Motilāl Tribhovandās Fozdār, B. A. LL. B., called the ब्रह्मानंदकाव्य.

Brahmānand

Bhāt by caste,[1] was born in a small village near Dungarpur, and was known as Lādu Bārot. He passed his childhood at Bhujnagar where he studied पिंगळशास्त्र (prosody) and other poetic works in Vraj Bhāshā. Being a Bārot, he had naturally the gift of being able to write poetry. While travelling in Kāthiāwād, he happened to go to Gadhadā, where he fell in with Sahajānand, and became his disciple at once assuming the name of Brahmānand (V. S. 1860). He was master of at least three languages, in which he wrote under different assumed names. In Chāraṇi (a bārdic dialect peculiar to Bhāts and Bārots) he wrote as Lādu, in Hindi as Shrirang and in Gujarāti as Brahmānand. He charmed the Nawāb of Junāgadh by his verses into allowing him to found a Swāminārayaṇ temple in that Mahomedan city in V. S. 1884. It is called RādhaRamaṇ temple. Mahārājā Sayājirao Gāikwād of Barodā also honoured him. It was he who by order of Sahajānand went to Vadtāl and founded in V. S. 1881 the famous temple of Lakshminārayāṇ there (V. S. 1881). He died at Muli in Kāthiāwād in A. D. 1832, V. S. 1888,

1. Some say he was Chāraṇ. His father Shambhudān was addressed as गढवी. Before he assumed the name of Brahmānand as a consequence of दीक्षा (initiation into the monk's order) he too was addressed as गढवी by Sahajānand Swāmi.

while acting as the head of the local temple (Mahant). About eight thousand miscellaneous Padas besides other works about nine in number, is said to have been his literary output. His forte was preaching (उपदेश), and for driving his preaching home he has used a number of illustrations and instances which show his marvellous grasp and knowledge of social problems, manners and customs.[1] His power over words, the content of his vocabulary is such that the very reading of his verses produces in the reader an indefinable emotion[2] of pleasure and satisfaction. The Pada given in the footnote, besides being on the lips of the people, embodies the principles which he wants to impress on his hearers.[3]

His forte was preaching or उपदेश

1. See especially his Shringār (erotic) lyrics.
2. To realise this read his कृष्णकीर्त्तननां पदो.
3. आ तन रंग पतंग सरीखो, जातां वार न लागेजी;
असंख्य गया धन संपत्ति मेली, तारी नजरो आगेजी.
अंगे तेल फुलेल लगावे, माथे छोगां घालेजी;
जोवन धननुं जोर जणावे, छाती काढी चालेजी.
जेम उंदरडे दारु पीधो, मस्तानो थई डोलेजी,
मगरुबीमां अंग मरोडे, जेम तेम मुखथी बोलेजी.
मनमां जाणे मुज सरीखो, रसीओ नहि कोई रागीजी;
बहारे ताकी रही बिलाडी लेतां वार न लागेजी.
आजकालमां हुं तुं करतां जमडा पकडी जाशेजी;
ब्रह्मानंद कहे चेत अज्ञानी, अंत फजेती थाशेजी.

Muktānand (born A. D. 1761, died A. D. 1824), was originally the chief disciple of Rāmānand. When Sahajānand came to Māngrol in Kāthiāwād, during the course of his travels, he found him holding an important position under Rāmānand. Sahajānand also lived under the same head for about eight or nine months and was ultimately appointed Gûrû in place of Rāmānand. Muktānand then became his disciple and till the day of his death which took place at Gadhadā about two months after that of Sahajānand, the latter entertained the very warmest feelings of affection and admiration for him. Just as Brahmānand stood up for उपदेश (preaching) so Muktānand did for ज्ञान (knowledge).

Muktānand

His *forte* was knowledge or ज्ञान

This body is like the colour of Sappan wood, it will disappear in no time. Before your very eyes innumerable persons have gone away leaving their riches and wealth behind. You who rub sweet smelling oils on your body (use cosmetics), put on aigrettes, make a display of your youth and wealth, and strut about with expanded chests (like athletes) resemble a drunken rat, waving his head to and fro with intoxication. You stretch your limbs in pride and give vent to all sorts of unmeaning utterances, thinking that there is no one on the earth to be compared with you, in seeking pleasures and in gratifying the senses, not knowing that outside is a cat crouching in readiness, to make a meal of you in no time. While you are thinking of "I and Thou," in a day or two the myrmidons of Death will carry you away. Therefore does Brahmānand tell you, O ignorant one, take heed in time or else you will be disgraced in the end.

How he renounced the world

Before he became a Sādhu he was known as Mukunddās, under which name he has written some verses called MukundBāvani. From the early age of thirteen he had conceived a fascination for Vairāgya, and when he saw that his parents would not permit him to renounce the world he pretended to be mad and ran away from Dhrāgandhrā, his native place. After living in company of various Sādhus at Vānkāner and Sardhār, he ultimately came under the influence of Rāmānand at Māngrol, who was so satisfied with him that he gave him a very high post under him.

His ṢatiGitā

Amongst his works which in addition to about nine thousand Padas are numerous, his UddhavGitā has taken a front place. SatiGitā (A. D. 1824) is equally entitled to that honor. In it the poet has described the different kinds of women, married and widowed, and minutely laid down their duties and responsibilities. Married women are divided into corrupt (कुलटा) and chaste (सती) and all those who are unmarried he calls widowed (विधवा). That class includes those who do not burn with their husbands, on account of Jnān, Vairāgya or Bhakti, or on account of their confidence in themselves that they would be able to observe all the duties of a widow, or because they have a son.

It also includes the woman, who being of an ascetic disposition has no inclination for the enjoyments of the world and hence considers Hari only as her lord. The woman who considers man as below her and therefore remains unmarried, one to whom Tapas is dear and who is emancipated from desire, one who from her childhood worships Hari is a widow too.[1] All these women are like Sannyāsis—ascetics or hermits. The whole poem—and it is pretty long—in very minute detail describes the various offices which married and widowed women have to fulfil. Their practices and their observances are given at great length and it is, on the whole, an entertaining, informing and instructive work, its great beauty being its simplicity of language.

Niśkulānand

Niśkulānand (alive in A. D. 1821) was a native of Cutch, and belonged to the Viśvakarmā (architect) caste of Brāhmins, and was known in his pre-Sādhu days as Lālji. He too was a companion of Sahajānand. He has written about twenty-two poems and three thousand Padas. The most salient feature of his poetry is his insistence of Vairāgya (retirement from the

1. It will be noted with what boldness of thought the poet contemplates for a Hindu woman lifelong spinsterhood and dedication to God like the nuns of Christian Europe.

world), and as a specimen of his verses on that subject, some lines are quoted in the footnote from a very popular Pada.[1]

ManjuKeśānand

Ā very large portion of ManjuKeśanānd's writings is still unpublished, lying in manuscript form at Vadatāl. Judging from the very few Padas published, he seems to have entertained a great dislike for false Gûrûs. He says: "You are fools and ignorant men, because you lose a game already won," i. e., having secured the boon of being born a human being, in itself a great thing, instead of improving the occasion, you listen to the sermons of false Sādhus, who see

1. जनुनी जीवो रे गोपीचंदनी, पुत्रने प्रेर्यो वैरागजी;
उपदेश आप्यो एणी पेरे, लाग्यो संसारीडो आगजी.—जननी०

धन धन माता रे ध्रुव तणी, कह्यां कठण वचंनजी;
राज-साज सुख परहरी, वेगे चाल्या वंनजी.—जननी०

भलो रे त्याग भरथरी तणो, तजी सोळसें नारजी,
मंदिर झरूखा मेली करी, आसन कीधलां बहारजी.—जननी०

Ail honour to the mother of Gopichand who preached to him the beauty of Vairāgya. She instructed him in such a way that he felt the world to be like a burning fire. All honor to the mother of Dhruva who spoke harsh words to him so that leaving his kingdom and his happiness he betook himself to a forest... .. .. .. Admirable is the retirement of Bharthari, who left his sixteen hundred queens, who left his palace and his balconies, and took up his residence outside (in the streets).

no sin in corruption and adultery, and are misled and miss the benefit of your position.[1]

Devānand

Devānand is the one poet of this group best known to and most popular with those who do not follow the tenets of Sahajānand. His Padas have been carried from village to village and city to city, by those itinerant beggars who claim to ask for something in charity in return for their having sung to you some holy words or chanted a pious verse.

and his garbis

His Garbis, like those of Dayārām, are set to music and sung by the women of Surat and Barodā in the fine moonlight nights of the first half of Aświn every year. Every native of Gujarāt must have at one time or other heard one or other of the following verses from the lips of some travelling mendicant or strolling minstrel, and been struck by their truth and sincerity as well as by their "spiciness."[2]

1. नर तन पामी, हार्यो जीती बाजि मूढ अज्ञानी;
खोटा संत तणी शीखामण, तें अन्तरमां सत्य मानी॰
कामी क्रोधी गुरु तुने एम कहे छे, तारा देहमांही प्रभु रहे छे,
तुं बहारथी शुं शोधे छे?.........नर तन पामी॰
एम कही परनारी संग करे, करी चेला तेनुं द्रव्य हरे;
तेनुं पाप हैयामां नव धरे.........नर तन पामी॰

2. (a) कर प्रभु संगाथे दृढ प्रीतडी रे, मरी जावुं मेली धनमाल;
अन्तकाळे सगुं नहि कोईनु रे.

Mulji Bhatt

Mulji Bhatt was alive in Samvat year 1881, A. D. 1825. His father's name was Bhāi Bhatt, and he belonged to Ahmedābād. His poem is called **नरसिंह महेताना पितानुं श्राद्ध.**

संस्कारे संबंधी सर्वे मळ्यां रे, ए छे जूठी माया केरी जाळ. अन्तकाळे०
मारूं मारूं करीने धन मेळव्युं रे, तेमां तारूं नथी तलभार. अन्तकाळे०
सुख स्वप्ना जेवुं छे संसारनुं रे, तेने जातां न लागे वार. अन्तकाळे०

Love God only, you have to leave your riches here and die; at the hour of death, there will be no relative (to help you). No one, however dear, will help you. Destiny has brought to you your relatives, but it is all a false net of Māyā (delusion). You accumulated wealth, saying "it is mine, it is mine," but really not even a pie of it belongs to you. Worldly happiness is a dream, it vanishes in no time... .. ..

(b) दुनिआमां डाह्यो डहापेणे दुःख पामे.

One who considers himself wise, suffers in this world by his wisdom.

(c) अज्ञानी ! तारा अन्तरमां देख विचारी,
अंत समे कोई काम न आवे, सगां कुटुंब नरनारी.—अज्ञानी०

जोवन धननुं जोर जणावे, फाटी आंखे फरतो,
काळ कराळ कठण शिर वेरी, दिलमां केम नथो डरतो? रे.—अज्ञानी०

माल खजांना मंदिर मेली, मुआ भूप मदमाता,
श्वान शुकरना देह धरीने, घरघर गोथां खाता रे.—अज्ञानी०

आज अमुलख अवसर आव्यो, हरि भजवानुं टाणुं,
देवानंद कहे देह मनुष्यनो, न मळे खरचे नाणुं रे.—अज्ञानी०

O you fool ! look into your heart and ponder over this. At the last moment, no one, neither your relatives, family nor wife will be of any use to you. You parade before the world your youth and riches and strut about with defiant eyes, but why are you not

Besides Mirānbāi, the flame ot Bhakti has been kept alive by other women,[1] who flourished towards the latter end of the last century. It is true that they cannot be named in the same breath with the Rājput Queen of Mewād, nor looking to the long interval of time that separated them could continuity of inspiration be presumed in the case of these lesser lights. Mirān's performance was bold, unequalled, original. There was nothing in her literary surroundings to create or even nurture that emotional poetic sense which manifested itself so vividly in her work. Intense religious emotionalism from inside made her burst out into sweet song. Not so with these latter day poetesses. The very atmosphere which they breathed was charged with the spirit of their writings. Their male confreres were actually—unlike as in the days in which Mirānbāi lived—engaged in the very work which they merely shared with them. But

Poetesses,

and their creditable work

afraid of death, that terrible and cruel foe that hovers over your head? Even powerful kings had to die leaving their riches and treasures and palaces, and (because of not having worshipped God) be reborn as dogs and pigs, driven from one door to another. To-day you have got an invaluable opportunity and to-day is the time for Hari Bhajan. Devānanad says, that even if one were to spend a fortune, one would not be able to secure human birth.

1. One of them Sursenā, the daughter-in-law of Narsinh Mehtā has been mentioned before, sec pages 46 footnote and 51.

all honor is due to them, as when there was darkness all around, so far as female education was concerned, they by means and efforts, best known to themselves, procured the light of learning sufficient to enlighten their minds and scatter brightness outside. Divālibāi, Rādhābāi, Krishṇābāi, Puribāi and Gavribāi, though judged by an absolute standard have turned out verses of a very mediocre, if not of quite an inferior quality, are still entitled to honourable mention for doing that which, all over the world, very few women have done.

Divālibāi

Divālibāi was the daughter of a Brāhmin living in Dabhoi. From her poems it appears that after the death of her husband she probably returned to her father's house, and he in the great famine of Samvat year 1847 (A. D. 1791), finding himself unable to maintain both of them, left her in the care of an aged Sādhu and disappeared. In her verses she calls this Sādhu, Dādā Gūrû Bhagvān. They lived for sometime at the village of Golvā and then at Barodā. She often went to Ayodhyā on pilgrimage with him. The Sādhu was a Rāma-bhakta or devotee of Rāma, and in his society, in Divālibāi too was generated a love for Rāma. Her pure life and intense devotion procured her many followers, one of whom built for her a temple for the worship of Rāma (RāmaMandir). In spite of her

and her Gûrû

having left the world, individuals suspecting her chastity were not wanting. One such scandal-monger, however, met with such an accidental and instantaneous death that people thought her reputation completely vindicated. In spite of it however she came to the conclusion, that life in a Rāma Temple at Barodā would greatly interfere with her devotional worship of the deity, and she left the city for good for Ayodhyā.

Her pilgrimages

The Sādhu had taught her the whole of the Rāmāyaṇ, and consequently all her poetry is taken up with the depiction of incidents in the life of the Prince of Ayodhyā. His birth, marriage and coronation have furnished her with themes on which she has dilated in about five hundred short poems. Her portraiture of the instincts of a woman is indeed very faithful. When in his old age, Daśarath, the father of Rāma, found that his three queens were in a position to continue his line, he was so pleased that he asked them to desire anything from him and he would give it. And, though so highly situated, what did they demand? It is common knowledge amongst women that, when they are pregnant, they crave for actual rubbish, earth, ashes and such deleterious substances. And what was the surprise of the king, when yielding to that common failing

Her faithful picture of women's characteristics

of their sex, one demanded a handful of earth, another tiles and the third ashes ?[1]

Her verses are pure in thought and simple in language

Looking at her poetry from a higher plane, it must be said that it is pure as she has selected as her hero the pure personality of Rāma, thus presenting a refreshing contrast to other poets who selected the amours of Krishṇa for their theme. Its language is simple, and it inculcates the principle that the worship of Rāma alone is the way to salvation, that Rāma is pleased merely by Bhakti—by recitation of his Bhajans—that those saints who adore him are free from caste prejudices, that they do not hanker after money perquisites or alms, that Rāma loves good conduct, and that in his eyes, rich and poor, married persons and widowers are equal.

he welcomes widowhood

She was so immersed in her devotion to Rāma that she even welcomed her widowhood, as giving her an opportunity to concentrate her mind on one thing only unperturbed by other worldly

1. These instances can be multiplied. For instance, the dialogue between Rāma and Sitā, on the eve of the coronation day, as to what colour she should choose for her Sāri for that auspicious occasion, when she rejects one colour after another, and ultimately selects rose, is such as can strike a woman only.

ties or considerations.[1] Her poetry is an echo of her life simple and pure.

Rādhābāi

Rādhābāi was a Dakshni Brahmin lady of Barodā. She was the pupil of a Sādhu, Avadhūtnāth, and a devotee of RādhāKrishṇa. When in Barodā, she lived in the temple of Rāmanāth, but she often went away on pilgrimages to the north and to Dwārkā. She was alive in Samvat year 1890 (A. D. 1834) and died about twenty three years later.

Her beauty and voice attract people

She is described as of a fair complexion with a beautiful figure, always dressed in white. Having a very good command over several musical instruments, and possessing a sweet voice, she is said to have attracted a large following of Vaiśṇavas singing to the accompaniment of music. Her Garbis and poems are recited by many.

Language of her verses mixed

A defect in her poetry is its language, which is neither unadulterated Gujarāti, Marāthi nor Hindi. It is a curious mixture of the three, and unless one

1. She says:—

मटे भवोभवनां दुःख, रामजी कहीए रे;
आ जनम पाम्यां सुख, रामजी कहीए रे.
थई विधवा पाम्यां भजन, रामजी कहीए रे;
एवी विधवा जुगोजुग, रामजी कहीए रे;
दीवाळी करीए तमारुं भजन, रामजी कहीए रे.

knows all the three languages, it is difficult to follow her. She has narrated several features of the life of Krishṇa and written short biographies of some saints like Vithobā, Karmābāi, Mirānbāi, Jnāneshwar, Tukaram and others.[1]

Being a great traveller, she has given us in a descriptive way, particulars of some places she visited. Her poetry is rough but full of force and directness. She is supposed to have died in A. D. 1857.

Krishṇābāi

Krishṇābāi was a Nāgar Brāhmin by caste and belonged to Vadnagar. Her "Lullabies for Krishṇa" (कृष्णनां हालरडां) and "The Bodice of Sitā" (सीताजीनी कांचळी) are well-known to women of Gujarāt. The story in respect of the Bodice is common knowledge. Marich, a colleague of Rāvaṇ, in the shape of a golden deer attracted Sitā's attention in the forest near Panchavati, and yielding to the weakness of her sex, she thought of making a bodice of the skin of that deer. For that purpose

1. Note the mixed language of the following:

तुकाराम बडा,(a) सारा भक्त;(b)
थई गया बडा(a) सशक्त;(c)
जाकुं(a) जाणे सघळा जक्त(b)
जे(b) इठुबामें हे(a) रक्त; तुकाराम तोळ्या.(c)

(a) **Hindi.** (b) Gujarāti. (c) Marāthi.

she sent Rāma to chase it and when some time after she heard cries of distress she concluded that they must be those of her husband, whom she had sent on the chase, much against his will as he did not want to leave her alone. On going away Rāma had extracted a promise from his brother that he would on no account leave Sitā unguarded. But thinking her husband in distress, she forced Lakśman to go to his succour by means of taunts and thus unwittingly left the field open to Rāvaṇ for her abduction. The dialogues between Sitā and Rāma and Sitā and Lakśman are couched in such homely but forcible language that they present a vivid picture of what an obstinate wife, a yielding husband and a dutiful brother are like.

Her verses well known

Puribāi[1] has celebrated the marriage of Sitā in verse. The poem is named SitāMangal, and is both simple and dignified.

Puribāi

Gavribāi, born in Samvat year 1815 (A. D. 1759) hailed from Dungarpur, and was a Nāgar Brāhmin by caste. She was married at the age of five or six, and lost her husband a very few days after her marriage. She

Gavribāi

1. An ārticle on Puribai in साहित्य-a Gujarāti monthly now extinct—of April 1926 states that she was born in Samvat Year 1737 and died in 1808.

thereupon took God to be her husband, and by dint of perseverance learnt to read and write and studied the Bhāgvat and other philosophical treatises, at the instance of a Rāmānandi Gūrū. She was able to attain Jnān (knowledge) and Vairāgya (asceticism). She was able to practise Samādhi (*i. e.*, concentrate her mind on the Supreme Being and enter into a spiritual trance). Her ascetic mode of life and her ardent devotion to Krishṇa, attracted the attention of the princes of Dungarpur, Jeypur and Benāres. The prince of Dungarpur built a temple of Bālmukund in V. S. 1836, for her, where she used to stay and pray to Krishṇa. In V. S. 1860 she changed her residence from her native place to Benāres, where she died in V. S. 1865 on Chaitra Sud (Rāma) Navami. This is the only Vedānti poetess in Gujarāt, her counterpart being Akho. Unlike his style, hers is such as can be understood even by the uneducated. Her illustrations are homely. For instance she compares the pervading of the Parabrahma in the Universe to the existence of smell in a flower, or to that of light in the sun. She has composed about six hundred fifty two Padas.[1]

honored by princes

1. A very instructive paper was read on "The Poetesses of Gujarāt" by Lady VidyāGavri Ramanbhāi Nilkanth, B. A., before the Third Gujarāti Sāhitya Pariśad at Rājkot in 1909. I have drawn upon the paper in preparing this account.

Dayārām

Of the three monarchs who share the throne of Gujarāti letters, Dayārām has been reserved till the last. Just as the van was gloriously led by Narsinh, the centre by Premanand, so the rear is brought up by Dayārām. In reaching its full stature, in being able to touch the stars, Gujarāti literature is equally indebted to all three and in the precious poetry of Dayārām the waning Lamp of Gujarāti classical verse, making a last splendid effort, produced a final flash before its light vanished.

and his place in Gujarāti literature

His mode of life

Dayārām has furnished an apt subject of controversy by his life, worldly and literary. There have been those who have not looked with approval on his connections with the other sex, which they think were not Platonic relationships, and there have been others who have defended them on the ground of domestic expediency. In his literary life, he has been compared to Hāfiz, the Persian Anacreon, to Byron, the gifted poet of England with loose morals, and to Surdās, the devotional Hindi poet.

A collection of her Gujarāti and Hindi poems is published by Mr. Kamalāshankar Gopālshankar Bhachech of Ahmedābād, recently. It is aptly named गवरीकीर्तनमाला. In this book her life and some remembrances of hers are given. A manuscript copy of her poems is lying with The Gujarāt Vernācular Society, Ahmedabād.

His early life and study

Dayārām,[1] whose original name was Dayāshankar, which he is said to have changed to Dayārām on his ceasing to be a follower of Śaṇkar and passing into the Vallabhāchārya fold, was born in V. S. 1833 at Chān-

1. A number o attempts have been made to ascertain the particulars of the life of this poet, the pioneer being Kavi Narmadāshankar. Of the others, the sketch given by Ichhārām Suryarām Desāi who too tried to obtain first hand information, is fuller and more detailed than that of Rao Bahādur Hargovandās Dwārkādās Kāntāvālā, published in the Prāchin KāvyaMālā. Mr. Tribhovandās Shet's Life of Dayārām is merely a compilation based on the three sketches, with here and there, a statement thrown in by way of elucidation.

Even at present Dayārām does not lack in students of his life and works also. The following four works have added much to our knowledge of his life, learning and works and led to the modification of opinions held as to his mode of life.

(1) Dayārām, by Jagjivan Dayālji Modi (1918), in the Gāikwad JnanManjuśā Series.

(2) 'Bhakta Kavi Shri Dayārāmbhāi nun JivanCharitra,' by Mr. Shankaprasād Chhaganlāl Rāval, published by Nārandās P. Shah Dabhoivālā (1920). It is based on materials supplied by the publisher who had secured them from Joshi Chhotālāl Girjāshankar, the son of the poet's Shishya (pupil) and from notes prepared by the late Mr. Mulchand T. Telivālā B. A., LL. B., a well known scholar of Pushtimārga philosophy and an authority on Dayārām's life and works.

(3) Dayārām's 'Āntar Jivan or Divya Akshar Deh' by the late Mr. Mulchand T. Telivālā and Prof. J. G. Shāh (1931). In this work lectures delivered by various scholars on the occasion of Dayāram's Jayānti are also published.

(4) RasikVallabh by Prof. J. G. Shāh (1933) published by the Gujarāt Vernacular Society, Ahmedābād.

dod, on the banks of the Narmadā in A. D. 1777,[1] and was a Sāthodarā Nāgar Brāhmin. He was left an orphan at the early age of thirteen, his father having predeceased his mother by a year. He had then acquired a rudimentary knowledge of accounts, and reading and writing Gujarāti, and was on the point of being sent to Barodā to supplement it by a study of Sanskrit when his father died.[2] Thenceforth he lived with an aunt of his till he was about 19 (or 20) years old. He left Chāndod for Dabhoi on her death and lived there for the most part of his life.

He was never married

The tradition is that he was betrothed when he was about eight years old, and that the girl whose name was Gangā died within two years of the betrothal. No one there-

1. It has now been conclusively established by close students of Dayārām's works that he was born in V. S. 1833 (A. D. 1777), and not ten years earlier (V. S. 1823) as was stated previously. Diwān Bahādur Keshavlāl H. Dhruva gives certain proofs from Dayārām's own works which are convincing on the point. Vide his lecture दयाराम विषे कंईक delivered in 1928 under the auspices of the Forbes Gujarāti Sabhā at Bombay.

2. Although he had no opportunity for direct study of the Puraṇās, Sanskrit dramas, poetry, and Vedānt he must have acquired knowledge of these subjects, either through some Gûrú or through listening to Kirtans (hymns), recited in Mandir-kathās (temple preachings and recitals). He must have picked up Vraj Bhāśā literature during his travels in North India. He knew Marāthi and Punjābi also. One thing is certain, viz., that he acquired all the varied knowledge he displays in his poems late in life.

after was found willing to entrust his daughter to him, his poverty being one of the causes. He too was unwilling to marry, because he considered himself as a devoted wife of Krishṇa. He died an old bachelor.

As a youth, from the age of fourteen and upwards, he seems to have imitated the juvenile escapades attributed to his favourite ideal, Krishṇa. The women of Chāndod (a place of pilgrimage on the Narmadā) are known all over Gujarāt for possessing a number of attractions special to their sex. They are fair, well-built (they know how to swim), beautiful, full of grace, boldness and charms. It is alleged by some critics of his life that Dayarām's sole delight was to make mischief with them, and with that view he gathered round him a band of likeminded mischievous boys, who made it their business to throw pebbles at or use other devices to tease those women who frequented the ghāts on the banks of the Narmadā to fetch water.[1] The modest among them would ignore the pranks played by the boys, but at times the latter met with those who were a match for them. One

His juvenile escapades

1. This pleasant occupation of paying uncalled for attention to women is not confined to Chāndod alone. Almost all ghāts similarly situated, and the neighbourhood of wells, are infested with bands of youths, gaily inclined, who take delight in whiling away their leisure moments in the manner of Dayārām.

day, a woman of the goldsmith caste, had the chatty on her head broken by Dayārām. Losing her temper, she caught him by his 'dhotar' and demanded from him the price of her pot. Dayārām was not possessed of a single pie, and seeing his own mistake, begged hard to be released. But the woman would not budge an inch. Some of his own castemen thereupon, urged him to commit further violence, saying should a Nāgar yield to a goldsmith? This taunt put some spirit into the boy and in the excitement of the moment, he slapped his assailant. Some one carried the news to her husband, who came running to the spot, hammer in hand. But in the meanwhile, Dayārām had managed to get his loin-cloth freed from her grasp and run away. While everybody thought that he had committed suicide by drowning in the river, he had hidden himself in Karnāli, a village within a stone's throw of Chāndod. There he fell in with a Sādhu, Keśavānand, whom he entreated to accept him as his disciple. The Sādhu declined, on account of his extreme youthful age. The boy misconstrued his motives, and sang them in a Lāvṇi (song), wherein he maintained that Sādhus eschewed young men as their disciples, as they were afraid that such youths would alienate from them–the Sādhus–the affections of young women, whose company they were fond of enjoying in secret. When it was recited before Keśavānand, he merely laughed and said that the boy was an ignoramus. He did not know the virtue and strength of Sādhus and that he would be made to see it some day. Two months later, Dayārām happened to swim over to Karnāli— when Keśavanand caught him, and at night, through the instrumentality of his spiritual powers made him see Krishṇa, in body. This miracle converted him into a devotee of Krishṇa.[1]

and their consequence

The spirit of mischief did not leave him even when he grew older. It is usual for pilgrims to proceed to Chāndod to bathe in the sacred river at the time of an eclipse. The ladies of H. H. The Gāikwād Fatehsinhrao's family had once come down to Chāndod for such a purpose. Guards were placed on the road to keep off males, while the Zenānā went for their bath. Dayārām took it into his head to disobey the order, and continued to sit on the ghāt, in company of a small boy, who knew very well how to play on the Sitār and who possessed a sweet, musical voice. Dayārām took up his own guitar or Tambura, and played on it. The ladies were so charmed with the singing and playing that they came forward and held out some gold coins, thinking that they must

His mischievous spirit

1. He is said to have aknowlodged Keśavānand as his Gûrû from this time, and composed a Pada, गुरु म्होटा, गुरु म्होटा, in respect of it.

be some beggar Brahmins. Dayaram declined to take them, saying he would not accept anything till he was sure that the donor was a person from whom he could with self-respect accept a Dakshinā (perquisite). The Rāni thereupon removed her veil and offered him gold mohurs. Dayārām generously said "give them to the boy." On the news reaching Barodā, an invitation was sent to him from the Court to go there. He complied with it, but owing to some political disturbance he was not given a warm reception, and he determined thereafter never to trust princes or their servants.

His handsome appearance

The poet was blessed by nature with attractive features. Fair, tall, slim and well-built, with a voice beautifully adapted for singing, he had added to these attractions several others which were in every way calculated to make havoc in the ranks of the fair sex.[1]

1. He is thus described by Kavi Narmadāshankar: Dayārām was thin and taller (than myself). His face was not round, but like mine, long. The nose was straight and pointed-acquiline at the end. His eyes were grey, but very restless, and forehead though receding from above the temples still projected forward a little, the moustaches were full and curved at the ends. He grew no whiskers. The colour of his skin was fairer than wheat, still it was so transparent that the red colour of the juice of pan leaves could be seen through his throat when he chewed them. The Sāthodarā Nāgars have the reputation of being dandies, (रंगीला):

and refined taste in dress

In dress his refined taste bordered almost on dandyism. He got his turban dyed at Nadiād, and paid as much as five rupees for each dyeing, the ordinary rate being from four to eight annas!

His silk bordered dhotars cost him from ten to twelve Rupees each, while the fine transparent malmal (Dacca Mull) cloth of which his coats were made was supplemented by emboroidery work of thread at the sleeves and neck. His tailor's bill was very high. He paid as much as three Rupees for the making of an angarkhā-coat and if the fit was not proper, it was not unusual for him to visit his wrath on the tailor with something more effective than words. In arranging the front folds of his dhoti he

साठोदरा केम जाणीए? बांकी पाघडीए,
भाणां वेची भोजन करे, जमे दाथडीए. (A proverb)

How to identify a Sāthodarā? by turban worn awry. He sells his (metal) pots, and dines off earthen plates.

So much refinement and taste could not fail to make their mark on the other sex, and his biographers have given at least four to five instances of high born ladies, who in their old age were not ashamed to own their past intimacy with him.

Some of his own castemen excused these liaisons on the ground of Dayārām being a companion of Krishṇa (Krishṇa had eight companions called अष्टसखा, Dayārām was said to be the ninth), whom he had sent specially into the world to demonstrate what RāsaLilā was.

was so finical that he used to spend half an hour over the operation ! His Dupatta (scarf or shoulder cloth) and embroidered shoes were the acme of daintiness.

attract women towards him

Till forty, his tastes and his looseness of morals had not deserted him, but thereafter he settled down to a life of sobriety,[1] selecting the company of one of his most faithful admirers, a goldsmith's child-widow Ratanbāi, who kept house for him, nursed him through his worst illness–and he was often ailing–and who survived him several years. This episode in the poet's career, though originating in an improper connection, is still one of the most redeeming features in their joint lives. From several autobiographical fragments, preserved by his followers, it appears that she was left a widow and an orphan at the age of nine, and was much oppressed by her relatives-at-law He picked her up on the banks of the Narmadā, and for thirty years they lived together through good report and evil. He

Relations between Ratanbāi and Dayārām

1. The cause of his return to sobriety is said to lie in the following incident. As was usual with him while at Barodā, he once put up in the house of an admirer of his. His wife was devotedly waiting on him but Dayārām took the services in another light and wanted to force her into intimacy. She cried out, and Dayārām had at once to take to the stairs and run away. The experience proved to be a great eye-opener.

said that in a former birth, she had been his wife and he had rejected her as she used to treat him badly! She was expiating for it by her widowhood in this birth. Except that he was unable to eat the food she cooked,[1] owing to the difference in their castes, she was for all practical purposes the mistress of his household. Owing to his sharp temper and also owing to her toleration of the excitability of his nature due to prolonged and complicated illness[2] Ratanbāi was often subjected to physical pain,[3] but she quietly bore it all. On one occasion, however, she could not bear his abuse and assaults and had to leave his roof. Dayārām's position then became intensely pathetic, and through intervention of a friend she was induced to

Sharp temper

1. Dayārām was an excellent cook himself, and he knew how to prepare several toothsome dishes. He used to cook for himself and her. Nāgars are proverbially experts in wielding their pens (कलम), ladles (कड़छी) and बरछी (a short javelin). As a Vallabhāite Marjādi Vaiṣṇava it was considered a devout action to cook and present dainty dishes to his beloved Krishṇa.

2. A catalogue of Dayārām's ailments would almost make a medical hand-book.

3. Once Dayārām was being led by her: his eyesight had become feeble and he used to move about with his hand on her shoulder. He somehow or other slipped, and losing temper he soundly cuffed her ears, but she, good woman that she was, unmindful of his assault busied herself in bandaging his sprained ankle and soothing him.

come back, specially as the poet had taken the bereavement so much to heart, that she was told that unless she agreed to come back he would die. His last and fatal illness brought out her best qualities as a nurse. During the last seven or eight years of his life his eye-sight got worse and worse, and for the last two or three years before his death he was blind.

Ratanbâi's last days, clouded and sad

He himself in describing her, has bestowed on her the epithet "sharer in my weal and woe." Thrice did he take her with him on pilgrimage, and even there she served him so well that he felt himself unable to express his full obligation to her. His last words of advice to his followers were that they should look after her when he was no more, but unfortunately she was not spared annoyance at the hands of the poet's relatives after his death. Actually, the poet was a poor man, yet he had managed to leave her a small sum, of which she was deprived by a cousin of his. She died in distress and penury about fourteen years after him.[1]

1. After the publication of the First Edition (1914) of this book the allegation that the relations between Dayârâm and Ratanbâi were immoral has been subjected to some scrutiny and it has been pronounced to be baseless on the following grounds: (1) That the poet was past his prime i. e., past fifty when Ratanbâi first elected to serve him. (2) That she herself was forty-five then. (3) That she was a Marajâdi Vaiśṇav like the Kavi (footnote p. 228) and hence her

Dayārām's explanation of his irregular life

It is not as if Dayārām was unaware of the scandal created by his mode of life. He was directly asked by some as to what he meant by retiring with young women alone, and allowing them to almost worship him. He said he knew scandal was being talked about him, but so it was about Krishṇa at Mathurā. The women did come to him and in spite of his protests, placed flowers before him, shampooed his feet, and altogether treated him as if he was a god. But his feelings towards them were pure.[1]

suitability to help him. (4) Further that Dayārām was so poor that he could not afford to give away any very large sums (as alleged) to her during his life time. He could provide for her a legacy of Rs. 25/- only at his death as shown by his last will and testament. It may be pointed out that the source, from which Ratanbāi is stated to have been forty-five years of age then, has not been disclosed, nor has any proof been forthcoming that the Gúrúcharitra Vārtās on the authority of which statements have been made in Vol. V of the Brihat Kāvya Dohan and which have been followed here, are forgeries. Only an emphatic statement is made there that it was not possible to agree with what the late Mr. Ichhārām S. Desāi had said in Vol. V of the Brihat KāvyaDohan (pp. 198-202), and Dayārām Jivan Charitra by Shankarprasād Rāval pp. 39-40, also Dayārām (p. 30) by J. D. Modi. At best the matter may be left in doubt. He may have led as good or as bad a moral life as any ordinary member of society. It is not necessary to look very closely into it, as it would not affect his title as the most popular poet of Gujarāt.

1. See pp. 20-21 of Vol. V. Brihat KāvyaDohan. गुरुचरित्रनी वार्ता चोथी.

His sole object was to lift them out of their state of worldly sins and make them one with Krishṇa. He composed a poem admitting his adultery, but it was an audultery with Krishṇa: "the beloved of Krishṇa was this slave girl" (his hummble self).[1]

His advice to shun Women

He was fully aware of the evils arising out of an inordinate love for feminine society, and he has in an admonitory poem warned persons if they desired happiness, to give women a wide berth.[2] Besides, he has taken to task downright one of the Mahārājās of his time because of his alleged misconduct.[3]

Dayārām, a great traveller

Between the age of twenty and forty, Dayārām was almost always on the move. He had thrice visited the four great centres of Hindu sanctity, Badrikāśram, Jagannāth Pûri, Rāmeśwar and Dwārkā. Seven times did he visit the sacred shrine at Nāthadwār and four times drink the waters of the Jamnā. He also had performed that most difficult but meritori-

1. दयानी प्यारी कृष्णजी कहावे, कृष्णनी प्यारी आ दासी;
रसुं, रमाडुं, प्रेमे पोढुं, जारी कृष्णसुं, नही तो उदासी;
ए व्यभिचार नित करीए रे, एथी भवसागर तरीए रे.

2. जे कोई जन कल्याण चाहो, ते स्त्रीनी संगत तजजो रे.

3. See pp. 300 and 301 post.

ous feat of a Hindu pilgrim, taking the waters of the Ganges on his shoulders from the river at Benāres, and bathing with them the idol of Śiva at Rāmeśwar. To Dākore, he travelled often from Dabhoi and his journeys were always undertaken on foot. At Dākore, a celebrated character, Ichhārām Bhatt, of Petlād heard his songs on the banks of the Gomti, and being very pleased with them advised him to add to his pious devotion by going on a pilgrimage, and he did so accordingly. On his return, Dayārām saw him again, and was given a blessing, and Ichhārām foretold that he would turn out to be a famous poet. In fact, he said Dayārām was no other than an incarnation of Narsinh Mehtā. His faith in Vaiśṇavism was sincere and deep, and on the first evening of his arrival at Śri Nāthadwār, he sang of and described the details of dress and ornaments on the body of Krishṇa, as seen by him in a vision, in such a charming style, that the head of the shrine, the Mahārāj— sent for him and presented him with a costly piece of cloth.[1] For three months did he continue to sing and play before the idol, and his fellow pilgrims

1. The Mahārāj kept him there specially for three months, under orders of the god, as he said. One day, the god was so pleased with him that he showed him in a vision the actual RāsaLilā—a performance witnessed by Narsinh Mehtā too. Dayārām was greatly pleased at this mark of special favour and sang it so graphically that the Mahārāj bestowed on him that precious piece of cloth.

were so charmed by his devotional music that they used to shower presents on him, all of which he gave away to the shrine.

Vicissitudes of travel

Dayārām has left some descriptions of the suffering he underwent during the course of these peregrinations, as well as the miracles he witnessed. After worshipping the Mahākāleśwar at Ujjain, his party was proceeding towards Nāsik. For five days, they met with nothing untoward, but on the sixth day, at a distance of about twenty kos from Āsirgarh, while taking their midday meal, they were visited by what appeared to be a band of pilgrims. The two parties, then, travelled together for five or six miles, till they came to a lonely spot, where the so called pilgrims fell upon Dayārām's friends and began to rob and murder them. Three were killed and the rest taken as prisoners to Hyderābād. After committing some excesses there they returned to Āsirgarh. There they called upon the poet to pay Rs. 500 as the price of his release. He said he was an orphan, had no family, and no relatives who could honor his hundi. He knew only his god Krishṇa, who might honor his letter as he had done that of Narsinh Mehtā. No one believed him and for five months, his trials continued. He dreamt one night that Krishṇa was thus punishing him for the desire he had once expressed at Vrindāvan, to leave the scene of his (Krishṇa's) revels and return home. During this dreamy state, he says he solicited his god by means of a poem[1] and he awoke. He thereafter saw the head of this band of robbers, and faithfully told him his life history and began to sing devotional songs. The robber chief was charmed, and promised to let him go in three days. Every night the chief listened to his songs, and true to his word, either through the influence of his god, or the charm of his Bhajans he allowed him to depart, giving him money to defray his travelling expenses. At Bālāji in the Madrās Presidency, the Mahant of the temple was in the habit of extorting money from pilgrims, and would not allow them to leave till they had satisfied his demands. Dayārām was also set upon, and being unable to pay absconded at night. The Mahant sent men in pursuit, who brought him back. He was not allowed to go till four days after during which time, on inquiry, the Mahant was fully satisfied that Dayārām had no money. He thence went Rameswar where he entered into a controversy with a Sādhu, who was a follower of Śiva, as to whether Śiva or Krishṇa was the greater. The Śadhu called Krishṇa an adulterer and Dayārām called Śiva a wretch of an ascetic (जोगटो).

1. श्रीजी! शरण पड्याने शीद संतापो?

O Shriji! why do you annoy one who seeks refuge at your feet, that is, him who has surrendered his all to you?

The Sādhu losing temper, assaulted Dayārām with his lāthi (stick). But a miracle happened, the lāthi was suspended in midair, and the Śadhu became dumb-founded. Dayārām says that every one present said that it was Krishṇa who was holding it aloft. His oppenent, thereafter, gave up his contention, and acknowledged that Hari (Krishṇa) and Hara (Śiva) were but one and the same. It took him nearly seven years to finish the pilgrimage.

His dislike of Vaiśṇava Mahārājās

Although he was a keen Vaiśṇava, he had a great horror of bowing his head befor the Mahārājās[1] in abject subjection, like the rest of their followers. He had taken a vow of Pāki Marjād,[2] but that did not make him pay any very exaggerated respect to those who were at the head of the creed. Twice had such Mahārājas had to eat humble pie in trying to force Dayārām to bow to their orders. Once his own Mahārāj, Purushottamji, from Bundī Kotā had to come on a visit to Dabhoi and while there misled by his followers he forbad Dayārām

1. The high priests of the Vallabhāchārya sect are so called.

2. One who takes this vow, which is an element in the observance of the extremest form of Vaiśṇavism, can eat food cooked by himself alone. He has to eschew the touch of many things and of all persons, excepting on the penalty of a bath after such contact.

the temple.[1] This is a very severe penalty on a Vaiśṇava. Dayārām thereupon composed a poem, satirizing the Mahārāj. It was read by some of those who had incited him to place the ban. They informed him of it. The Mahārāj was greatly struck by his boldness, and went to call on him at his house, but Dayārām shut the doors in his face, and returned to him the necklace of Tulsi beads, the emblem of his being a Vaiśṇava. The Mahārāj saw his mistake and admitted it, and returned him the necklace. On another occassion when another Mahārāj came to Dabhoi, all the Vaiśṇavās went to him to pay their respects (in coin), but not so Dayārām. He was specially sent for, but he sent word that he

and their open insults

would come only on condition that his seat should not be lower than the Mahārājā's, as he was in no way inferior to him. The Mahārāj took great offence at this, but still complied with his demand. Dayārām, before starting, had sent a man of his to inquire whether his gādi (seat) was placed just like the Mahārājā's and was told that it was so. On his arrival, when he was going to sit on the gādi, a follower of the Mahārāj at once took it away and Dayārām's wrath knew no bounds. He abused the Mahārāj to his face, took off the necklace there and then and tore it in two, and threw the pieces

1. Such a kind of punishment for Vaiśṇavas even now exists.

into the hands of the very man who had gone to call him on behalf of the Mahārāj, saying contemptously, "here is your necklace worth two farthings." The Mahārāj felt some remorse at his own action, and called on Dayārām at his house, but he met with the same fate as his predecessor and had to return without seeing him. Dayārām fully believed, and he said as much, that it is not by means of this outward emblem of Vaiśṇavism—putting on a necklace of Tulsi beads—that one can be called a Vaiśṇava. His views as regards the duties of these spiritual leaders were very correct, and much in advance of his times. He knew that they were really responsible for leading their followers into wrong paths. He narrated an incident, once witnessed by him, in connection with a debauched Mahārāj of Kākroli. This man was in the habit of considering all his female followers as legitimate instruments for gratifying his lust, and his behaviour when in their midst was most improper and openly indecent. Dayārām could not brook to see him touching them lustfully, and he said that the eyes which should really rest on Thākurjee were resting on undesirable places, but such persons always met with their deserts at last. This Mahārāj, under the impression that he was the husband of all the women in the world once behaved improperly with the wife of a cadet of the Mahārājā of

and exposure of their immoral conduct

Udaipur, and the court at Udaipur coming to know of it at once despached a hundred horsemen to capture the delinquent, who on hearing the news hastened to Kākroli from Girirāj, where he had been philandering with his female followers. Dayārām conceived great hatred for them, he says, from the day he witnessed this misonduct.

All the same his faith was deep-seated

His dislike for such leaders of the creed is not to be taken as an index of the faith he had in the creed itself. His works bear an eloquent testimony to his deep-seated belief in the tenets formulated by Vallabhāchārya.

He lived in different places

He passed his time mostly at Dabhoi, Barodā and Dākore. He visited Surat also, but his stay in Broach in his very young days, is doubted by some of his biographers.

Dayārām's poverty, resources, and spendthriftness

Dayārām was poor all his life. His chief source of income was the perquisites reverently given to him by his admiring disciples. As he had an admirable and musical voice, many were the gatherings to which he was invited. He earned about Rs. 200 per year in this manner, but he was so improvident that he spent all he got. He was both an epicure and a dandy, and besides, his numerous pilgrimages must have taxed his resources to their utmost. When an Indian dies, a dinner is given to his caste men by his heirs. Dayārām thought that he would forestall his demise, and give the customary dinner.[1] His numerous disciples at Dabhoi, Chāndod, Broach, Umreth, Nadiād and other places came to know of it, and sent him money to enable him to defray the expenses. The presents amounted to Rs. 2,000 and he spent nearly Rs. 4,000 ! Such was his happy-go-lucky nature. The only assets left by him after his death were his books. Ratanbāi had to sacrifice a large portion of her scanty resources, to meet the charges of his funeral, and defray other expenses.[2] Dayārām would have liked to have royal patronage, but was too proud to bend or bow to the noble or the wealthy to secure it. He was proud to say that his head bowed only to Krishṇa. He had left all his cares to Krishṇa.[3]

1. Generally it is customary for the heirs of a deceased person to give a grand dinner after his death. But some people, mostly wealthy or without any heir, prefer to give such a feast during their life even (called जीवतक्रिया). It is considered a meritorious act.

2. His last will and testament made in S. Y. 1898, about eleven years before he died, seems to show as if he possessed about Rs. 600 in cash. See a copy of it at pp. 316-17 of Dayārām Jivan Charitra by S. C. Rāval.

3. चित्त ! तुं शिदने चिन्ता करे? कृष्णने करवुं होय ते करे.

A large following of admirers had gathered itself round the poet, from every conceivable part of Gujarāt, and from every caste, ranging from the proud and cultured Nāgar Brāhmin to the humble or unlettered Soni (goldsmith).[1] Two of his most devoted disciples Amratrām Pandyā and Dāyābhāi, a Sāthodarā Nāgar, although they held high posts, renounced the world, to sit at his feet. Raṇchhod was his last disciple. The discipleship began when Dayārām was sixty and Raṇchhod only fifteen. He went to Dayārām, to sing some of his songs. The poet was so pleased with his voice and his mode of singing, that he instantly gave him a place amongst the ranks of his followers, and afterwards placed him at their head. When the boy was threatened by his creditors, after the death of his father, Dayārām undertook to satisfy them and he did so. His advice both to him and Girjāshankar was, that they should earn their livelihood by singing his songs. Dayārām possessed nothing more precious than his books and his Tamburā. The former he bequeathed to Raṇchhod, and the latter to Vasantrām, on his death-bed,

Dayārām's many disciples

1. The names of the most noted amongst them are: Joshi Raṇchhod, an Audich Brāhmin, Manordās, a Lād Baniā of Broach, Girjāshankar Joshi and Lakshmirām Desāi, Brāhmins, Trikamdās, a Baniā, Ghelābhāi Amin, a Pātidār, Vasantrām, Lallubhāi, Kāyasthas, Mohanbhāi, a Pātidār, Pritamlāl, a Zārolā Baniā, and Nāraṇ, a Soni.

and Vasantrām worshipped it as if it was a god. The minute description given by his friend Chimanlāl as gathered from the lips of those who watched and nursed him in his last days, brings into prominent relief, the touching part played by Raṇchhod, Vasantrām, Ghelābhāi and Ratanbāi. The two former were unremitting in their efforts to soothe his last moments by singing and music, and Ghelābhāi and Ratanbāi by washing and cleaning him. The services they rendered were such as even Dayārām's nearest relatives would not have performed. At Barodā, Dabhoi, Dākore, wherever he chanced to be, his followers always recieved him with open arms. But in spite of all this devotion and admiration, Dayārām kept his head cool. He was asked by Raṇchhod permission to worship his Pādukā[1] (wooden sandals) after him, which would have been tantamount to founding a new creed. He stoutly resisted the demand, saying "Who am I? You should never talk of it again."

and their exemplary devotion to him

Haribhat of Barodā, who already has been mentioned, was for a time, a rival of Dayārām. He used to compose songs and poems on the same lines as Dayārām's, and this made the latter very angry. Moreover, the followers of each began to laud their own favourite

Dayārām's rival

1. This is a kind of deification of the owner of the sandals.

to the skies and this gave greater publicity to Haribhat's works. Dayārām was resolved to put him down, and in a day composed one hundred poems, an output which completely beat Haribhat, and when

and his discomfiture

one of Dayārām's songs[1] was thereafter sung, in the wellknown house of the leading citizen of Barodā, Haribhakti, the audience with one voice acclaimed it and said that there could be no comparison between Haribhat and Dayārām.

Dayārām's mastery over music

Dayārām's great mastery over the science of music and singing was put to an unusual test once. He was pressed to be present at a party, where his two disciples Raṇchhod and Girjāshankar were performing to the accompaniment of the music of Narghān[2] and Sārangi recitations of some of his own Padas at Barodā. During the course of the entertainment, Girjāshankar happened to play a wrong time on the Narghān, and a Bāvā (ascetic) who was sitting amongst the audience twitted him on it, putting Girjāshankar to shame. Dayārām could not bear it, and so he said, every one was liable to err, and

1. मानीती मोहन तणी, ओ वांसलडी! रे.

2. These are two drumlike instruments, played by the palm and fingers of the hand.

so was Girjāshankar, and after all, that mistake was not of any very great moment. The Bāvā demurred and said that he who had acquired mastery over his craft should never err. Dayārām, impetuous as he was, there and then challenged him to demonstrate his unfailing mastery. The latter accepted the challenge, and seizing hold of the Narghān began to play to the accompaniment of Dayārām's singing. Dayārām by means of various tricks, tried to make him deviate him from the correct time, but the Bāvā was a thorough master of his art, and baffled all his attempts to make him play the wrong time. The contest lasted long, and became very lively, and a large concourse of men was attracted to witness this musical duel between two masters. The night was passing into dawn, but the combatants were still evenly matched. Dayārām was already losing heart, but at last he made a final grand effort, and sang a song full of such intricate ताल (measures of time), that the Bāvā was thrown off his guard and for once played wrongly. The crowd cheered and clapped but Dayārām rose to the occasion, and congratulated him, saying he had never seen such a perfect player before, and as a token of his regard for his knowledge and ability, as impulsively as he had thrown out the challenge, took his gold necklace from off his neck and made a present of it to the Bāvā.

Put to test

His triumph

Dayārām's chronic ill-health

For nearly a dozen years prior to his death, Dayārām was a martyr to chronic illness. In his youth, extensive travel is supposed to have done his constitution some good. His ordinary food consisted of double the usual quantity, but latterly, at times he used to subsist upon half a pound of milk only. The multiplicity of his diseases has already been noticed, but so strong was his will that in spite of all if he once settled down for an entertainment with his Tamburā or to worship, for five or six hours at a stretch, he would become entirely forgetful of his malady, and concentrate his attention on the subject in hand. At the end of it, a reaction would set in, weakness of the kidneys and laxity of the bowels would supervene and out of sheer exhaustion, he would lie down and rest. The entreaties and persuasions of his friends and followers to place himself under medical treatment, always proved fruitless. His reply to them was the stock reply of all Hindus: "The body has to bear pain and it does its duty in doing so. I am (my soul is) unaffected by it."

Dayārām's last illness

A somewhat detailed diary of the last fifteen days of his fatal illness has been published in his biographies. The pain he suffered was immense, and even Ratanbāi's nursing was unequal to alleviating it. As long as his strength lasted he struggled to observe the usual routine of the worship of his household gods, but he had ultimately to give in and be content with listening to hymns recited by Raṇchhod and others. He suffered from hernia, fistula and hydrocele, but though racked with pain he consoled himself by composing poetry. Every day made him weaker, and when he saw that his end was near he gave minute instructions (1) as to the way in which his dead body was to be laid on ground which was to be made holy by being covered with the sands and the waters brought by him from the Jamnā, mixed with cowdung procured from the stables of Śri Nāthadwār, and sprinkled with the waters of all the holy places preserved by him specially for this occasion, and spread over with pieces of Tulsi wood and its leaves, (2) as to the person who was to light the funeral pyre. He gave strict injunctions that no one was to weep after him, but that his bier was to be carried to the burning ground amid great rejoicings. By special permission, obtained from him during his lifetime, his body was covered over with a shawl, instead of the ordinary red funeral cloth. The use of such costly stuff is in vogue only in case of rich and

very painful

Minute instructions about his funeral

distinguished people, and Dayaram disliked the show, but he had to yield to the earnest entreaties of Ghelābhāi, who insisted on his being allowed to show this last mark of respect to his Gûrû. His very last moments were happy and he passed away while unconscious. Nearly two hundred men followed his remains to the burning ground. He died at 9 A. M., on the 9th of February, 1852 A. D.

Routine of daily life

Dayārām was an early riser. He would leave his bed at about five in the morning and take an early bath, after which he would be engaged in the worship of the likeness of Śriji and the idol of Bālamukund, till about ten. It is strange that in spite of weak kidneys and bowels, the four hours that he spent thus were free from pain. He was very particular about not being interrupted at the time of worship. If any one disturbed him, so much the worse for the intruder: sometimes he got a thrashing. At about 11 A. M. he would start cooking, the materials for which would be kept ready by Ratanbāi. Thereafter both of them would sit down to take their meal together.[1] In the afternoon he would sit down alone to work, viz., composing poetry and no one was allowed to trespass on his retirement. In the evening, the men of Dabhoi would gather round him, and he would

1. He used to take only one meal during the day.

then give full reins to his devotion, and in their company, dance, clap, jump and sing. At times, he was so overpowered by his emotions that tears would actually flow from his eyes.

Dayārām's nature, irascible

By nature, he was irascible. There was a vein of vanity running in him in his early days, which later gave way to sobriety. Independent in spirit, money had no attractions for him, and he never truckled to any one or bent knee or head to any individual, to get money, patronage or favours. Generous to the verge of improvidence, he left nothing behind him but his books, and he was conscious of the fact that they were worth millions.[1] In spite

1. He had made this remark to Raṇchhod, whom he had asked to sing the songs composed by him, as they would appear to be worth millions to those who understood them. But he was not so sure that the literature produced by him would survive long. During the last illness, he was once found staring out of the window at some object, for a very long time. Vasantrām and Ratanbāi were near him, and the former asked him twice or thrice what was there on the road to attract his gaze. Dayārām pointed out a broken brick, and said that he had been seeing it there for the last six months, and that every day it was losing in size, as particle after particle was falling away from it. He was afraid that his works also would meet with the same fate. Vasantrām assured him that it would not be so, and that he would preserve them. Dayārām rejoined, "How long will you live? No one can say what will happen after you are no more." Looking to the extreme popularity he enjoys even now it cannot be said that his fears have been realised.

of his short temper, he was able to make many friends, and the devotedness of Ratanbāi whom he abused, beat, assaulted and drove away, furnishes a proof of the fact, that there must have been some traits in his character, some sterling virtues, which made him lovable in spite of his bad temper.

His likeness

The fact that he could accompany himself on the Tamburā and other (Indian) musical instruments and sing, added to the attractions with which he was endowed by nature must indeed have made his personality remarkable. There is one likeness of him said to have been left with Ratanbāi, which she refused to part with, as she said that she daily worshipped it before taking her meals. The other likeness, from which copies are procurable is said to be a copy of the original. It was in possession of Raṇchhod, his last and favourite disciple.

His works

His works are numerous, and the unprecedented popularity that he enjoys to-day is really based on a very minor portion of those works. His garbis which describe the revels of Krishṇa with the "sylvan girls"-Gopis-of Gokul Vrindāvan, are, after all, a drop in the ocean of his whole output, and he has to be judged on the point of study, scholarship, powers of exposition, and his faith, by other poems, and not solely by these erotic and emotional ditties. In Gujarāti, his works come to forty-eight, in Vraj[1] to forty-one, besides seven thousand miscellaneous Padas in Gujarāti, twelve thousand in Vraj, two hundrad in Marāthi and forty in Punjābi, fifteen in Sanskrit and seventy-five in Urdu. Very few of these are obtainable.

and *impromptu* songs

Some put down the total number of his works at one hundred and thirty-five, and some at two hundred and eight and the number of miscellaneous verses at one lac and a quarter. Many of these have not been committed to writing, as he was in the habit of composing and reciting *impromptu*, and if no one was near to write them down, they were lost. The women of Dabhoi and Chāndod even now sing some songs of his composing which have never yet been collected.[2]

1. Many Gujarāti poets from the earliest times, such as Narsinhà Mehtā, Bhālaṇ and others, have written in Vraj (Hindi). The late Mr. Dayābhai Derāsari's book called गुजरातीओए हिन्दी साहित्यमां आपेलो फाळो, published by the Gujarāt Vernācular Society, Ahmedābād is a useful guide in that respect.

2. The following are his Gujarāti works:

१ गीतामाहात्म्य.	८ प्रश्नोत्तरमालिका.
२ रसिकवल्लभ.	९ श्रीकृष्णनाममाहात्म्यमंजरी.
३ अजामिलाख्यान.	१० श्रीकृष्णनाममाहात्म्यमाधुरी.
४ वक्त्रासुराख्यान.	११ श्रीकृष्णस्तवनचन्द्रिका.
५ प्रेमरसगीता.	१२ श्रीहरिभक्तचन्द्रिका.
६ प्रबोधबावनी.	१३ श्रीहरिभक्तरत्नमाळा.
७ काळज्ञानसार.	१४ श्रीहरिनामवेली.

His Hindi works

Out of the very large number of his Hindî compositions, the **शतसैया** (Śat Śayyā) stamps him as a profound Sanskrit scholar and shows he was well versed in the philosophy of the Vallabhi sect. He has given such a masterly exposition of the Śuddhādwaita school of metaphysics in that work, that it simply exacts admiration for the study of a scholar, self-made in every sense of the word. The commentaries on the poem

१५ श्रीगुरुदेवचन्द्रिका.
१६ प्रेमप्रशंसा.
१७ शिक्षा तथा परीक्षा.
१८ भक्तिपोषण.
१९ भक्तिदृढाव.
२० स्तवनमाधुरी.
२१ सत्यभामाविवाह.
२२ रुक्मिणीविवाह.
२३ दशमलीला.
२४ रासपंचाध्यायी.
२५ भ्रान्तिभंजन.
२६ अन्यायमर्दन.
२७ मोहमर्दन.
२८ ईश्वरनिरीक्षण.
२९ पुष्टिपंथरहस्यमणीदाम.
३० चिन्ताचूर्णिका.
३१ प्रमेयपंचाव तथा स्वान्तःकरणसमाधान.
३२ श्रीकृष्णनामामृतधारा.
३३ क्षमापराधषोडशी.
३४ षड्ऋतुवर्णन.
३५ बारमास.
३६ भक्तवेल.
३७ चोरासी वैष्णवनुं धोळ.
३८ ब्राह्मणभक्तविवाद नाटक.
३९ वाणाधरी अन्तरनिष्ठ संवाद नाटक.
४० मनमतिसंवाद.
४१ पुरुषोत्तमपंचांग.
४२ श्रीयमुनास्तवन.
४३ श्रीकृष्णअष्टोतरशतनामचिन्तामणि.
४४ श्रीकृष्णनामावली.
४५ विनयबत्रिसी.
४६ अष्टपटराणीविवाह.
४७ ओखाहरण.
४८ नरसिंहमहेतानी हुंडी.

The plays written by Dayārām are mere dialogues, miscalled plays (नाटक). So says the late Harilāl H. Dhruva in his Essay on भरतनाट्यशास्त्र.

are written by him in prose–in Gujarāti–and they but serve to confirm the favourable opinion already formed of his abilities.

Many poems short

Many of his poems are very short, and some consist of a few lines only. He has "sown from the sack and not from the hand," but the sack was not very large. There are others, Sāmal for instance and Premānand, whose collected works would form as large a library as Dayārām's. But we are more concerned with the quality of the output than its quantity.

Threefold division of his work:

His work is naturally divided into three parts: 1. Religious or religio-philosophical, 2. Ethical or moral and 3. Erotic or Śringāric. The first takes up by far the largest space in his publications, and the curious reader is referred to his own works, such as the RasikVallabh[1] and the ŚatŚayyā to completely follow the trend of his beliefs and tenets.

1. Religious

The most prominent feature of his faith, religion or philosophy is HariBhakti, devotion to or worship of Hari, which is subordinated to every other consideration.

1. Mr. G. M. Tripāthi considers it to be a key to his works and beliefs. RasikVallabh is ably edited by Prof. J. G. Shāh M. A. and published by the Gujarāt Vernācular Society (1933).

resembles work of Sufi poets

Like the poets of Sufism—Hafiz and Mowlānā Rûmi,—he too preaches the cult of love.[1] If anywhere absence of selfishness were to be found in the world it would be in the pure love of a lover for his beloved, in the pursuit of which he braves all dangers and ignores all difficulties. The poet says, make Hari your beloved, place yourself in the position of his lover. Live for Hari, do everything for Hari. Efface yourself for or in Hari. The world is deceitful (full of Māyā), do not pursue its pleasures, but wean yourself away from their temporary bliss and momentary gratification, and devote yourself to Hari. The orthodox form of this Bhakti is ninefold,[2] and the poet has enlarged on all the nine stages. Excepting Mr. G. M. Tripāthi's book called **दयारामनो अक्षरदेह**, there is no other work in Gujarāti expounding Dayārām's philosophy, to which those who are interested in the Śuddhādwaita tenets of Vallabh may turn with much advantage.

1. The present writer has in a small pamphlet called दयाराम अने हाफेझ shown the points of similarity in the cult and poetry of both these poets.

2. श्रवण, कीर्तन, स्मरण, पादसेवन, अर्चन, वंदन, दासत्व, सख्य अने आत्मनिवेदन.

Some add a tenth, the crown of all the stages, called पराभक्ति or प्रेमभक्ति.

His poems on morals or ethics,—pūre and simple, for it must be noted that Dayārām was capable of completely forgetting his amatory self and write on morals, Vairāgya and Jnān—preponderate in number over his love lyrics. Their great charm lies in the felicity of the language in which they are couched. In spite of their subject matter, a complete antithesis to love, Dayārām did not find it at all difficult to clothe them in as clear and happy a language as his love-songs. The play of words, the interplay of ideas, the execution in short of the whole branch of his work on Niti (morals) and Bhakti is as brilliant as that of the other branch which has made him so popular and so famous.[1]

2. Ethical

on a par with other popular poems

1. One test of popularity, viz., the Padas (songs) being chanted by wandering minstrels, itinerant bards and beggars on the roadside, is more than fulfilled by these songs of Dayārām, and the following may be mentioned as some of them.

(a) वैष्णव नथी थयो तुं रे, शीद गुमानमां घूमे?
        हरिजन नथी थयो तुं रे.

(b) फूल्यो शुं फरे छे रे, भूल्यो भवकूपमां पड्यो,
मनुष्यदेह मोंघी रे, ग्वांयो मणि हाथे चढ्यो.

(c) गर्भवास राख्यो रे, किरपा तने बहु करी,
सदा सुख आप्युं रे, तेने केम गयो विसरी!

(d) साचुं ने सगपण रे, तनज नन श्याम तणुं,
बाकी सहु जूठुं रे, कशुं नहि काम तणुं.

3. Erotic,

The third part is that which has immortalised him. It consists of a large number of garbis (lyrics). They fulfil both the requirements of a lyric, in as much as "each poem turns on some single thought, feeling and

(e) श्रीवल्लभ विठ्ठल श्री जी, स्वामी ! सामळीआ वहाला,
सवकुं समजो छो. अन्तरजामी ! नंदलाला रे.

(f) व्रज वहालुं रे, वैकुंठ नहि आवुं,
मने न गमे चतुर्भुज थावुं,
त्यां नंदकुंवर क्यांथी लावुं ? व्रज वहालुं रे.

(g) जे कोइ जन कल्याण चाहो ते स्त्रीनी संगत तजजो रे.

(h) जे कोई प्रेम अंशी अवतरे, प्रेमरस तेना उरमां ठरे.
सिंहण केरुं दूध होय ते, सिंहणसुतने जरे;
कनकपात्र पाखे सौ धातु, फोडीने नीसरे--प्रेमरस०
सकरखोरनुं साकर जीवन, खरना प्राण ज हरे.
क्षारसिंधुनुं माछलडुं ज्यम, मीठा जळमां मरे—प्रेमरस०
सोमवेली रस पान शुद्ध, जे ब्राह्मण होय ते करे;
वगळवंशीने वमन करावे, वेदवाणी उचरे—प्रेमरस०
उत्तम वस्तु अधिकार विना मळे, तदपि अर्थ नव सरे;
मत्स्यभोगी बगलो मुक्ताफळ, देखी चंचु ना भरे—प्रेमरस०

(h) He alone who is born with the love-element in him, will be able to assimilate love. It is only a lion-cub that can digest the milk of a lioness; her milk will tear off and destroy every other metal cup excepting that of gold. Sugar will keep alive the sugar-eating bird, but if you give it to a donkey, it will kill him. A salt-water fish if kept in fresh water will die. It is only a Brahmin who can drink (with impunity) the *Soma* juice, a bastard will vomit it out: so say the Vedās. If you get a good thing without being fit for it, it will not serve your purpose. A fish-eating crane, even if it sees pearls will no eat them.

situation," and can be, rather, is meant to be, sung to a musical accompaniment. He sings of carnal love with an enthusiasm and power that is wonderful. These lyrics are said by his admirers to have a religious meaning. They say that the object of his yearning is not the woman addressed, but the deity, that the only way he could express his intense devotion and his ecstatic bliss was in terms of human, sensual love, that Persian poets have sung of the deity and divine worship under the guise of singing the joys of wine and women. This is how they are being explained away. The French poet Paul Verlaine wrote lines of ardent devotion and submission to God; at other times he wrote grossly erotic verses. Algernon Swinburne wrote in the same way too. Now no one would credit Verlaine and Swinburne with expressing their devotion to God when they composed their lyrics. It is a moot point also whether Hafiz can be interpreted as singing of divine things when he wrote burning words about his *Sāki* (cupbearer) and *Māshuk* (beloved)-and many will take leave to doubt that the women of Dayārām's lyrics symbolized the deity.

some of them tried to be explained away

Some of his poems *are* erotic pure and simple. The sentiment is so obviously that of a cunning and clever voluptuary,

Some incapable of such an explanation

if not a debauchee that no amount of argument can convince the reader, that the words are to be taken in an allegorical sense.[1] One Gujarāti critic writes: "His poems on Krishṇa and the maids of Gokul are a stream of burning lava, of realistic passion and love, and if lewdness of characterization does not take away from the merits of a poet he is a very great poet indeed."

Samples of verses containing undisguised Sringar

Samples of the garbis[2] given below, illustrate the undisguised

1. For instance the following verses

गोळ पोताने खूणे खाइए, करीए दीठो अदीठोजी;
प्रकट करी बजारे बेठां शुं, लागे छे अति मीठो !

Enjoy your sweets on tho sly-secretly. They do not add to their sweetness by being eaten in public.

2. (a) आवोने मारे घरे माणवा हो जी, राज ! आवोनी मारे घेर माणवा.
प्रेमरस प्यालो पीवा ने पावा, जोबन तुरीने पलाणवा हो जी राज०
पडती राने पधारजो प्रीतम ! कोई नथी बेटुं जाणवा हो जी राज०

This garbi is found in the works of Devānand also.

"Come to my house, O prince ! to enjoy yourself, come to my house. Come there to drink and make (me) drink the cup of love and to ride the steed of youth. Come at nightfall and no one will notice it."

(b) कई संगे लपटाणा, वालमजी ! कई संग लपटाना ?

"With which lady have you entangled (enjoyed) yourself, my love ! with which ?

(c) वळतां वहालमां रे, नचाव्यां लल्चाव्यां लोचन.

× × × × ×

रमीशुं रातडी रे, आवजो अलबेलाजी घेर,
कहेजो मातने रे, गाय एक खोवाणी छे आज,
जाउं छुं शोधवा रे, बांधजो पाणी पहेली पाज,
सासरीआं थकी रे, मारो आवास छे एकान्त,

× × × × ×

राखीश दीवडो रे, माणीशुं मनमानी मोज.

× × × × ×

While going away he darted his amorous glances at me .. .. Do come to my house, my love, we will enjoy ourselves at night. Tell your mother that a cow is missing and you will have to go in search of her, thus keep an excuse ready for your absence from home. My own apartments are away from those of my husband's relatives. .. ..

I will keep a light burning (to guide you) and we will enjoy ourselves to our heart' content.

(d) काचना फानसमां, दीपक जेवो चळके रे,
सुन्दरीनां नेणमां तेवो रतिरस झळके रे.

Just as a light shines brilliant in a glass lantern, so does the light of love flash out from the eyes of a woman.

(e) By way of variety a song which Krishṇa addresses to a gopi is given.

तमारो तमारो, प्यारी! मन माने ते कहोनी;
नथी चूक्यो, पण चूक्यो छुं, मने दंड गमे ते दोनी;
गुनेहगार जाणी मुजने, बे भुज पाशे बांधो रे;
तेथी अधिक करो तो मुजपर, नेनबाण बे साधो रे;
नाशी जईश जाणो तो मुजने, उर किल्ले चढावो रे;
कहो तो धीज पतीज करुं, शिवपिंडी हाथ धरावो रे;

× × × ×

हेत धरी हैडासुं लीधा, मंदिरमां पधराव्या रे;
प्रेम सहित पर्यंके पोढ्यां, उमग्यो रतिरस भारी रे;
ए जुगल रूप तणी लीलापर, जाय दयो बलिहारी रे.

I am yours, I am yours, my beloved, you may give me any names you like. I have not erred but still I say I have erred, punish me as you like. Consider me to be an offender, and bind me with the rope of (your) two hands; if you want to punish me still more aim the two arrows of your eyes at me. If you are afraid of my fleeing away, hoist me up on the castle of your bosom. I will assure you of my sincerity in any way you like. I will, if you wish, take a vow by placing my hand on the image (लिङ्ग) of Śiva .. .. (She was so pleased that) Out of sheer affection she took him to her bosom and carried him home. They slept on the bed with great affection and enjoyed the happiness of love with delight. Dayo is prepared to sacrifice himself for the revels of this pair.

(f) The following dialogue between a Gopi and Krishṇa shows the ingenuity of the latter.

मुजने अडशो मां आघा रहो, अलबेला ! छेला ! अडशो मां,
अंक भर्यानां सम खाओ तो, अधर तणो रस पाऊं;
कहान कुंवर काळा छो, अडता, हु काळी थई जाऊं- मुजने०
तुं मुज अडतां श्याम थाश तो, हुं क्यम नहि थाउं गोरो,
फरी मळता रंग अदलाबदली, मुज मोरो तुज तोरो- मुजने०

Do not touch me, O my dear, do not touch me. I will make you drink the nectar of my lips if you swear not to embrace me, because, O prince Kahān ! you are dark, and if you touch me I am afraid I might become dark too. (Krishna says) If you think, by my touch, you would become dark, why might not it happen that by your touch-embrace—I might become white, and on our embracing each other again you may get back your color and I mine ? (He thus calls for two embraces where she objected even to one).

Śringār of Dayārām.[1]

Dayārām's *forte* his language.

Dayārām's strength is his language. It is simple, chaste, classical and expressive. His songs are superior to those of others, both on account of their language and their rhythm. To appreciate

1. One school of critics of "the lewdness of Dayārām's writings" while admitting that his Śringār is undisguised, suggests that the key to discover the underlying spiritual idea is furnished by the principles of the Pushtimārga which are that the Lord is to be wooed by भक्ति.

तेमनां काव्योमां जे शृंगाररस छे ते लौकिक रति नथी, परंतु श्री कृष्णना आलंबन-विभाव पर रचायेली माधुर्यभक्ति छे. आ भक्तिरस दयारामनी प्राणनाडीमां वहे छे, अने ते कंई मात्र वैखरी वाणीमां शृंगारना रुपमां वहे छे एम नथी.

vide Diwān Bahādur Narmadāshankar D. Mehta's lecture (1929) quoted at pp. 392–393–395–399 of Dayarām's Ântar Jivan.

His contention is that the erotic descriptions found in Dayārām's poems are not those pertaining to worldly pleasures (लौकिक रति), but to that sweet devotion (माधुर्यभक्ति) which hangs on the yearning of the devotee's soul to become one with Krishṇa or which yearns for companionship with him (सखीभाव). Dayārām considers Krishṇa to be his lover and himself his beloved steeped in love to the point of madness.

The subject is highly technical and therefore controversial, and requires deep and important study.

The present writer presided recently (August 1937) at the 101st Birth anniversary meeting of Dayārām Jayanti at Bombay, and pointed out that Dayārām had like his predecessors, Mirānbāi and Narsinh Mehtā, followed what was set out in the Bhāgvat, Harivansh,

their lilt, they must be heard, when ladies of well-known skill lead the garba-circles of Surat or Barodā. The audience and the singers are simply carried beyond themselves, and by the enthusiasm engendered by the rhythmical clap of hands and measured voices of the leader and the led, one, for the moment, forgets the objectionable feature of the songs, which does not lie deep.

Navalrām's estimate of Dayārām's work very sober

Dayārām's works have been reviewed and criticised often and by many. The soberest and the sanest review, however, is that of Navalrām, a wellknown critic and reviewer. His poetry is greatly subjective, but speaking of passion and love, he thinks his poems are defective in so far as they do not "paint pictures." "One third of them consists of pure emotion, and the rest is superficial embellishment, which to the experienced eye of the real poet appears to be tawdry and useless." "He is inferior to Premanand even in Śringār ... ... Where every word of a sentence is in its proper place, where if

Vishṇu Purāṇ and other allied Sanskrit works as to the incident of the Rās Lilā and the relations between Krishṇa and Gopis. They did not mean to stress the physical aspect of it but to allegorise the same. In doing so they had naturally had to describe in graphic terms and in details the different stages and conditions of sexual enjoyment, but that therefore, they should not be charged with possessing loose morals.

one word were changed or taken away, the picture drawn by it would be spoiled, where even though there be the embellishment of rhyme, it would appear to be so skilfully done as to appear as if it were a part and parcel thereof, where there is no useless amplification, but merely a word to the wise, where there would be conciseness but not such as would make even a learned man desire to add a word to it, where not a rule of prosody would be violated—such poetry, full of meaning and significance does not exist in our language. Only Sanskrit and English contain such poetry." Judged by this standard, therefore, Dayārām fails to be considered a master poet in Navalrām's eyes, in spite of his immense popularity, the reason of which, he thinks, is the subject matter of his poems, namely, the life and loves of Rādhā and Krishṇa.

If it were to be believed that Premānand[1] did write the plays that are attributed to him, then the

1. Those who contend that the prose dramas which are now ascribed to Premānand were written by him, should produce for inspection the ancient manuscripts from which they have been published, so say those who doubt their genuineness When Dr Johnson was asked to accept the Ossian translations of Macpherson as translations of very ancient Gaelic original poems, he demanded the production of the original manuscripts by the ancient Gaelic scribes—these not being forthcoming Johnson held Macpherson's translations to be forgeries, and until the manuscripts of Premānand's prose drama are produced—their genuineness will remain open to doubt.

statement that till the beginning of the nineteenth century Gujarāti literature consisted merely of poetry with only a negligible quantity of prose, has to be modified. The prose works of Premānand betray a language so very modern in style, that one would be constrained to say that during the last four hundred years, the language had undergone no change, grammatical, syntactical or idiomatical.[1] But if side by side with that of Premānand, the prose written by Dayāram and his followers be considered, it will be found that the latter, even though written later, betrays some archaic features which are wanting in the style of Premānand. So the problem arises, how can prose written later in point of time, betray such characteristics, which in their very nature

Dayārām's prose might throw some light on that written earlier

1. This cannot be said to be a correct conclusion. The following extract taken from a copy of the Panchatantra, made during the time of Sāmal and Premānand, should enable the reader to gauge the difference between the prose of the plays and the prose prevalent then. I am indebted for the extract to Mr. Ranjitrām Vāvābhāi, who has given it in his Introduction to Gujarāti prose in a book called the साहित्यरत्न:

त्यांहां गुणनिध्यांन नामे राजा छि. तेने १०० पुत्र हवा राजपुत्रने भणाविवानुं उपाय घणुं करी पण जे भणावे तेहनें मारीनें सघला घरि आव्या ॥ पछीं राजा च्यंतातुर थयो. तारी प्रधानि पूछुं स्वामी तुनें सी चंता छे ॥ वलतु राजाइ कहु ॥ प्रधान मुनेहुं मोटी चंता छे ॥ वलतुं राजाइ कहु ॥ जे सघलाज मूर्ष पूत्र ॥

जेहना पूत्र मूर्ष होइं ॥ ते पुरुष वांझियु वारु ॥ पण मूर्ष पुत्रथी तो ऐकु अर्थ ना सरइ ॥

could not be absent from the prose of an earlier period. The following sentences are taken from a small fragmentary writing of a disciple of Dayārām.

जात्राळुओनो मोटो संग हुतो, तेमां अनेक स्त्रीपुरुषोनां जुट ने जुट आवतां हतां, तेओ पुरण पुरुषोत्तमरूप धारीने आ बाळकोने प्रणाम करवाने एटले पगे लागवाने जती हती अने पुगनी जे खावानुं ते धरावती.

पण जीव जे एकज पदार्थ पर च्होंटेलुं रहे ते श्रेष्ठ जे मोटुं छे ते द्रूयम कहेतां बे स्थळे भमतूं रहे छे तेनो ओद्धार थतो नथी.

ते वातो तुषार जे हीम तेनी पेठे ठंडा थई जाय छे, ने शिष्यने तपावे कहेतां बाळे छे.........

Another instance is taken from Dayārām's own writing, his prose commentary to his Sat Sayyā.

एक दुर्वानामां गोपी जंन छे, ते पोतानी सखी प्रत्ये पोताना व्रेहे तापनुं दुःख कहे छे के अली ! मारा विरहनी व्यथा जे पीडा ते जेने हुं कहुं छुं, ते सांभळतां तेनुं शरीर तपी जाय छे, तारे मारा हृदेना तापनुं शुं कहेवुं ? पण अहो कहेतां एक मोटुं आश्चर्य छे, जे ते हृदयमां मनमोहन जे नंदलाल ते वसे छे तो ए पण सीरे कहेतां टाढे रह्या, एटले शो भाव के जो तपता होय तो आवीने दर्शन केम न आपे ?

The peculiar characteristic of this style is that the writer always tries to explain one word by its synonym, or a phrase by its equivalent, somewhat like this in English: he felt cold, that is, he felt the absence of heat, he went home, i. e., to his native place. This feature is still found in the speech of those Purāṇis who even now read out and explain such sacred works as the Bhāgvat and the Purāṇas. It is just a survival of this old style, and their Kathā is one running speech most thickly interspersed with double phrases like those underlined above. In Premānand's prose this feature is absent. Could it have come into vogue between his and Dayārām's day ?

APPENDIX to CHAPTER VII

The following list of Dayarām's Works is prepared by Mr. Natvarlāl I. Desāi B. A. and arranged according to subjects.

भक्तिविषयक काव्यो

–श्री भगवद्गीतामाहात्म्य (पद्म पुराणमांथो अनुवाद)
–भक्तिपोषण
–चिन्ताचूर्णिका
–काळज्ञानसारांश
–परीक्षाप्रदीप
–शिक्षा
–अकळ कळा
–भक्तवेल

उपदेशनां काव्यो

–मनप्रबोध (कक्को)
–प्रबोधबावनी
–चातुरचित्तविलास (समस्याओ)
–प्रश्नोत्तरमालिका
–मूर्खलक्षणावलि
–सारावलि
–हरिभक्तिचंद्रिका

श्रीकृष्णनी लीलानां पदो

–श्रीकृष्णजन्म
–पारणुं
–बाळलीला (कुंवरने वारो व्रजराणी !)
–दाणचातुरी (दाणलीला)
–मुरलीलीला
–कमळलीला
–पत्रलीला
–रूपलीला
–कात्यायनीनो गरबो
–मोहिनीस्वरूप
–रासलीला
–रासपंचाध्यायी
–श्रीकृष्णना व्यानंनुं धोळ
–श्रीकृष्णक्रीडा
–श्रीकृष्णस्तुति

व्रजयात्रा संबंधी काव्यो

–व्रजमहिमा
–यमुनाजीनी स्तुति
–व्रजविलासामृत (व्रज)

श्रीकृष्णविरहनां काव्यो

–प्रेमरस गीता
–प्रेमपरीक्षा
–चेतवणी
–चातुरीनो गरबो
–स्नेहविलास

तिथि-मास-वारनां काव्यो

–पंदर तिथिओ (१) (सुणो ओधवजी !)
– ,, ,, (२) (पडवे प्राणजीवन)
–रसियाजीना महिना
–वाहलाजीना महिना
–बार मासनी गरबी
–सात वार अने मानचरित्र
–षड्ऋतुवर्णन

चरित्रकाव्यो

–मीरांचरित्र
–नरसिंह मेहेतानी हुंडी (मराठी)

श्रीकृष्णना स्तवननां पदो

–श्रीकृष्णस्तवनमंजरी
–अपराधक्षमास्तोत्र
–श्रीकृष्णनाममाहात्म्यमंजरी
–श्रीकृष्णनामचिन्तामणि
–श्रीकृष्णअष्टोत्तरशतनाममाळा
–श्रीकृष्णअष्टोत्तरशतनामचिन्तामणि
–श्री शेषशाइजीनुं धोळ
–श्रीशेषशाइजीनुं वर्णन
–हरिनाममाळा
–श्रीकृष्णस्तवनामृत (व्रज)

श्रीकृष्णना विवाहनां काव्यो

(सामाजिक काव्यो)

–अष्ट पटराणीनो विवाह
–रुक्मणिनो विवाह
–सत्यभामानो विवाह
–नाग्नजितीनो विवाह

राधाजी साथे विवाहनां काव्यो

–राधाजीनुं स्वप्नुं
–राधाजीनुं माता प्रत्ये कथन
–राधाजीनां वखाण
–राधाजीनो विवाहखेल
–राधा अष्टोत्तरशतनाम
–श्रीकृष्ण-उपवीत

सीमन्त

–रुक्मणि सीमन्त
–कुंवरबाइनुं मोसाळुं

भागवतना ग्रंथो

–श्रीमद्भागवत स्कंध, प्रकरण अने अध्यायानुक्रमणिका (हिन्दी)
–श्रीमद्भागवत दशमस्कंधानुक्रमणिका (गुजराती)
–चोवीश अवतारनुं धोळ
–अजामिलाख्यान

संवाद काव्यो

—हनुमानगरुडसंवाद

—मन–मतिसंवाद

—ब्राह्मण-भक्तविवाद नाटक

—गुरु–शिष्य संवाद (अप्रकट)

गुजराती गद्य

—सतसैयानी गुजराती टीका

—हरिहरादिस्वरूपतारतम्यकथन

—प्रश्नोत्तरमालिका

पुष्टिसम्प्रदायना ग्रन्थो (गुजराती)

—रसिकवल्लभ

—चोराशी वैष्णवो

—वल्लभनो परिवार

—पुष्टिपथरहस्य

—मायामतखंडननो गरवो

श्री पुरुषोत्तम पंचांग

—श्री पुरुषोत्तम अष्टोत्तरशतनाम

—श्री वल्लभ अष्टोत्तरशतनाम

—श्री विठ्ठल अष्टोत्तरशतनाम

—श्री राधा अष्टोत्तरशतनाम

—श्रीव्रजभक्त अष्टोत्तरशतनाम

पुष्टिसंप्रदायना ग्रन्थो (व्रज)

—सम्प्रदायसार

—कलेशकुठार

—रसिकरंजन

—पिंगळसार (अप्रसिद्ध)

—सिद्धान्तसार

—श्रीकृष्णस्तवनामृत

—भक्तिविधान[1]

—पुष्टिपथसारमणिदाम

—विज्ञप्तिविलास (some choice quotations from his सतसैया)

दयारामनाव्रजभाषा (हिन्दी)मां रचेला ग्रंथो

सतसैया

व्रजविलासामृत, (व्रज चोराशी कोशनी यात्रानुं वर्णन)

वस्तुवृंददीपिका (१ थी १०८ वस्तुओ नामोनो कोश)

1. It is not known who has incorporated भक्तिविधान of Shobhachand into Dayārām's original work. It seems his followers or disciples might have wrongly or by mistake inserted it into Dayārām's poems; or wrongly counted it as one of Dayārām's poems.

वृंदावनविलास	श्रीकृष्णस्तवनचंद्रिका
श्रीकृष्णअकलचरित्रचंद्रिका	पुष्टिभक्तरूपमालिका
काशीपुरीनी लावणी	

कवि दयारामे सारोद्धार करेला ग्रन्थो

(१) **ओखाहरण.** This poem was originally written by Premānand in 29 cantos; which he himself increased to 36 by adding the last 7 cantos describing the various ceremonies and customs observed by Gujaratis generally on marriage occasions. This poem became so popular in Gujarāt that many poets after Premānand went on adding to it and brought it upto 52 cantos; the last addition was by Dayārām who brought it to upto 64 cantos. He has, however, put his name at the end of some of the added cantos as their author rather than pass them off as those of Premānand. Other poets have, however, not refraind from adding to it, and increased the number to 92 and even to 108 cantos.

Besides the above list of published books the list of books still unpublished given by his followers is a fairly large one; but unless one actually sees and examines them critically one cannot vouchsafe their genuinenees.

The number of his small poems called (पद) Padas is very large. He has written such small poems not only in Gujarati, but also in Vrāj (Hindi as spoken round about Mathurā i. e. Vrajmandal), Mārwādi, Marāthi, Punjābi, and a mixture of all the prevalent chief languages spoken in India during his time. In all these works and poems, there is one common thread running viz., that of absolute devotion to Lord Śhree Krishṇa.

कवि दयारामना जीवननां वर्षो

विक्रम संवत.

१८३३ मां जन्म भादरवा सुदी ११
१८४१ मां उपवीत(जनोइ)धारण
१८४१ मां विवाहसंबंध (पाछळथी तुटी गयो)
१८४३ मां कविना पिता प्रभुरामनो स्वर्गवास
१८४५ मां कविनां माता राजकोर उरफे महालक्ष्मीनो स्वर्गवास
१८४७ मां कविए ब्रह्मसंबंध कराव्यो; पुष्टिमार्गीय वैष्णवी दीक्षा लीधी
१८५० मां भागवतना बारे स्कंधोनो अध्यायवार सार रच्यो
१८५१ मां भगवद्‌गीता गुजरातीमां रची
१८५१ मां एक वैदकना ग्रंथनो उतारो कर्यो
(१८५३–५८ मां पहेली यात्रा भरतखंडनी कीधी)
१८५३ मां डाकोरना भक्त इच्छाराम भट्टजी साथे मेळाप
१८५३ मां तेनी आज्ञाथी वडोदराना एक संघ साथे यात्रा करवा गया.
१८५८ मां मनमरजाद लीधी
(१८६१–६५ मां भरतखंडनी बीजी वार यात्रा करी)
१८६१ मां पाकी मरजाद लीधी
१८६२ मां पत्रलीला काव्य लख्युं
१८६३ मां अजामिलाख्यान लख्युं
१८६५ मां यात्रा करी पाछा फर्या
१८६६ मां डभोईमां स्थायी मुकाम कर्यो

१८६७ मां **भागवत दशम स्कंधानुक्रमणिका लखी** जेठ वद ११
१८६९ मां वैष्णव घेलाभाई मजमुदारनी शंकानुं समाधान
१८७१ मां चांदोदनुं घर वेच्युं
१८७२ मां **सतसैया** रची पूरा कर्या श्रावण शुद ८
१८७४ मां फत्तेहसिंहराव गायकवाडनी मुलाकात।
१९७४ मां **वस्तुवृंददिपीका** रची श्रावण वद ८
१८७७ मां सयाजीराव गायकवाडनी मुलाकात
१८७९ मां **श्री भागवतानुक्रमणिका** रची फागण वद २
१८८० मां **सारावली** रची श्रावण सुद १२
१८८२ मां **व्रजविलासामृत** रच्यो आसो सुद ९
१८८३ मां रामानुजी अनन्ताचार्यनो मेळाप
१८८४ मां **रसिकवल्लभ** ग्रंथ लख्यो श्रावण सुद ११
१८८५ मां भरुचवाळा चीमनलाल साथे मित्रता बंधाई
१८८६ मां अमदावादवाळा व्यास माधवरामे पूछेला सवालनो जवाब कवितामां आप्यो. आज अरसामां अमदावादवाळा कवि कृष्णरामे दयारामने उद्देशीने केटलांक काव्यो रच्यां छे
१८८७–८८ मां भरतखंडनी त्रीजी यात्रा
१८८७ मां श्रीनाथजीनी सातमी अने छेल्ली वार झांखी करी
१८९० मां **गीतामाहात्म्य** रच्युं श्रावण वद ८
१८९० मां वैष्णव कृपाराम माधवराम मजमुदारने त्यां शंका समाधाननो एक प्रसंग
१८९८ मां पहेलो मंदवाड. भविष्यनी व्यवस्था लखी मागशर वदी १३ आमां सहि दयाराम तरीके नहि पण दयाशंकर तरीके जोवामां आवे छे
१९०६ मां मुंबइ आव्या हता एम केटलाक वैष्णवो कहे छे
१९०९ मां भगवत्पदप्राप्ति महावदी ५

CHAPTER VIII

THE INDIGENOUS LITERATURE OF KĀTHIĀWĀD.[1]

Peculiar ballad literature of Kāthiāwād

There is an indigenous ballad literature peculiar to Kāthiāwād; it is peculiar in two respects: firstly, language, and secondly, the glimpses it gives of the social life of the people of the province, wild, romantic and chivalrous. It has been preserved up till now, like the texts of the Vedas in early days, not as a written record, but by oral tradition.[2] No sustained action has hitherto been taken to collect and publish the many poems and verses, which illustrate the conditions obtaining in old Kāthiāwād, rich in colour, full of martial prowess, and quivering with emotion. Out of many incidents a few of the most celebrated, will be referred to here. The ballads are written in a style called दुहा and सोरठा or couplets, and

1. This Chapter originally appeared in *East and West* of July, 1913. With the kind permission of the Editor it is reprinted here after being revised.

2. "A more important side of Gujarāti Literature is the corpus of bardic histories none of which have, so far as I am aware, been published." Grierson's Linguistic Survey of Indiā, Part I, p. 333.

it is these दुहा and सोरठा which are recited by the simple folk of Kāthiāwād, its peasants and its shepherds while at work or leisure. This is done with considerable feeling, particularly when they commemorate events which have shed an abiding lustre on the lives of their countrymen and countrywomen. It has not been possible to discover the author of these ballads, nor indeed is it known whether the ballads were the work of many or of one. Only one thing is certain, viz., that these ballads are old and very popular.

Halāmaṇ Jethwā and Sona Rāṇi

The दुहा of Halāmaṇ Jethwā, the spirited recitation of which maintains many Bhāts or bards even to-day, are an instance in point. They describe the difficulties of young lovers, whose efforts towards being united in marriage were thwarted by a near relative. Sona Rāṇi was the daughter of Rāṇā Rājsinh of Bālambhā. She had made up her mind to marry only such a person as would be able to answer her riddle:

घणवण घडयां, एरणे अड्यां [एरण आभड्यो] नहीं,[1]

"What is that which has been made without hammer or anvil?" The family priest was sent to

1. There is a supplementary line added,

गोत्यां नव जड्यां, मळे तो मोकलजो.

various courts to see if he could get any one to solve it. After many failures, he at last tried Ghumli, at the foot of the Bardā mountains. The local chief, a scion of the famous Jethwā clan of Rājputs, Rāṇā Shiyāji tried his hand at the solution but failed. But his young nephew Halāmaṇ, could read it at once.

सरवर सात (स्वात) तणां मळे तो मोती नीपजे.[1]

Pearls are produced if rain drops fall into the mouths of oysters during the time when the Sun is passing through the Swāti Nakshatra (fifteenth mansion of the Hindu Zodiac). His solution was "Pearls," which are fashioned without being hammered or placed on an anvil. In the ordinary course the priest would have gone and reported the matter faithfully to princess Sona and her union with Halāmaṇ would have been the result, but seeing a beautiful prize about to be snatched away from his hands Rāṇā Shiyāji bribed the Brāhmin to substitute his name instead of Halāmaṇ's as the reader of the riddle, and accordingly it was arranged that the bride should go, with a proper equipage in charge of the

1. Some substitute the following reply;

माता मेरामण वसे, पिता वसे आकाश,
जोइये तो जूनां मोकलुं, नवां तो आसो मास

The mother lives in the ocean, and the father in the clouds. If you want them, I would send you old ones now, the new ones would come in Âso.

priest to Ghumli, and be married to the Rāṇa. Till the bride's party came to the place, Halāmaṇ was under the impression that he was the chosen bridegroom, but his eyes were opened by a trusted follower of his, who told him that his uncle had decided to marry the princess. He was sorely disappointed, but yielding to an impulse of respect for his elders, he said he would not interfere. On the other hand, it so happened, that a squabble took place between the maidservants of Sona Kunvari, and Rāṇā Shiyāji, at a well while drawing water, and they began to taunt and abuse each other.

The Rāṇā's maid said:

बांधी मूठी लाख लिये, उघाडी वा खाय,
हलामण दुहा पारखे, सोन शियाने जाय.[1]

"Who knows what is in a shut hand? When opened it may be empty or may have a lac of Rupees. Halāmaṇ reads the riddle, but Shiyā gets Sona for his bride."

This startled the poor maid so much that she at once ran to her mistress, and told her what had happened. She called the priest, whom she suspected of foul play, and under threat of punishment made him confess his guilt. She now knew what

1. Another reading is,

बांधी मूठी लाख, उघाडी वा(सर) खाय,
हलामण दुहो पाल्टे, सोन शिया वेर जाय.

had taken place, and made up her mind to thwart the Rāṇā's designs. Accordingly when he sent her presents of ornaments and dresses, she threw them away and sent word with the servants—

सुंडलीभर्यो शणगार, मने शियानो शोभे नहीं,
हलामण भरथार, शियो अमारो सासरो.

"That it did not behove her to accept the basketful of presents from Shiyāji, as he was her father-in-law, while Halāmaṇ was her husband."

When his servants reported this incident to him Shiyāji lost his temper at the insult. He thought that there must be the hand of Halāmaṇ in it. He sent for Halāmaṇ and ordered him to quit his dominions forthwith. Halāmaṇ obeyed, but while leaving he met a servant-girl of Sona, by whom he sent a message:

देशवटो धरार, साचो दीधो, शिये जेठवे,
हवे जईं भणजे जुहार, हांवे गयो हलामणो.

"Shiyā Jethwā has sent me away at once, hence, I am going to Hāmbā in Sind. Tell your mistress this and present her with my respects."

On hearing this, Sona exclaimed:

उतारो अंगार, मने जातां लागे जेठवो,
मारी उरमां मार, क्यां हाल्यो गयो हलामणो ?

"I feel this house burning me like fire, now that

Halāmaṇ Jethwā has gone. O Halāmaṇ ! having wounded my heart, where have you gone ?"

The painful incident rendered her faint, and it was with difficulty that her maids were able to bring her back to consciousness, when the Rāṇā called on her to learn his fate. She shut herself up in a room and refused to see him, saying he should not have any evil designs on his daughter-in-law. This added to his anger, and he was preparing to ravish her, when a servant brought him news, that the Sindhis had attacked the borders of his territory, and his immediate presence there was necessary to beat them back. This unexpected contingency upset his plans, and he had to leave at once, after giving orders that Sona should on no account be allowed to go out. However, after his departure Sona did leave the town, saying she wanted to visit a temple. At some distance from the town, she and her maid managed to get rid of the driver and the maid taking his place drove away towards Hāmbā.

Meanwhile Halāmaṇ was living at Hāmbā with his aunt, but his life was not happy. Like a distracted lover, he was wandering in the jungle from place to place, and like King Pururavā in the famous drama of Kālidās, Vikramorvashi questioning every tree and bird if they had seen his beloved. The दुहा that he addressed them are very well known for their pathos:

व्हाला वियोगी वांस ! अहीं शी अवगणे आवीओ ?
भणने मारी भोंयना, मने संदेशो कांई सोननो ?

Seeing a bamboo tree, he was reminded of his native country, where bamboos grew in abundance. He felt it-was in exile like him, but still he thought it might be knowing something about his beloved. He says, "My dear exiled bamboo ! what fault has brought you here ? O you ! who come from my native place, have you a message from Sona for me ?"

The bamboo replies:

काप्यो लई कवाडीये, पछे झीक्यो झखु मांय,
कोढे लेवाणो आज, तेथी शुद्ध न रही सोननी.

"I was cut down with an axe and thrown into the sea. The waves rendered me senseless, so I know nothing of Sona."

He addresses a fisherman, then:

जालीडा ! नांखने जाळ, मीठा मेरामण मझे,[1]
करम छे कपाळ, के बोंतेरसें बरडे रह्यां ?

"O fisherman ! throw your net into the sea, and then let me see, if my good fortune has come with me, or been left behind at Bardā."

His aunt to console him proposed a marriage to a Sindhi beauty, but he declined, saying, Sona only will I wed.

1. There is a variant which reads better, हलामणना नामनी.

In this unhappy state of mind, he sat on a stone in a jungle. A serpent came from under it, and bit his toe. The poison began to do its work, and Halāmaṇ thought that his last moments were approaching, and that he would die without seeing his lady-love. So he bewailed his fate thus:

वळजे सोन सुजाण, हुं सूतो छेल्ले साथरे,
पामी नथी तुं प्राण, अध घडी आरामनी.
मनहर तारुं मुख, में जाण अजाणे जोयुं नहि,
आशा रही उर मांय, अंते पाम्यो आ गति.

"Come this way, dear Sona! I am lying on my last bed. O my soul! you have not had even half a moment of solace. I have neither consciously nor unconsciously seen your beautiful face, my hopes have remained in my heart, and at last I find myself in this plight (*i.e.*, am dying)."

After leaving the territory of the Rāṇā, Sona and her maid, on their way to Hāmbā, were passing through the jungle and halted for rest and refreshment. The maid went to find water, and whilst wandering about came to where Halāmaṇ was lying unconscious. She recognised him and ran to her mistress with the news. Sona came to the spot, and seeing the unhappy fate of her lover, fainted away. After great exertion the maid brought her back to consciousness. But her lamentations were heartrending:

हांबानी हद मांय, में वहाली वस्तु विसारीयुं,
हैडा केरो हार, जे हतो हलामण जेठवो.
हांबा डुंगर हेठ, में हलामण हिंचोळयो नहि,
आशायुं रही अनेक, मने जेठवो जोवा तणी.

"I have lost a thing dear to me within the limits of Hāmbā; it is the necklace of my heart, one whose name was Halāmaṇ Jethwā. Alas! I could not rock Halāmaṇ (to sleep) at the foot of the Hāmbā mountains. I had many hopes of meeting Jethwā, but they all remained unfulfilled."

Taking him to be lifeless, she thought it incumbent on her to cremate the dead body decently, and she asked her maid to gather together fuel, so that she might prepare a pile for that purpose, and also burn herself with the lord of her heart, like a true *Sati*. She says:

हांबानी हद मांहि आज पीठीभर्यो पोढाडीओ.
मींढळ छूट्यां मसाण, हुं हारी बेठी हलामणो.
हलामणने हिये, खोडचं खडकीआं,
हवे करवा स्वर्गे साथ, मारे बळवुं, बरडाना धणी.

"I have laid, within the boundaries of Hāmbā, one on whom the (yellow) colour of turmeric paste applied at the time of marriage is yet fresh (*i. e.*, one who was soon to marry). The mindhal nuts tied (to our hands) have been untied on the burning ground, (since) I have lost Halāmaṇ. On the body of Halāmaṇ wood has been piled. I will mount the pyre, and with the lord of Bardā I shall ascend to heaven."

The wails of Sona and her maid attracted the attention of a serpent charmer, who came upon the scene. He examined the body of Halāmaṇ and found that life was not extinct, and that there was a chance of reviving him. The serpent charmer took out the antidote he had against snake poison and applied it to the wound. Soon Halāmaṇ regained his senses, and was both surprised and delighted to see Sona there. The rest of the tale is easily told. They married, and as Shiyāji died shortly after, they went back to their native country, and lived happily.

जेवी सोन सुजाण, तेवो हलामण हीरलो,
तन बे एक ज प्राण जुगते जुगतुं जोडलुं.

Just as Sona was clever, so was Halāmaṇ shining (like a diamond). They had two bodies, but one soul: they were a fit pair in every way.

Ujali and Meha

Another such couple is Ujalibāi and Meha Jethwā of the same Bardā hills. Ujali was the daughter of a Chāraṇ, and the natives of Kāthiāwād revere Chāraṇ ladies as they revere a goddess. Reports of Ujali's unparalleled beauty made Meha Jethwā anxious to see her. When he saw her, they fell in love with each other and the prince of Ghumli promised to marry her. But the Mahājan of the place–his own subjects–knew better. To them, the union of a Chāraṇi-lady–a goddess–with a Rajput appeared to be a gross act of sacrilege, and they were prepared to prevent it at any cost. They therefore waylaid Meha Jethwā, on his way back from a meeting with Ujali. Meha saw them cruelly beating an old cow, and it struck him as an unusual thing to see Hindus ill-treating a cow. He asked them the reason of it, and they said, that if their king thought there was no sin in a Rajput marrying a Chāraṇi woman, they too thought there was no sin in beating a cow. He realised the enormity of the offence he was on the point of committing, and promised them to abstain from it.

On the day fixed for the wedding, as there was no call from Meha, Ujali became impatient, and went over to Ghumli. She wanted to see Meha, but was not permitted to do so. She sent a message to him, and was told in reply that Meha would not marry her. This broke her heart, and she passed the rest of her life in performing acts of piety and in devotion.

There are many दुहा depicting the various stages of their love and the disenchantment of Ujali. The following are some couplets from the messages sent by her:

हतुं अने हारवीउं, मोती महा दरिये,
काळो पहेरी काछ, अमने सागर शोधवो पड्यो.
मेहनी मेडी हेठ, उभी अरदासां करां,
मोंढुं देखाडने मेह ! जीवतां रहीए जेठवा !

× × × ×

आभपरेथी उतरी, चारण भूखी छे,
क्यां जाऊं जेठवा ? मोरी मत मुंझाणी छे.

× × × ×

मुंझव में, हमने ऊंडे जळ उतारीने,
अम मरते तुंने, जस नही आवे जेठवा !

'I had a pearl, I lost it in the great ocean. I had to put on black garments and search the ocean. I am standing underneath the balcony of Meha, and entreating. O Meha! show me your face, so that I might live, O Jethwā!.........The Chāraṇ woman has descended from the sky, and is hungry. Where should I go, O Jethwā? my senses are confused...... O Jethwā! do not abandon me after taking me into deep waters. If I die, it will not redound to your credit."

To these pathetic entreaties, Meha sent this reply:

चारण एटला देव, जोगमाया करी जाणीए,
चारणथी मन मळे, बूडे बरडानो धणी.

"To us, all the Chāraṇs are gods, and all the Chāraṇis goddesses. If he were to love (and wed) Chāraṇ (ladies), the ruler of Bardā would die."

Odho Jam and Hothaldé Padamani, Lākho and Fulāndé, these two couples have also furnished food for romance.

Rāṇakdevi and Siddhrāj

The courage of Rāṇakdevi, the wife of Rākhengār, the ruler of Junāgadh, whom Siddhrāj Jayasinh, of Anhilwād Pātāṇ had attacked (in the eleventh century A. D.) and defeated, to deprive him of his beautiful consort, has passed into history. Rākhengār was betrayed and killed through the treachery of his nephew, and Rāṇakdevi was forcibly taken away by Siddhrāj. But coming near Wadhwān, she managed to burn herself as a *Sati* with the permission of Siddhrāj.

A number of fine and spirited couplets are attributed to her, in praise of Girnār and in praise of her lord:

(१) माणेरा ! म तुं रोय, म कर राती आंखडी,
कूळमां कागे खोय, मरतां मा न संभारीए.

(२) उतर्यो गढ गिरनार, तन आव्युं तळाटीए,
वळतां बीजी वार, दामो कंड नथी देखचो.

(३) उंचो गढ गिरनार, वादळथी वातुं करे,
मरतां रा खेंगार, रंडापो राणकदेवडी.

(४) मारु पाटण देश, पाणी विना पूरा मरे,
सरवो सोरठ देश, सावजडा सेजळ पीए.

(५) वायु वाय सवाय, वाये वेळु परजळे,
उभो त्यां सिधराज, सत जोवा सोरठियाणीनुं.

(1) "Weep not my child, make not your eyelids red, think not of your mother when facing death: disgrace not your ancestors by showing weakness." (2) "I descended the hill of Girnār, and my body reached its foot. I will never again see Damodar Kund" (the lake at the foot of the hill). (3) "The fort of Girnār is so high that it touches the sky. By the death of Rākhengār, Rāṇakdevi becomes a widow." (4) "The country round about Pātaṇ is waterless, its people die of thirst but prosperous is the land of Sorath, where even tigers drink their fill." (5) "The winds are hurricanes, they are so hot that they burn even sand. There Siddhrāj was standing to watch the miraculous power of the lady from Sorath."

Rā Mandalik's unhappy fate

Rā Mandalik III, another ruler belonging to the same family as Rākhengār's–the same who put Narsinh Mehtā's faith to test—forgetting his duty (धर्म) as a king, to protect his subjects like his children tried to lay violent hands on a Chāraṇ lady, Nāgbāi. Nāgbāi cursed him in very bitter terms, prophesying that he would lose his kingdom, and Mahomedans would rule where Hindus exercised authority so long. The prophecy came true, as in A. D. 1473. Mahmud Begadā invaded Junāgadh and Rā Mandalik had to embrace Islam.

गढ गरवानां राज, संतापी चारण, पामीश नहिं,
काया थाशे कोढणी, मुं संभारीश मंडलिक !

× × × ×

दरवाजे दरवाण, राहना रहेशे नहि,
भमतो मागीश भीख, मुं संभारीश मंडलिक !
झालरना झणकार, शंख संभळाशे नहि,
मुल्लां पढशे नमाज, मुं संभारीश मंडलिक !

× × × ×

पोथां ने पुराण भागवते भळशो नहि.
कलमो पढशे कुरान, ते दी मुं संभारीश मंडलिक !

"If you make a Chāraṇ maid unhappy, you will not be able to rule the mighty fort (of Girnār). Your body will be attacked with leprosy, then you will remember me and my curse. ... At the gates, there will be no gate-keepers of the Rā, and you will have to wander about as a beggar; you will then remember me and my curse. You will hear no more the ringing of the gong, nor the sounding of the conch. Mullas will say their prayers there (in the temples), and then you will remember me and my curse. You will no more be able to read religious works, the Purāṇas and the Bhāgavat, but the Kalamā of the Koran will be read (in your territory), and on that day O Mandalik! you will remember me and my curse."

These burning words, uttered from the bottom of her heart by a woman, whose modesty was outraged by one, who stood to her in the capacity of a father, are often quoted as a warning to unscrupulous rulers. The decline of Hindu sway in Junāgadh is said to be the direct result of Rā Mandalik's improper conduct.

Adventures of other heroes

The adventures of many local heroes like Ebhal Vālo, Jetho Vālo, Ugo Vālo and Khetā Makvān, have been perpetuated in fragmentary verses. The higher and more well known clans of Rajputs, the Zālās and the Parmārs, have also inspired poets by their courage and chivalry.

Didactic and ethical verses

There is quite a store-house of didactic and ethical verses in the literature composed by saintly peasants, who are known by the appellation of Bhagats. The following specimens are chosen at random from a miscellaneous collection:

आशा ऊंडी खाड, पहाडथी पूराय नहि,
हेम मेरु सम होय तोये मन माने नहि.

"Hope is like a deep ravine, which cannot be filled up even with a mountain. No one is satisfied even if he possesses (a pile of) gold, as high as Mount Meru."

देशमां ढंढेरो फेरवो, प्रीत म करशो कोय,
करो तो काळज आपजो, (नकां) नित बरझोळा होय.

"Have it proclaimed throughout your country, that no one should fall in love; but if one does so, he must give up his heart or otherwise there will be unhappiness every day."

धूता होय सलक्षणा, वेश्या होय सलज्ज,
खारां पाणी निर्मळां, ए त्रण चीज अकज्ज.

"It is impossible to expect cheats to be virtuous, prostitutes to be modest, and salt water to be clear."[1]

In many poems we find references to the natural scenery of Kāthiāwād, and to the life led by its humble inhabitants—the Rabāris and the Chārans—the shepherds, goatherds and cowherds—very pointedly made.

Utterances of Bhadali prognosticating weather

The भडळीवाक्य—the utterances of Bhadali[2]—is a string of aphorisms, prognosticating (specially) the state of (wet) weather, based on certain phenomena in nature. It is the Bible of the agriculturist. If a certain state of weather prevails on a certain day or in a certain month, the condition of the coming monsoon is prophesied to be hopeful or disappointing: this is what is found in the collection. The statements are as concise and definite as the *Sutras* of the Dharm Śāstras. An exact counterpart to them is

1. Compare सलज्जा कुलटा नारी (नष्टा), निर्लज्जा च कुलाङ्गना। (लोकोक्ति).

2. The only daughter of Hudad, a well-known astrologer of Mārwād. He had no son, and so he taught his science to his daughter.

found also in the very early literature of Bengal, where the collection is called—**बारमासी.**

१. श्रावण पहेलां पांच दिन, मेह न मांडे आळ,
पियु पधारो माळवे, हमे जशुं मोसाळ.
२. पूरव ताणे काचबी जो आथमते सूर,
भडली वायक एम भणे दुधे जमाडुं कूर.
३. शनि आदीतां मंगळां, जो पोढे जदूराय,
चाक चढावे मेदनी, पृथ्वी परले थाय [करके पाज बंधाय].

1. "If rain does not begin to pour down five days before Shrāvaṇ then a wife should say to her husband, you had better go to Mālwā (to earn), and I to my father's house, meaning that the monsoon would fail, and they should shut up their house.

2. "If at sunset, a rainbow be seen in the east, then Bhadali says, that she would be able to feed people on rice and milk, that is, the monsoon would be prosperous.[1]

3. "If the god Jadurāy goes to sleep on a Saturday, Sunday or Tuesday—*i. e.*, if the Āshādi Ekādashi (the eleventh day of the first half of the month of Âshād, on which day the god Jadurāy is supposed to go to sleep, and sleep for the next four months)

1. This is like the English proverb:—
A rainbow in the morning
Is a shepherd's warning,
A rainbow at night
Is a shepherd's delight.

falls on any of these days of the week—the rains would be so abundant, that people would go mad, and the earth would be drowned (and a bridge made of bones)."

Those who have put these prognostications to the test, have found them true, almost invariably. The weather-wisdom contained in the verses is the result of observation and experience spread over a very long time, and cultivators all over Kāthiāwād turn to it intuitively, and base their calculations on it. The verses are collected and published, but owing to absence of editing, many of them have become obscure, and cannot be understood, and owing also to variation of readings, it is very difficult at times to determine the correct text or interpretation. It is most desirable that some one acquainted both with the science of meteorology and the provincialisms of Kāthiāwād, should bring out a corrected and annotated edition of the भड्ळीवाक्य. It would be a boon greatly appreciated by the general public.

found to be correct

Those who have heard the shepherds and cowherds of Kāthiāwād, while grazing their flocks or herds on opposite banks of a stream or river reciting दुहा, narrating some incident in the amorous life of Krishṇa and Rādhā—the shepherd on one bank reci-

Effect of hearing recitation of couplets

ting a couplet, and the shepherd on the opposite bank answering back—would never forget the charm of the situation, which is heightened when this feast of song happens to take place in a lonely jungle, with the rain falling in a slight drizzle, and nature wearing a green robe matching the very description of scenes and spots in the lines sung. The illiteracy of the reciters does not prevent them from entering fully into the spirit of the song. This floating literature has not yet been caught by the printer's art, although very valuable from various points of view.

Folklore

The folklore of Gujarāt, Kāthiāwād and Cutch, and specially of Kāthiāwād has been receiving earnest attention of Gujarāti scholars, and a couple of them, Jhaverchand Meghāni and Gokuldās Rāichurā have rescued and published a large number of folk tales and songs, thus helping their resuscitation and preservation. The present state of folk literature in Gujarāt will be found described in an article published in the June A. D. 1937 issue of the 'Modern Review' of Calcutta and reprinted as an Appendix to this work. So far as efforts to collect folk literature are concerned the Weekly Paper "गुजराती" and the Forbes Gujarāti Sabhā have been taking interest in the matter and the latter got the two volumes of folk tales in Kāthiāwād by Mr. Hargovind Premshankar published some time ago.

Besides this Jayshankar P. Pāṭhak, the late Ranjitrām Vāvābhāi (who collected and published गोपकाव्यो) and Popatlāl T. Adāljā have also contributed their mite to its advancement.

The folklore of Cutch is also considerable in quantity and closely allied to that of Sind. A fine sketch of the state of this branch of literature in Cutch will be found in the Introduction contributed by the late Mr. Nārāyaṇ V. Thakkur to the Chronicle of the Chandravamshiya Rājputs and called the Kalādhars of Cutch.[1] The Chronicle is a treasure house of romance and folklore and a valuable contribution to the history of the subject so far as Cutch is concerned.

---

1. Edited by Dulerai L. Karāni (1934).

APPENDIX

FOLK LITERATURE IN GUJARAT

I

FOLKLORE IN GUJARĀT: GENERAL

Traditional learning of backward people: this is what folklore deals with. This traditional learning is composed of the beliefs and customs, stories and songs, art and ritual of early and uncultured people. As there are aboriginal and uncultured people all over the world, each country has got its own folklore. In a vast country like India, each province has got its own folklore. But unfortunately very little has been done for tracing the origin of the various branches of the lore and their resemblances with the lore of other provinces. There is no Society in India like the Folklore Society of England nor a book of the calibre of the Golden Bough of Sir James Fraser.

Gujarāt, including Kāthiāwād and Cutch, being a very ancient province does possess folklore, Kāthiāwād more than Gujarāt. It is teeming with songs and stories. The essential features of a folksong are that it must originally have been sung by the peasantry and that it must have been passed down the years orally and not in written word. It must have been sung while the singers are at work or play. Incidentally one learns from it much about the old tendency of popular thought, customs, manners and traditions, as it is usually based on local legends or incidents of common life. Where deeds fade, legends remain and legends shape even new deeds.

The present state of Folklore Literature in Gujarāt is hardly satisfactory, as there has been till now very little sustained effort made either towards research or preservation of what has been obtained by scattered work. There is a Folksong Society in England and it has recorded several thousand authentic folksongs. Though a few folktales—Gujarāt and Kāthiāwād Deshni Vārtā, Kāthiāwādni Juni Vārtāo,—were collected and published several years ago, the fact remains that the work was not continued and it is only lately that a couple of research workers in Kāthiāwād have made it their business to explore that treasure-house of folktale and songs and give them a permanent form. Jhaverchand Meghāṇi has specialised in it and recorded much which otherwise would have remained unrecorded and ultimately perished. Gokuldās Rāichurā, the other worker has made it his business during his numerous tours over the whole of Kāthiāwād to take down legends from the mouths of Mers and other uncultured tribes and publish them. Gujarāt proper is slowly taking to it.

The different provinces of India, however, claim a common heritage for a part of this ancient lore, and that heritage is Sanskrit Literature. Loka-Kathā (Popular Legends) in Sanskrit deals with folk-stories or folktales, and the earliest of such collections made by Guṇādhya is known as Brihat-Kathā, the Great Story. It is in Paishāchi Prākrit. In the second century, a scholar from Sorath, Pādliptāchārya, made a collection in Sanskrit and called it TarangLolā. Later collections such as Kathā SaritSāgar of Somadev (XI Century), the Brihat-KathāManjari of Kshemendra, and books like Vaitāl-Pachisi, SinhāsanBatrisi, ShukSaptati, which have been translated into various old and modern Indian languages, Hindi, Marāthi, Bengāli, Gujarāti and those of the South, evidence this common heritage. Jātak stories which depict previous lives of Buddha are, it is said, in reality folktales current amongst people long before the coming of the Buddha.

However, that was in the past. In the present times every province has become active and scholars are systematically engaging themselves in the collection of folksongs etc. Rām Naresh Tripāthi, the compiler of KavitāKaumudi is a well known authority on Hindi folksong. Behāri and Bhojpuri Grāmgit (village songs) have also been collected and published. Prof. Devendra Satyārthi is collecting and publishing the folksongs sung by country women in the Punjāb. Bengāl, of course, does not lag behind. Thus there is a stir everywhere. In England folksongs spread through the agency of the wandering gypsy and the itinerant ballad singer. Here too it is the wandering beggar and the itinerant minstrel who carry the folktale in song from place to place, with or without the accompaniment of music.

The common types of folksongs, for instance, in England are love-songs which tell a story at greater or shorter length.[4] Folksongs also depict various aspects of country life. Folksongs of Gujarāt and Kāthiāwād, in common with the rest of the country, possess these very features, in addition to others, which are peculiar to the domestic life of India, such as early marriage and its sequel-rough treatment of the newly wedded bride, mostly a child, by the sister-in-law and mother-in-law. Songs sung by women at weddings also accentuate this feature of the home life of the Hindu. These songs have been passing from mother to daughter, and nobody knows who has composed them. A good many wedding songs in Gujarāt and Kāthiāwād are identical line by line, with those of the Punjāb. That points to the course of migration of certain races which settled in Kāthiāwād. The legends of the loves of Rādhā and Krishṇa, furnish another common feature universally adopted over North, East, West and Central India.

The women of India from old days take certain vows and fulfil them. They are called Vrit. They take the vow with certain objects and pray to the relative gods and goddesses to grant them. These vows are taken in either or both stages of a woman's life, maiden and married. A large amouut of folklore and tales has gathered round this practice, and fortunately also been published at least in Bengāl and Gujarāt.

English scholars have led the way in this matter, as in several others. Sir Richard Temple collected and published the Legends of the Punjāb, and Mr. Enthoven, the Folklore Notes of Gujarāt, compiled from notes collected by the late Mr. Jackson. In Gujarāt Thākardās and Bhils, who are its oldest dwellers, when properly approached prove of great help in this matter. Rām Nārāyaṇ Pāthak and Umāshankar Joshi are greatly interested in collecting materials from these communities, and the Bhil Sevā Mandal which comes in intimate contact with them can rescue a lot. In addition to ordinary folklore, they possess a lore, which is of a mystical kind. The supernatural appeals to them. The workings of the supernatural forces, which they cannot account for and understand form the staple of their songs and also the powers of the Meladi Mātā, an inauspicious goddess. The loves of Rādhā and Krishṇa also find favour with them. In north Gujarāt the limits of Idar march with those of Mewād, Dungarpur, Vānswādā and other Rājputānā States. Here live numerous small Jāgirdars who were independent rulers in old times. Civil wars were the order of the day resulting in chaos. The hills and hill fastnesses roundabout offered ideal places for ambushes and fights. Popular folksongs have commemorated many such incidents.

Grierson, the well known scholar of Indian languages had very early noted the absence of publication of this important side of Gujarāti Literature: *viz.*, the corpus of bardic histories. Bards sing ballads in which story telling forms an important item. The martial life of the clans of Kāthiāwād and their chivalry have been versified since ages: these ballads consist of Duhās, couplets or Sorathās, longer stanzas. It is difficult to find out their author or authors.

Verses relating to the story of Halāmaṇ Jethwo and Sona Rāṇi, of Ujali and Meha, of Rāṇakdevi and Siddharāj—both of them historical figures,—Odho Jām and Hothalde Padmaṇi, Lākho and Fulānde, are very interesting and typical of the life of the old Kāthiāwādi. Adventures of local heroes like Ebhal Vālo, Jetho Vālo, Ugo Vālā, Khetā Makwāṇi and of Robin Hoods like Jogidās Khumāṇ and Bhimā Jat, are perpetuated in stirring language. The folktale of Suhini Mehār is one out of many secured by Jhaverchand Meghāṇi; hearing it recited from the lips of Meghāṇi whets one's appetite for hearing many more such tales. Hearing Duhās recited by Gokuldās Rāichurā, is an unforgettable pleasant experience. Meghāṇi's five volumes of Rasadhār and Rāichurā's Collections at present hold the field. In reciting them, they of course follow the method of the professional story-teller.

So far as folksongs and folktales are concerned it is both the matter and the manner of reciting them that constitute their charm. Folksongs as said before are mostly Duhās or Sorathās, some are long poems. The former are generally sung by goatherds, shepherds, cowherds—*i. e.*, those living in jungles and forests in close communion with nature;—they divide themselves into opposite groups and then begin singing them. In the rainy season with a drizzle falling, when one party recites a couplet from one bank of a river intervening between the grazing grounds of two herds and is answered by the other from the opposite bank, in the particular lilt and drawling manner affected by these villagers, the incident is not easily forgotten by one who is fortunate enough to witness it. Similarly for the long poems recited by bards (भाटचारण). The bards have their own way of telling a story and reciting a poem. The twang and the singsong practised by them cannot be transferred to a talk. A bard uses words which strikes more by their sound than their sense. A good deal of alliteration and very many mnemonic words, constitute the beauty of bardic recitations, so says one who sixty years ago, underwent the expense and trouble of getting these bards to recite to him in order to put their performance on paper. Brij is generally the bardic language, but the recitation is interlarded with poetical quotations in Gujarāti. Their mnemonics consist of half obsolete and half dialectic words: they give to the recitation individuality and rough picturesqueness. Bardic Duhā and long poems are also written in Mārwādi more correctly called Rājasthāni. Bardic lore has expressed itself in a peculiar dialect, a mixture of Sindhi, Rājasthāni and Brij languages.

The same collector divides those who belong by birth to the profession of the story teller into Bhāts, Chāraṇs, Rāvalyas and Turee among Hindus and Mirs and Lunghās among Musalmāns. Bhāts and Chāraṇs are bards of the Rājput, Rāvalyas of the Kāṭhi princes and Āhirs of shepherd tribes and the Turees of the low castes like Dheds. Among Bābi Musalmāns there are besides Mirs and Lunghās, Dhādees who are specially their family bards and leeches.

They say that what the Bābis earn, the Dhādees eat. But besides these professional story tellers there are others also who recite stories with the ease and accomplishment of *bona fide* professionals. One must have come across many such including women. Prof. B. K. Thākore has mentioned the instance of one Zakkalbāi Bhāvsāreṇ, the wife of a neighbouring Dhobi at Rājkot, who used to come to his mother to help her pass her lonely nights, when she had to be by herself, his father being away, by reciting to them stories of Ebhal Vālo, Jesal, Todi Rāṇi, the Rās of Junāghad, Jethawās of Ghumli and Sumrās of Cutch and Sind, with the assistance of Duhās and Sorathās. Indeed she told them so well that they all lost the count of time.

These story tellers have their own fashion of telling stories. Some tell them piecemeal. Some tell them with intervals for smoking Hookāh and partaking of opium. Bard story tellers, if they know that you are going to make some use of their story demand a consideration, which may be reasonable or otherwisc. Further there are so many versions of one and the same story and repetitions occur so often, that one has to prune the weed from the flower, and cut them out to make the story intelligible and continuous. Woman's "wiles" form a branch of this kind of folktale and it must be said to the credit of these reciters that one finds very little indecency or even vulgarity, in the way in which they present these "wiles." Men and women are made to talk in the genteel way, but all the same, nothing is sacrificed to the reality of the situation. A tiff on womanly virtue between a barber and his wife, might border on the coarse but never on the indecent.

Folk dance and folk medicine are equally important branches of the Folklore of Gujarāt. The use of milk to ward off diseases among cattle, preparations for transforming an old man into a youth or for inducing pregnancy in a woman, and other such instances of human credulity are found in the folk medicine of all old countries like Egypt and India.

Bhil dance is a very ancient institution. Some of the dances are danced by both men and women, the former with swords or sticks in hand. They do dance in a circle, but their movements are like waves, advancing and receding. They must be seen to be appreciated.

Songs sung by women like lullabies, as well as spiritual or religious songs called Bhajans, are also parts of this lore. Bhajan Literature is very vast. These lyrics describe spiritual ecstacy. Balladic Bhajans narrate events relating to piety, renunciation etc.

The Supplement to the well known Persian History of Gujarāt called the Mirāt-i-Ahmadi is a storehouse of folklore. Legends relating to Mahommedan saints and their Durghas are found in very generous proportions in its pages: it will repay the labour of study.

II

FOLKLORE OF GUJARAT: TALES

In the previous section I had spoken of the characteristics of the Folklore of Gujarāt generally. In the present section those characteristics will be illustrated with tales.

Youthful love forms one of such characteristics. Here is a story illustrating that side of human nature.

Sindh, Cutch and Kāthiāwād in old times were very closely connected, and therefore the folk story of the loves of Suhini and Mehār, rescued by Jhaverchand Meghāṇi and ably edited, may be taken as typifying this particular phase of folklore in the three provinces. The scene is laid on the banks of the Indus. Mehār meaning a buffalo-herd keeper, who tended the buffaloes and donkeys of one Tolā, a potter of Sadāpur on the Indus, was really a cultured youth from Bokhārā, and the son of a millionaire. He was on his way to the Mogul Court and had put up at the serai of the place where Suhini's father sold earthen pots. He happened to go to Tolā's place to purchase pots and saw Suhini. He fell in love with her at once and abandoned the idea of going to Delhi, and entered into Tolā's service as a herd keeper. He knew neither herd keeping nor milking and was therefore often rebuked by his master. Suhini, however, pitied him and always came to his rescue, though every now and then taunting him for his awkwardness and inefficiency. For these very shortcomings, however, she began to like him, though in the beginning she did not know who he really was. The liking ripened into friendship and later into love. They often met in the forest and Suhini's father felt scandalised by the rumours he heard of their secret meetings. He, therefore, dismissed Mehār, who left Sadāpur and built himself a hut on the river bank opposite. He would catch a fish from the river, fry it, cross over every night, meet Suhini and they would partake of the meal together. Whatever the state of the weather, whether the waters of the Indus were quiet or stormy, Mehār would not miss a single night. One day it so happened that he could catch no fish. He, thereupon, cut off a slice of flesh from his thigh, fried it and took it to his beloved, who ate it with great relish and said that she had never eaten such a tasty fish in her life. During their talk she learned later what it was, and then she said that it was now her turn and that she would cross the river over, thereafter, to his bank. Her father, however, took steps to marry her off to an uncouth, ugly youth of his own caste, but Suhini did not acknowledge him as her husband and continued her nightly visits. She did not know swimming well, and the river was full of strong eddies and whirlpools which would suck down any mortal. She used to swim over with the support of a well-baked chatty: पाको घडो. Her persistence proved too much for her parents, and they therefore thought of doing away with her, and with that object, substituted a not well baked—Kāchā—pot one night in place of her usual well baked—Pākā one. Half way, the unbaked earth of the pot proved treacherous and gave way. She thus lost the support and began to feel exhausted. She could have cried out and called on Mehār to come to her rescue, but she thought of the wound on his thigh, which had not yet healed and refrained, but when the last moment came involuntarily she cried out. Mehār heard her cries, and jumped into water to meet her. But before he could reach her she had gone down. Exertion reopened Mehār's wound and it began bleeding and he too succumbed. Next morning two dead bodies were thrown up by the Indus. They were buried together and the tomb built over them called Suhini's Tomb is still standing at Sadāpur. The whole pathetic story is embellished by stirring couplets in the dialect of the locality.

The legend of Mehār and Suhiṇi is one of pure love. The story of Rāṇakdevi, the beautiful consort of Rā'Khengār of Junāghad and Siddharāj, the ruler of Gujarāt, who had invaded Junāgadh, is one of pure passion, met with spiritual courage. Junāgadh was taken by Siddharāj through treachery of Rā'Khengār's nephew and after Rā'Khengar was killed Siddharāj desired to possess his widow and made her various tempting offers. She refused to yield to him and so he took her away forcibly. 'But coming near Wadhwāṇ she became Sati and that too with the permission of Sidharāj, who was by then convinced that he would never be able to displace her love for Rā'Khengār. The verses attributed to her as having been recited at the time when she mounted the funeral pile are very pathetic and prophetic. She had a son, and she admonished him thus: Weep not, my child, make not your eyelids wet, nor red, think not of your mother, when facing death; disgrace not your ancestors by showing weakness. When being taken forcibly away by Siddharāj, she bids adieu to Girnār, in these words: "I descended the hill of Girnār and my body reached its foot. I will never again see Dāmodar Kund (the lake at the foot of the hill). The fort of Girnār is so high that it touches the sky. By the death of Rā'Khengār Rāṇakdevi becomes a widow. To her Sorath was everything: Pātan, the capital of Siddharāj, nothing. The country round about Pātan is waterless, its people die of thirst, but prosperous is the land of Sorath, where even the tigers drink their fill. Siddharāj was watching her burning, and she thus alludes to it. The winds are hurricanes, they are so hot that they burn even sand. There Siddharāj was standing to watch the miraculous power of the lady from Sorath. I regret it is not possible to convey in English the force and rhythm of the original couplets.

The story of Halāmaṇ Jethawo and Sona Raṇi, is placed both in Kāthiāwād and Sind, thus establishing their close folklore connection. It is the story of a courageous girl like Suhini, proving steadfast to her vow and refusing to be deflected from her purpose in the face of various troubles and tribulations. Sona Rāṇi was the daughter of Rāṇa Rājsing of Bālambhā. She had taken a vow to marry only such a person as would be able to answer her riddle which was this: "What is that which has been made without hammer or anvil?" As usual the family priest was sent to various Durbārs to see if he could get anyone to solve it. After many failures he at last tried Ghumli, at the foot of the Bardā mountains. The local chief, a scion of the famous Jethwā clan of Rājputs, Rāṇa Shiyāji tried his hand at the solution, but failed. His young nephew, Halāmaṇ, however could at once read it. The answer was "Pearls," which are fashioned without being hammered or placed on an anvil. The riddle was couched in verse and his reply was in verse also. He said, the mother lives in the ocean and the father in the clouds; this refers to the belief amongst Hindus that if rain drops fall into the mouth of oysters during the Swāti Nakshatra (Fifteenth mansion of the Zodiāc), pearls are formed. In ordinary course, the priest would have gone and reported the matter faithfully to Princess Sona and her union with Halāmaṇ would have been the result, but seeing a beautiful prize about to be snatched away from his hands, the Rāṇā bribed the Brāhmin to substitute his name in place of Halāmaṇ. The Brāhmin did so, and accordingly it was arranged that the Princess should go with a proper equipage in charge of the Brāhmin to Ghumli and be married to the Rāṇā. Till the bride's party came to Ghumli, Halāmaṇ was under the impression that he was the chosen bridegroom. But his eyes were opened by a trusted follower who told him that his uncle had decided to marry the Princess. He was sorely disappointed but yielding to an impulse of respect for elders, remained silent. On the other hand, it so happened, that a squabble took place between the maid servants of Princess Sona and Rāṇā Shiyāji at a well, while drawing water, and they began to taunt and abuse each other. The Rāṇā's maid said mysteriously, Who knows what is in a shut hand? When opened it may be empty. Then she let the cat out of the bag and boldly proclaimed the truth in order to wound the feelings of her opponents. She said: Halāmaṇ reads the riddle and Shiyā gets the bride. Sona's maid told her mistress as to what had happened. Sona called the priest whom she suspected of foul play, and he confessed his guilt. She now knew what had taken place and made up her mind to thwart the Rāṇā's plans. Accordingly when the usual wedding presents of ornaments and dresses came to her from the Rāṇā, she threw them away, sending word that it did not behove her to accept presents from the Rāṇā when Halāmaṇ was her husband: the Rāṇā was her father-in-law. The chief on being informed of this insult at her hands flew into a rage, and sending for Halāmaṇ asked him to leave the limits of his State at once. Halāmaṇ obeyed. On his way he met a servant girl of the Princess and sent a message with her to Sona that he was being banished and going to his aunt at Hāmbā in Sind. She was very much upset, and when the Rāṇā called on her, she shut herself up in a room and refused to see him, saying a father-in-law should not have any evil designs on his daughter-in-law. This added to his anger and he was preparing himself to assault her when word was brought to him that Sindhis had attacked the borders of his State and that his immediate presence was necessary to beat them back. This unexpected contingency upset his plans, and he had to leave at once, which he did after giving orders that Sona was on no account to be allowed to move out. She however, under pretext of having to visit a temple, did move out and when at some distance from the town she and her maid managed to get rid of the driver who was driving them to the temple. The maid took his place and they drove away towards Hāmbā. Meanwhile Halāmaṇ was living at Hāmbā a very unhappy life. Like a distracted lover he was wandering in the jungle from place to place, and like King Pururavā in the famous drama ot Kālidās, questioning every tree and bird if they had seen his beloved. The couplets that he addressed them are very pathetic. His aunt tried to console him by proposing marriage with a Sindhi beauty, but Halāmaṇ declined saying Sona only will I wed. In this disconsolate state of mind he was sitting on a stone in a jungle. A serpent came from beneath it and bit his toe. The poison did its work and he thought he would die without seeing his lady love. Now it so happened that after leaving the territory of the Rāṇā, Sona and her maid on their way to Hāmbā while passing through the jungle had halted there for rest and refreshments. The maid set out to find water and while looking about found Halāmaṇ lying unconscicus. She recognised him and ran to her mistress with the news. Sona came where he was lying and fainted. The maid however brought her back to consciousness and then her lamentations were heart-rending. She said, I have lost a thing dear to me within the limits of Hāmbā: it is the necklace of my heart, etc. Thinking that life was extinct, she made preparations for cremating the dead body and burning herself with the lord of her heart. She sang, "On the body of Halāmaṇ wood has been piled. I will mount the pyre and with the lord of Bardā I shall ascend to heaven" The wails of Sona and her maid attracted the attention of a serpent charmer. He came upon the scene and examined the body, and found that life was not extinct, and that there was a chance of reviving him. He took out an antidote and applied it to the wound. Soon Halāmaṇ regained his senses and, was both surprised and delighted to see Sona there. The rest of the tale is easily told. They married and as the Rāṇā died shortly after they went back to their native country and lived happily. Their loves are thus commemorated in a couplet:

जेवी सोन सुजाण, तेवो हलामण हीरलो,
तन बे, एक ज प्राण, जुगते जुगतुं जोडलुं.

Just as Sona was clever, so was Halāmaṇ shining like a diamond. They had two bodies but one soul. It a was fit pair in every way.

A real outlaw (Robin Hood) of Kāthiāwād is always conceived as chivalrous towards women and generous to the poor. Jogidās Khumāṇ of Kundlā under the Bhāvnagar State became along with his old father, an outlaw against the ruler Vajesangji because of certain villages of their Jāgir having been confiscated. The incident is a recent one, about a hundred years old (round about Samvat Year 1875); his eight brothers had agreed to the sequestration, he alone held out, and with his three sons, one of them being Jogidās, began to harass State subjects. Jogidās as the leader of the band was the hero of numerous romantic incidents out of which he always came out with flying colours. He had secured the blessings of a Mahomedan saint whose holy peacock was shot and eaten by the Sindhi troops sent to watch Jogidās' village and who on their way to Bhāvnagar were defeated and killed by a ruse practised on them. One of such incidents reflects great credit on Jogidās' keen sense of chivalry. Nānibā, the Rāṇi of Vajesangji was going in a covered carriage from Bhāvnagar to Dadvā, her brother's home. She had of course costly ornaments with her and Ragho Chāvdo, expert thief of Akadiā got news of it. He therefore made up his mind to rob her on her way and fasten the robbery on Jogidās, the declared enemy of Vajesang. At sunset, accordingly, Ragho and his horsemen suddenly attacked her escort and killed many of them. Then Ragho called upon Nānibā to give up her box of ornaments. She asked him who he was. He said Jogidās' man. She said, Is it possible that Jogidās would rob helpless women? Would he eat prohibited food? Ragho said, Yes, yes, to a hungry stomach prohibited food is allowable. She retorted, that Jogidās was a lion and a hungry lion would never eat grass. Ragho, however, silenced her by threat ot violence. At this psychological moment, footfalls of running horses were heard and forty horsemen led by Jogidās came up. Ragho was delighted. He welcomed them. Jogidās in his turn, asked what the matter was. Ragho acquainted him with the situation and offered to go shares in the booty. Jogidās asked who the victim was and was told that she was the wife of his enemy Vajesang. He spurned the offer and rebuked Ragho, who though a Kāthi was a thief. Jogidās said that his differences were with Vajesang and not with his wife. She was like his sister, his mother, and even if she had got millions with her, it was to him like cow's flesh. Ragho then said, Jogidās! better leave here and let matters proceed. The latter demurred and challanged Ragho to touch the conveyance with his little finger even. The tussle resulted in a fight between their respective followers, and Ragho's party being worsted, he decamped. Jogidās then called upon the driver to consult Nānibā as to where she desired to go, to her husband's or her brother's house. He would see her safe there. Nānibā elected to go to Bhāvnagar and Jogidās escorted her as far as the frontiers of the State. He left her there but the grateful lady entreated him to go with her and said that she would intervene on his behalf and see his wrong righted. Jogidās said, No, I have not done this with any such expectation. I will myself see my wrong righted, either by piercing Vajesang's bosom with a sword or enclosing it in an embrace. Saying this he spurred on his horse in the darkness. Nānibā cried after him, Jogidāsbhāi! Jogidāsbhāi! but only the whistle of the night wind answered her. Vajesang and Jogidās were ultimately reconciled.[1]

1 Two Broadcast Talks from the All India Radio Centre at Bombay: in December, 1936 and January, 1937.

BIBLIOGRAPHY

(E—English. G—Gujarāti.)

(1. G.) Akhābhakta and His poems: by Ambālāl B. Jāni, B. A. (1907).

(2. G.) Akhākrit Kāvya:
Part I: by Diwān Bahādur Narmdāshankar D. Mehtā, B. A. (1931).
Part II: by Kavi Sāgar: (1932): both published by the Gujarāt Vernacular Society.

(3. G.) Akhāni Vāṇi: published by Bhikshu Akhandānand: Sastun Sāhitya Vardhak Kāryālaya (1924).

(4. G.) Ānand Kāvya Mahodadhi Series: Vols. I to VIII. published by Jivaṇchand S. Jhaveri, Surat. (1912–1927).

(5. G.) Articles on Akhā, Narsinh Mehtā, Mirānbāi, Premānand, and Dhiro; in Vasant, Samālochak, Buddhiprakāsh, Sāhitya, Gujarāt, Traimāsik of the Forbes Gujarāti Sabhā and other magazines.

(6. G.) Aprasiddha Gujarāti Grantho: (Quarterly), by Chaturbhāi S. Patel, Nadiad.

(7. G.) Bhakta Kavi Narsinh Mehtā: by J. P. Joshipurā (1908).

(8. G.) BhaktaKavi Dayārāmnun Āntar Jivan or Divya Akshar Deha: by Mulchandra T. Teliwālā B.A., LL.B., and Prof. J. G. Shah, M.A. (1931).

(9. G.) BhaktaKavi Dayārāmnun JivanCharitra: by Shankarprasād C. Rāvaḷ (1920).

(10. G) Bhālaṇ: by Rāmlāl C. Modi, Sayāji Sahitya Mālā, Vol. XXXIII (1919).

(11. G.) Bhim (Vishnudās): 1. Introduction to Harililā Shodash Kalā: by Ambālāl B. Jāni, B. A. (1930). 2. Introduction to Prabodhprakāsh: by Keshavrām K. Shāstri (1936): both published by the Gujarāt Vernacular Society.

(12. G.) BhojoBhakta: Introduction to BrihatKāvyā-Dohan Part VIII, by Natvarlal I. Desai B. A., published by The Gujarāti Printing Press, Bombay (1913).

(13. G.) BrahmānandKāvya: published by Motilāl T. Fozdār (First Editon 1902).

(14. G.) BrihatKāvyaDohan (Series): Vols. I to VIII. edited by I. S. Desāi, published by The Gujarāti Printing Press, Bombay.

(15. G.) Buddhiprakāsh: Several Vols: Monthly and Quarterly.

(16. E.) Classical Poets of Gujarāt: by Govardhanrām M. Tripathi, B. A., LL. B. (1894).

(17. E.) Dalpatrām HastalikhitPustakSangraha: edited

by H. T. Parekh, B. A., published by The Gujarāt Vernacular Society (1930).

(18. G.) DalpatrāmKāvyadohan, Parts I and II: published by The Gujarāt Vernacular Society.

(19. G.) Dayrām and Hāfez: by Diwān Bahādur K. M. Jhaveri, M. A., LL. B. (1901).

(20. G.) Dayārāmkrit KāvyaSangrah: edited by Kavi Narmadāshankar and published by I. S. Desāi, The Gujarāti Pinting Press, Bombay (1909).

(21. G.) Dayārāmkrit KāvyaMaṇimālā: Parts I to V: Published by N. P. Dabhoiwālā (1914 to 1929).

(22. G.) DayārāmKāvyaSudhā: edited by Praṇshankar V. Vaijnāth, and published by The Gujarāti Pinting Press, Bombay (1916).

(23. G.) Dayārām's Life: by Tribhuvandās B. Sheth.

(24. G.) Dayārām's Life: by Jagjivandās D. Modi, Sayāji Sāhitya Mālā, Vol. XIV (1918).

(25. G.) Dayārām's Rasikvallabh: by Prof. Jethālāl G. Shah, M. A., published by The Gujarāt Vernacular Society (1933).

(26. G.) Dayārāmno Akshardeh: by Govardhanrām M. Tripathi, B. A., LL. B. (1908).

(27. G. E.) Dictionary, Gujarāti–English: by Mancher-shaw Kekobād.

(28. E. G.) ,, English–Gujarāti: by Shāpurji. (1863).

(29. E. G.) ,, ,, by Mirzā Mahomed Kāzim and Nowroji Furdunji. (1846)

(30. G.) Diwāli Issues: 'Gujarāti' Weekly (1909 to 1937).

(31. E.) Early History of India: by Vincent Smith (1914).

(32. G.) GavarikirtanMālā: published by Kamalāshankar G. Bhachech, B. A. (1938)

(33. G.) Girdharkrit Rāmāyaṇa: edited by J. D. Mody and published by Sastun Sāhitya Vardhak Kāryālaya (1926).

(34. G.) Girdharkrit Krishṇalilā (Xth Canto. Bhāgvat): edited by I. S. Desai and published by The Gujarāti Printing Press, Bombay (1895).

(35. G.) Girdhar's Life: by Jagjivandās D. Modi, Sayāji Sāhitya Mālā Vol. XXX (1919).

(36. E.) Gujarāt and Its Literature: by The Hon'ble Mr. Kanaiyalāl M. Munshi, B. A., LL. B. (1935).

(37. G.) Gujarāti Bhāshāno Itihās: by Vrijlāl Kālidās Shāstri. Published by the Gujarāt Vernacular Society (1900).

(38. E.) Gujarāti Language and Literature: Philological Lectures: by N. B. Divatiā, B. A. Part I (1921) and Part II (1932).

(39. E.) Gujarāti Language and Literature: Vasanji Mādhavji Thakkar Lectures: by N. B. Divatiā, B. A. (1930).

(40. E.) Gujarāti Poets, Lectures: by Rev. H. R. Scott (1914).

(41. G.) Gujarāti Poets: (List) AryajnānVardhak: by I. S. Desāi. (1887):

(42. G.) Gujarāti Rājasthān.

(43. G.) Gujarāti SāhityaParishad Reports, Presidential Addresses and other Essays: Vols. I to XII (1905 to 1936).

(44. G.) Gujarāti (Weekly): Issues 21st and 28th July: (1912) Swāminārāyaṇ Sampradāy.

(45. G.) Gurjar Sākshar Jayanti: published by Jivanlāl Amarshi Mehtā. (1921).

(46. G.) Halāmaṇ Jethwo: Stribodh Issue: Jan. 1913.

(47. G.) Hand Book of Bengāli Literature: by R. C. Dutt.

(48. G.) Harililā Shodash Kalā of Kavi Bhima: Introduction: by A. B. Jāni, B. A., published by The Gujarāt Vernacular Society (1930).

(49. G.) HastLikhitPustak Nāmāvali: by A. B. Jāni, B. A. (Shri Forbes Gujarāti Sabhā Sangraha). (1929)

(50. G.) HastLikhit Pustak Savistar Nāmāvali: Parts I and II, by A. B. Jāni, (Shri Forbes Gujarati Sabhā) (1923 and 1929).

(51. E.) History of Benglāi Literature: by Rai Bahādur Dinesh Chandra Sen.

(52. E.) Indiān Literature: by Frazer.

(53. G.) Jain Conference Harold: Issues, March and April (1913): Articles on Old Gujarāti Language by Kavi Narmadāshankar.

(54. G.) Jain Gurjar Kavio, Parts I and II: Edited by Mohanlāl D. Desāi, B. A., LL. B. (1926) and (1931).

(55. G.) Jain Granthāwali: published by The Jain Śwetāmber Conference, Bombay.

(56. G.) Jain KāvyaMālā (Raichandra Series, Parts I and II): by Mansukhlāl R. Mehtā (1908).

(57. G.) JainSāhitya: A Short History: by Mohanlāl D. Desāi, B. A., LL. B. (1933).

(58. G.) J(Z)arthost Nāmā: by Meharbanoo and Beharāmrgor T. Anklesaria (1932).

(59. G.) Juni Gujarāti Bhāshā: by Prof. C. P. Patel, Sayāji SāhityaMālā Vol. 239 (1935).

(60. G.) Junun Narmagadya (Lives of Poets): by Kavi Narmadāshankar, published by The Gujarāti Printing Press, Bombay (1912).

(61. G.) Kahānad de Prabandh: by D. P. Derāsari, Bar-at-law.

(62. G.) KrishnaLilāKāvya (Keshavdās H. Xth Canto. Bhāgvat): by A. B. Jāni, B. A., Introduction by Natvarlāl I. Desāi, B. A. (1932).

(63. G.) KāthiāwādiSāhitya: by KānjiDharmasi(1913).

(64. G.) Lyric: Prayogmālā Series No. 5, by Prof. B. K. Thakore, B. A. (1928).

(65. E.) Linguistic Survery of India: Vol. IX, Parts I and II, by Sir George Grierson (1916).

(66. G.) MadhyaYugano SāhityaPravāh: published by the Sāhitya Sansad, Parts I to VII (1926).

(67. G.) Mahābhārat: different Parvas: (old Gujarāti, Ākhyāns) by K. K. Shāstri, published by The Forbes Gujarāti Sabhā (1913 to 1936).

(68. G.) Mugdhavbodh Auktik: The Prāchin Gujarāti Sāhitya RatnMālā, Edited by H. H. Dhruva, B. A., LL. B. (1888).

(69. E.) Miranbai: Story, by Bankey Behari (1935).

(70. G.) Mirānbāi: Life by Bhānusukharām N. Mehtā, Sayāji Sāhitya Mālā, Vol. XX (1918).

(71. G.) Mirānbāi: Life and Tenets by T. M. Tripāthi, B. A., Introduction to Brihat Kāvya-Dohan, Part VII (1911).

(72. G.) Nākar: Introduction to Brihat Kāvya Dohan Part VIII, by Ambālāl B. Jāni, B. A. (1913).

(73. G.) NarmaKosh: Introduction by Kavi Narmadāshankar (1874).

(74. G.) Narsinsh Mehtā: J. P. Joshipurā, M. A. Sayāji Sāhitya Mālā, Vol. 191, (1931).

(75. G.) Narsinh Mehtā Bhakta Harino: by The Hon'ble Mr. Kanaiyālāl M. Munshi, B. A., LL. B. (1933).

(76. G.) Narsinh Mehtā: Collected Works, edited by I. S. Desāi, The Gujarāti Printing Press, Bombay (1913).

(77. G.) ,, Life and Works: Introduction to the above book (76 G.) by I. S. Desāi, The Gujarāti Printing Press, Bombay (1913).

(78. E.) Notes on the Grammar of Old and Western Rājasthāni: by Dr. L. C. Tessitori, (April 1914).

(79. G.) Prāchin Gujarāti KāvyaSangrah: Part I (Gaikwād Orientle Series) (1921) by Chimanlāl C. Dalāl.

(80. G.) Prāchin Gurjar Kavio (Fifteenth Century): by Diwān Bahādur K. H. Dhruv, published by The Gujarāt Vernacular Society (1927).

(81. G.) Prāchin Gadya Sandarbh: by Muni Jinvijayji.

(82. G.) Prāchin Kāvya Trimāsik Series: Parts 1 to 38, by H. D. Kāntāwālā (From 1884 to 1894).

(83. G.) Prāchin KāvyaMālā: by H. D. Kāntāwālā Vols. I to XXXV, with Introductions.

(84. G.) Premānand (Essay): Diwān Bahādur K. H. Druva, B. A. (1905).

(85. G.) Premānand, Life: by Bhānusunkharām N. Mehtā, Sayāji Sāhitya Mālā Vol. VIII (1918).

(86. G.) Premānand JivanKalā: by Ambālāl B. Jāni, B. A., Introduction to Subhadrāharaṇ, (1919 and 1924).

(87. G.) Poems (of old Poets) in the Sāhitya Monthly: by H. D. Kāntāwālā.

(88. G.) Rājasthān: Gujarāti.

(89. E.) Rājasthān: Todd.

(90. G.) SāhityaRatna: by I. P. Khānsāheb and Narharilāl Trimbaklāl, M. A., LL. B.

(91. G.) Sayāji Sāhitya Mālā Vols. 8, 14, 20, 30, 33, 45, 133, 191.

(92. G.) SinhāsanBatrisi (Sāmal) Parts I and II: with Introduction by Ambālāl B. Jāni, B. A., (1924 and 1926).

(93. G.) Sāthinā Sāhityanun Digdarśan: by Dayābhāi P. Derāsari, published by The Gujarāt Vernacular Society (1911).

(94. G.) Thodānk Rāsdarshno: by the Hon'ble Mr. Kanaiyālāl M. Munshi, B. A., LL. B. (1923).

(95. G.) Traimāsik: (The Forbes Gujarāti Sabhā) Vols. I, II and III, (V. S. 1992 to 1994).

(96. E.) Vaishnavās of Gujarāt: by Pro. N. A. Thoothi (1935).

(97. G.) Vallabh: Gajendrashankar S. Pandyā, M. A., Sayāji Sāhitya Mālā, Vol. 133, (1928).

(98. G.) Vishnudās: Introduction to Brihat Kāvya Dohan by Natvarlāl I. Desāi (1913).

(99. G.) Vishnudās: Bhānusukarām N. Mehtā, Sayaji Sāhitya Mālā, Vol. 45 (1920).

(100. G.) Trikamdās, Poems: Introduction by Natvarlāl I. Desāi, B. A., Nayansukhrai V. Majmudār, B. A. (1930).

INDEX

(f.—Foot note)

C

M

N

R